S0-AYO-587

For Pete's Sake

All The Best
Joanne

Pete Wohler

For Pete's Sake

Going Through Hell and
Coming Out Whole

Pamela Chappell

Copyright © 2011 Pamela Chappell, Big Blue Water Productions

Cover design by Brennan and Rachel Sang.

Library of Congress Control Number: 2011900116
ISBN: Hardcover   978-1-4568-4865-1
                    Softcover   978-1-4568-4864-4
                    Ebook   978-1-4568-4866-8

All rights reserved. No part of this book may be reproduced or transmitted in
any form or by any means, electronic or mechanical, including photocopying,
recording, or by any information storage and retrieval system, without
permission in writing from the copyright owner.

This book was printed in the United States of America.

To order additional copies of this book, contact:
Xlibris Corporation
1-888-795-4274
www.Xlibris.com
Orders@Xlibris.com
91434

Dedication

For Peter, My Beloved

and

The One

Who Gave Him New Life

ACKNOWLEDGMENTS

IN LIVING THIS story and writing this book I called upon resources from nearly every corner of my life. I am deeply grateful to the many teachers who have influenced and inspired me over the years. Some I have known personally and some have been my mentors by way of books, conferences, and the like. They include Annette Covatta, Neale Donald Walsch, Louise Hay, John Denver, Wayne Dyer, Leona Washburn, Marchiene (Marty) Rienstra, Margie Towne Kivel, Linda Beushausen, Debra Basham, Claudia Mierau, Sherry Petro-Surdel, Nancy Lou English Grib, Nancy O'Donohue, all of my Goddess Sisters and the loving members of Unity on the Lakeshore of Douglas, Michigan. These wonderful people have helped me raise my consciousness in many ways that served me when I faced the challenges related in this book.

Pete and I are both indebted to the people, too many to mention individually, who supported us with CarePages postings, e-mails, cards, donations, gifts, prayers and their presence. Our family and friends were with us every step of the way and continue to bless us with their support. There is no way to thank these people enough, but I know that in God's way, they will be blessed one hundredfold for their kindness. We are also deeply grateful for the skill and caring of *absolutely everyone* at the University of Michigan Health Care System. Thank you to those who read the manuscript and gave me excellent suggestions.

A special thanks to my siblings, Connie and Terry, to Brennan and Rachel for the cover design, to Nancy Grib for her open heart and home, and to Doctors Haft, Romano, Pagani and Aaronson. They are the faces of God.

More than any person, we are grateful for the presence of Spirit in all things and all beings, and the comfort and strength that constant Presence provides for us.

For my part, I thank my darling Peter for having the fortitude and desire to live–to stay here, on this side of the veil, with me.

"Kindness is like a fresh breeze that
relieves the journey of tired souls."
–Mother Teresa

AUTHOR'S NOTE

SINCE MUSIC IS a constant blessing in my life and Pete's, it is not surprising that a number of songs are mentioned in this book. Those that are my own are available for your listening pleasure at <www.forpetessakethebook.com> with the password: <peteandpam>.

The postings and updates in this book are presented as originally written in Pete's CarePages except for some minor editing for continuity, mechanics, readability, brevity and relevance. There were more than 2,000 postings, each one a precious blessing. I include here just a sprinkling to represent all that was written.

A few journal entries were reconstructed from memory and several names have been changed, but most are real and included with permission. In some cases I have noted where postings originated, simply to demonstrate how far flung was our circle of support.

Acknowledging that my memory is not perfect, this is how I remember those thirteen months.

INTRODUCTION

IT HAS BEEN said that the best thing we can do for others is to thrive ourselves, and then be willing to explain or demonstrate by example what it is that we have learned that enables us to do so. One of my favorite John Denver songs has a line that comes back to me often: ". . . And when everybody's watching you, shine so bright!"

I don't think that I was shining or thriving during the events related in this book, but I *did* find reserves of faith, courage, and perseverance that I had not even known were there. Maybe that is what "shining" is. Maybe one of the blessings that will come out of this experience is a demonstration of resilience and the power of prayer–prayers that kept sweeping over us, like an endless warm front moving across the country. I know they made a difference in Pete's healing–that goes without saying–but they also made an immense difference to me. We did not face this challenge alone.

I want to be clear that this book is not about what remarkable things I did and how wonderful, strong and inspiring I am. People sent messages telling me those things, and at the risk of sounding more than a little self-serving, I have included some of those comments in this book. I do so because I want you, dear reader, to understand how powerful it is to lend support and encouragement to people in times of crisis. When friends saw me as courageous and told me so, something inside of me said, "Yes, I *am* courageous. I can do this." It gave me an image that I could step into. It was a catalyst for me to summon up the strength deep inside that was already there, waiting for me to notice it, try it on, and see how it felt. This book reveals the magical circle of love from family, friends and strangers alike that wrapped us in comfort and hope when we most needed it. It also tells about how anyone—yes, even you—can draw on faith, the support of others and the constant presence of God in all things to move through challenges and come out on the other side.

Pete and I have been enormously blessed. We sincerely wish the same for you.

CHAPTER ONE

Love Story

"THERE ARE ONLY two ways to live a life.
One is as though nothing is a miracle.
The other is as though everything
is a miracle."–Albert Einstein

THE AMBULANCE DRIVER, a wiry, dark haired young man with calm, hazel eyes, warned, "Don't try to keep up with us. Too many accidents happen that way." I nodded.

Numb and shaky, I got in my car and slipped onto the road behind the ambulance. The two lanes of M-43 twist and turn like a lazy snake, giving few opportunities for passing. With a truck ahead of me doing the speed limit, I knew it would be about a 50 minute drive to the hospital in Kalamazoo.

At the stoplight on Blue Star Highway, I pulled out my cell phone and quick-dialed Tom, our family doctor. He took care of both of my parents before they passed, and has been my own doctor for a long time. We've shared a great deal over the years and have become deep and lasting friends. I asked him if he would meet me at the hospital for moral support. "I don't want to be there alone," I said. Tom said he was on his way.

Clutching the steering wheel, I willed myself not to cry so I could see the road ahead. *What's happening with Pete's heart? Is he still breathing? Is he going to die?* At that point we had only been married for nine months. We were still riding high on honeymoon hormones. *Is it all going to come crashing down? Will he be taken away from me so soon? We just found each other! What's going through Pete's mind? Uh . . . Is anything going through his mind? I mean . . . is he even conscious?*

I said a prayer . . . a dozen prayers. Then I pleaded: *Please, please, dear God–I have to know. Is he going to make it?* I listened, listened *hard.* And then, with a simple certainty and an undeniable clarity, I knew. Without words, without images, a "knowing" settled down, deep inside of me. He would make it. Dear God, he would make it–but there were some things he would have to go through first.

That's what this book is about.

May 2004

"You will be singing somewhere and there will be a man in the audience who will hear you and fall in love with you through the music. After the performance he will come up to you and tell you how much he loved your music." This message came to me in a reading from Margie Kivel, a trusted friend of mine who is honest and gifted in her work as a psychic medium.

That October I was invited to sing at the Unity Church of Peace in South Bend, Indiana. The music director, Kathy Keasey, "Kat" for short, particularly liked my song, "One."

What if we are one, and there is no one else?
What if what I do to you, I'm doing to myself?
What if we are waves in some big rolling sea,
Grains of sand along the shore,
Part of something that is more than you and me?
What if we are one?

It took me a little over an hour to get to South Bend that Sunday. I remember noticing a handsome man sitting toward the back of the church on the left side.

He closed his eyes when I sang, and I wondered if he were deep in reverie, or if he just hadn't had enough sleep the night before. I sang two of my own songs, "One" and the "Peace Canon" that day, and the congregation clapped enthusiastically.

After the service, he came by my CD table and introduced himself as Pete Wehle (rhymes with "really"). He said that he loved my music, and that he was a singer too. My internal sensors came alive, blinking and beeping to beat the band, but I made every effort to appear nonchalant. He came across as very warm and kindhearted. Tall and athletic-looking, with a little gray at the temples, he resembled Randy Travis a bit, I thought, or no, maybe a mature Kevin Bacon. He took my card, and then he was gone. We had an instant rapport, and I was almost certain I would hear from him. At least I thought I would.

Later, as I was packing up, I heard the choir rehearsing in the sanctuary. They were hammering out Handel's "Hallelujah Chorus," phrase by phrase. Through the closed doorway, I heard one voice that stood out–a strong baritone, absolutely true to pitch, and warm in texture. I thought, *that can't possibly be the guy I talked with, could it?* Slipping into the sanctuary to get my coat, I saw him–Pete Wehle himself, singing his heart out, "Alleluia, Amen, Amen . . ." *Wow.*

❧❧

Pete didn't call me. I waited and waited. Had I misread the signals? Would I ever see him again? Two weeks passed. Nothing.

I had a dream about him: I was by the side of a swimming pool and other people were around, chatting and relaxing. I was watching Peter Wehle from across the pool. He had a kind face, an intelligence and a magnetism that drew me to him.

He didn't know I was watching. He took off his shirt to go into the hot tub, and as he went in I saw that he had "love handles"–a small roll of flesh around the waist. I realized that this was not the perfect body of an Adonis statue, and in a tender way, it endeared him to me even more. He was imperfect, just like me.

❧❧

Early in November I got a call from Kat asking me if I would like to sing at the South Bend church again. "Would I ever!" I said. "By the way, do you happen to have Pete Wehle's phone number? Is he married? Involved?" Kat assured me that Pete was not married and not involved with anyone. She thought he might be interested in dating.

I took a deep breath, and before my courage could evaporate, called him. "Hi. This is Pamela Chappell. I sang at your church a few weeks ago. Remember?"

"Oh, yeah. I remember. How are you?"

"I'm fine, thanks. Um, I am going to be singing at your church again on November the twenty-first, and I was wondering if you would like to have lunch with me after church."

"Sure. That sounds great."

I walked around smiling for days afterwards.

Pete and I had lunch at a little Greek restaurant in South Bend, and right from the start, he opened up his life to me. We talked for a very long time–about his two sons, my two sons, about our work, our childhoods. At one point he said to me, "You know, Pam, music has always been very important to me." Again, my internal sensors came alive–bing-zam-bang! Music is central to my life as well, and always has been, since my first public performance at age 8.

That Sunday was only four days before Thanksgiving. "The holidays are tough for people like us, divorced, with kids. How do you and your ex work that out?" I asked.

"Well, their mother usually has the boys on Thanksgiving Day and Christmas, and then I get them the day after."

"So, what are your plans for Thanksgiving Day this year?"

"I guess I really don't have any plans right now," he said.

"Well . . ." I dragged it out, as if the thought had just occurred to me, "How would you like to have a phenomenal Thanksgiving dinner?"

And so it was decided that Pete would join my family and me for our annual Thanksgiving celebration. For over two decades we have rented a retreat center and gathered for Thanksgiving weekend with ridiculous amounts of pies, turkey, potatoes, brownies, salads, ham . . . and also board games, guitars, newspapers, and stories to tell. Family, of both the immediate and the shirttail variety, come from as far as Kansas, Texas, Georgia, Ontario, and Montana. I live the closest—only about 70 miles away.

So Pete met the family early—my sons, my sister, brother, and their kids, and all the rest of the clan. I'll never forget my niece, Wendy, taking me aside and saying, "He seems like a really great guy . . . but what if he is a Republican?"

From that time on, Pete and I were an item. We talked on the phone daily, often several times, we drove back and forth to each other's homes, and we slipped into love like puzzle pieces. We fit.

That was autumn, 2004. Three years later we were married on the banks of Lake Michigan across the street from our home. Pete had moved in with me the winter before, and we had already settled into our life together in the house where I grew up. I was teaching workshops for teachers and singing and writing music as much as I could. Pete looked for work in Michigan and came across a business opportunity that seemed right for him.

When people asked me how things were going, now that we were married, my answer was always the same: "I think I'm the happiest I have ever been in my life." I was. I had met a man I could love deeply who loved me deeply right back, and I knew we could go the distance together. We laughed a lot, snuggled in front of the TV, watching movies, soaked in the sunsets, and sang together as we rode in the car. We were both on a spiritual path and loved our little Unity Church and its teachings.

Pete was my "roadie" when I had gigs, helping me haul my gear, selling CDs for me, and cheering me on. I went with him to his performances, running the sound system and grinning at him from the side of the room as he belted out Sinatra tunes. One fellow told me he didn't know whether it was more fun watching Pete sing or watching me, watching Pete sing.

Pete and I did a show together with our friend, Elfi, a talented pianist, arranger, and vocalist. It was a cabaret featuring standards from Cole Porter, Irving Berlin and, of course, Sinatra. Another time, we created a show for Valentine's Day, called "Songs in the Key of Love." It was a two-hour program of love songs, moving from the 20's through the 60's. It was really fun performing together, and our audiences loved it.

Pete and I talked often about feeling that God brought us together at just the right time in our lives. Before we met, Pete had gone through a time of depression. He drove for an expedite company then, delivering time-sensitive equipment and supplies all over the country. The hours were long, it didn't pay well, and in the winter the driving could be treacherous. He missed his sons, Paul and Sean, who lived with their mother. He was in a rough place emotionally at that time, feeling lost and unloved.

Pete didn't have cable TV in his mobile home, so, sports fan that he is, he was in the habit of going to the tavern down the road to watch football and baseball games. He tells of the guys he drank with there, always sitting in the same place, always griping about politics or the economy. One fellow would buy him a beer, and he would feel obliged to reciprocate, and on and on it went. Shortly before I met him, he grew concerned that he might be on the road to alcoholism, so he stopped drinking altogether.

As I mentioned, I had been single for a long time, nearly two decades. The workshops I taught were demanding, but sporadic, so I had time to kick back a bit and do some creative work, a wonderful thing after decades of work as a classroom teacher and later as an educational consultant. I was living on Lake Michigan in the house of my childhood, enjoying being on the water and writing and singing songs of my own. I was not wealthy in the way of money, but I had enough to pay my bills and travel a bit. I was very rich in the way of friends and family, though, and had finally found a way to be happy in my life as a single woman. I decided that if I were meant to be on my own for the rest of my life, I could live with that. It always amuses me that it was then that Pete showed up.

After we got married, Pete and I often lay in bed in each other's arms and talked about our purpose together. I remember both of us praying to God to use us. We were so grateful to have each other, we wanted to somehow share the love—to help other people. Little did we know that God would use us in ways we could never have imagined. Be careful what you ask for, they say.

CHAPTER TWO

Spiraling Down

*"BECAUSE OUR INNER guidance is always trying to
take us in the direction of our greatest growth
and development, it will sometimes lead
us right into the challenge that we
were hoping to avoid."*
–Shakti Gawain

ONE DAY IN late spring, just nine
months into our marriage, Pete
mentioned to me that he had been feeling dizzy when he was driving or sitting
at the kitchen table with clients, selling mortgage protection. He was one of the
top sales persons on his team. That evening he had a late appointment, and felt
so dizzy on the way home, he opened the windows and slowed the car down to
a crawl, just to stay on the road. I was in bed reading when he got home. Startled
by his ashen face, I said, "You look terrible!"

"I feel terrible," he replied, "and exhausted." He crawled under the covers
without shedding his clothes.

I checked his forehead for a fever. Finding none, I said, "We are going in to see Tom first thing in the morning and find out what's going on." I had no idea of how sick he was. That was June 3, 2008. Hold on, folks. The ride is about to begin.

I called Tom's office in the morning, and the receptionist said we could come right in. Tom examined Pete, asked some questions, and ordered some blood tests. He speculated that Pete might have a virus, or an allergic reaction to something in our home, but he wanted to see the test results before drawing any conclusions. We went straight from his office to the lab and had Pete's blood drawn.

Back at home an hour and a half later, I was doing dishes and Pete was working in our home office when I had a strong feeling that I needed to check on him. I've learned to trust my gut, so I went around the corner to the office. Pete was lying on his back on the wooden floor, his jeans wet at the crotch, remnants of his half-eaten sandwich scattered around him. Kneeling beside him, I called to him, "Pete! Pete, can you hear me? Pete!" His eyes were open, but he didn't respond at all. *Oh dear God, what's going on? What's happening?*

I continued calling his name, but he did not respond. Then, after a few moments he said, "I'm all right. I'm all right. I need to get these apps out." There were three applications for insurance policies on his desk. He said again that he needed to get them to the post office, but at that point, he didn't even seem to be able to move.

I called 911. *What to do? Unlock the front door. Give him an aspirin. Put a pillow under his head. Get a blanket on him. Uh–what else?* My mind ticked back all the things I had heard it was important to do in the case of a–what? Heart attack? Stroke?

Oh, dear God, is he going to be all right? Maybe he just fainted and I'm overreacting. No, he wouldn't have wet himself if he had just fainted. He's breathing. Thank God, he is breathing. Where are they?

After about ten agonizing minutes, three paramedics arrived. By then, Pete had become a little more coherent. He could answer me, and kept insisting that he was all right, but he needed to get those applications in the mail. Clearly he was not all right.

The paramedics moved very efficiently and with a calmness that was reassuring. One of them asked Pete if he could stand. He thought so, but when he tried, his knees buckled under him. Another one of the paramedics asked me about his medical history. How old is he? Height? Weight? Date of birth? Any history of heart disease? Stroke? High blood pressure? What about in his family? What exactly happened? The paramedic relayed data to someone at the other end of his hand radio. The other two men took Pete's blood pressure and did a quick examination, then lifted him onto a gurney, strapped him on, and wheeled him out the front door.

I grabbed my purse and car keys and stood there on the sidewalk. Cars passed, and people gawked out their windows at the ambulance. Once Pete was inside, I waited for what seemed like an eternity while they settled him in. Finally they left for the South Haven Hospital Emergency Room, and I followed in my car. We live in a small Michigan town, where nothing is more than five minutes away. I was grateful for that.

At the hospital a tall, stocky male nurse took Pete's vitals and the E.R. doctor, examined him. Pete was hooked up to an IV and given an EKG. Within minutes the doctor told me he wanted to have Pete transported to a hospital in Kalamazoo, about 45 miles away, where they have a cardiologist on site 24/7.

I held Pete's hand, and we said the familiar prayer together:

The light of God surrounds us.
The love of God enfolds us.
The power of God protects us.
The presence of God watches over us.
Wherever we are, God is, and all is well.

I followed the ambulance in my car. Pete tells me that the paramedic that rode in back with him showed him the shock paddles and said, "Do not pass out again or I'll have to use these, and you will *not* like it . . ."

Tom arrived in Kalamazoo before I did and met me at the E.R. entrance, giving me a hug and some reassuring words. We were ushered into a room crowded with at least half a dozen people in scrubs, all hovering around Pete's gurney, listening to his heart, filling in charts, adjusting machines, hooking up

IVs. Someone said in grave tones that Pete had lost consciousness again, twice. They asked me the same questions: date of birth, height, weight, family history, what happened, etc. Some of the staff avoided my eyes. I was the wife, and it didn't look good.

The cardiac doctor on duty said that he needed to do a heart catheterization to see if there were any blockages in Pete's heart. He said if necessary, he would put in a stent or perhaps a pacemaker, on the spot.

Tom and I were directed down a long, stark hallway to the waiting room. I was grateful for his calming presence. The doctor had explained that he would be inserting a thin plastic tube into a blood vessel in Pete's leg. Then, guided by X-ray, he would carefully thread the catheter into the coronary arteries and a dye would be injected. That way, he would be able to examine the blood flow to the heart, test how well the heart was pumping and determine if there were any significant blockages. The whole thing seemed like major surgery to me. I didn't know then, that in time a heart catheterization would come to feel routine.

Tom and I made small talk and the clock ticked away the minutes. As I waited, Tom went on a mission to find a sandwich for me. Finally after about two hours, the surgeon came to the doorway and showed us an X-ray. Pete's arteries looked good except for some 30-40% artherosclerosis–plaque buildup–in a few spots, not enough to cause the problem Pete was experiencing or to warrant bypass surgery. The doctor said that a pacemaker would be implanted the next morning. Tom gave me another hug and asked if I was all right. He had an early morning the next day, so I told him I would be okay, and he headed for home.

I followed Pete's gurney as he was brought up in the elevator to the cardiac unit. He was rolled to a spot by the window, hooked up to monitors and tucked in for the night. His new roommate gave me a wave of hello.

Although Pete was alert enough to say a few words, he appeared confused and overwhelmed. I explained to him what had happened, and told him that everything was going to be all right. I think I was trying to convince myself as much as him. "Get some rest," I said, and kissed him. "I'll be right here." He was exhausted, and drifted off right away. I sat down in a chair at the foot of his bed and took a deep breath, thinking I would stay there throughout the night, maybe catch a few winks in the chair. Pete's roommate was soon snoring softly, and the hospital corridors were silent as the clock on the wall approached midnight.

Relieved to know that Pete was in competent hands, I pulled a book out from my bag and settled in for a long night.

Within minutes, a stampede of nurses and technicians charged into the room. One of the nurses yelled at Pete to wake up. She yelled again, and tried shaking him, but he didn't respond. This petite, wide woman with gray hair and kind eyes crossed her hands, one over the other and started pumping on Pete's chest. A crash cart was wheeled in and Pete's roommate was wheeled out. I stood with my mouth wide open, watching the surreal scene. A young ponytailed nurse who looked about fifteen took me gently but firmly by the elbow, leading me out of the room and around the corner to the waiting room. "You wait right here," she insisted. Someone brought me a cup of water and promised they would let me know what was going on when they could.

I spilled the water. My knees felt like they might give way any minute. *This can't be real. It isn't happening to Pete! It isn't happening to me! Should I be calling someone? What if . . . No, I cannot go there. I have to stay positive. I have to believe that he will make it through this. I have been assured, after all. Haven't I?* That old battle of "I believe. Please heal my disbelief," reared up in me.

I sat down and took some deep breaths, trying to calm myself. A frail looking, ancient man sitting on a couch watched with curiosity. He nodded his head and then turned back to his newspaper. I prayed, asking God to heal Pete and to bring me peace and comfort. I waited, picked up a magazine, put it down, paced. After about ten minutes—a million minutes—a thin woman in scrubs came and declared triumphantly, "We brought him back!"

I was stunned. Back from where? I didn't know he had been "gone." Are we talking dead here? Later they told me that they pounded on his chest and massaged his heart for a full five minutes before it started pumping again on its own. In hospital-speak, he had "coded."

I was told that they needed to put in a temporary pacemaker right away so that Pete would make it through the night, and that a permanent one would be implanted in the morning. Eventually they let me go in and see him. He looked dazed and shaken. In moments, he was whisked back down to surgery.

A kindly, tall man was introduced to me as the chaplain. He was about 50, gray-haired, looking like Mr. Rogers in his buttoned-up sweater. "Would you like some company?" he asked. I wondered what his life must be like, hanging around the hospital through the long nights, waiting to see if someone might "need company." He came with me to the now-familiar waiting room on the first floor. We sat on the sofa and chatted a bit. I shared with him the Prayer for Protection created by James Dillet Freeman. We say it in our church every Sunday at the close of the service:

The light of God surrounds us.
The love of God enfolds us.
The power of God protects us.
The presence of God watches over us.
Wherever we are, God is, and all is well.

He asked me to teach it to him, so I wrote it out on a napkin for him. He was kind. I was numb. I told him I was doing all right, and thanked him. I just wanted to sit, meditate, and wait. He seemed to understand, and left. There was no one to call that late at night. I asked Spirit to be with me. I was okay. Was Pete?

After the surgery, Pete was returned to his room heavily sedated. I sat with him for a couple of hours, watching every breath, every rise of his chest. Finally I realized I was exhausted, so I grabbed an extra pillow and a blanket and went back down the hall to the waiting room. The two couches there were occupied by others trying to sleep, so I lay down on the floor and tried to sleep. Every hour or so I walked the dark, quiet halls back to Pete's room to see for myself that he was okay. It was a long night, but he kept on breathing.

The next morning we met Dr. Abel (not his real name), who would be putting in the pacemaker. He was an upbeat, rather cocky seeming guy with a Hawaiian print shirt and a cheeky sense of humor. He assured us that he had done thousands of these procedures and that there was nothing to worry about. Again, Pete was wheeled out of his room, and I returned to the waiting room. The pacemaker was implanted without any complications, and two days later Pete was discharged.

Both of us were more than a little nervous. In the hospital there were always well-established procedures, emergency equipment and someone there with answers to our questions. At home–well–it would be just us. I hoped that I was up to the task at hand. I have taken on a great deal of responsibility in various situations over the years, but–responsible for my husband's life? That was something else, altogether.

E-mail, Tuesday, June 10, 2008

Hi Kat,

Just thought you might want to know that Pete had a "cardiac incident" Wednesday night. His heart stopped beating. We were at a hospital in Kalamazoo by the time that happened (It's a long story.) and they were wonderful. Pete is now the proud owner of a pacemaker and is resting and recovering. We are both incredibly grateful to be alive!

Love,

Pam

E-mail Reply, Tuesday, June 10, 2008

Pam and Pete,

What a shocker! I am so glad that Pete is all right! I want to hear about it. Wow . . . it must have been a sudden thing. Thank God he's got you. I am praying that "the beat goes on." Please take care, you two.

Love,

Kat

E-mail, Thursday, June 12, 2008

Thanks, Kathy. We had a follow-up appointment today. The doctor is concerned about congestive heart failure. Pete has some fluid in his lungs. Looks like he will have to go in for another heart catheterization next Wednesday to see if they can figure out the source of the problem. The doc said it's possible they may have to put in a stent—but maybe not.

It's a difficult time for us, not really knowing what is going on or what we can expect in the near and distant future. Please continue to hold us in your prayers. Could you let Christine know about this for us? I don't have her e-address. Thanks so much.

I am having a few health challenges of my own. Will have a CT scan tomorrow. With me it's not as serious an issue—perhaps some asthma. Don't know yet. Will try to keep you posted.

Much love,

Pam

E-mail Reply, Thursday, June 12, 2008

Pam—

I'm so sorry for these health challenges you and Pete are undergoing. I know you both are receiving the right and perfect care and that all is well. Pete will be fine. He's strong and still young. You can both weather this. You have my prayers and love. God bless you.

Love,

Kat

E-mail Reply, Monday, June 16, 2008

Kat—

We're sort of planning one day at a time these days . . . Pete is still wiped out from the pacemaker surgery on June 5th. I guess it would be wise for you to see if you can get someone else to sing at church on the twenty-second. (Sigh—I hate to do this to you!) I just won't leave him alone for that long, and I don't know if he'll be up to traveling at that point. Please forgive me—I know you will—and I hope you won't have a hard time finding a replacement for me.

Warmly,

Pamela

In the days following the pacemaker surgery, Pete was still weak. He napped a lot, but he got up, showered, and dressed each day. We went for short walks across the street to sit on the bench overlooking the lake. It was June, and South Haven was bursting with late spring energy. It was good to be home.

One morning Pete and I went to the Shoreline Wellness Center where we used to work out several times a week. Pete made it only part way around the track, though. I took him home and he went straight to bed.

A few days later he rolled the dumpster to the curb for garbage pickup and found himself totally exhausted afterwards. I assumed that it would just take a while for him to get his strength and energy back, but he wasn't so sure that was all it was. He coughed–a lot. "Something's not right," he said.

I wasn't feeling well myself. A particularly nasty bout of bronchitis I had in May kept hanging on. My lungs felt inflamed, I had a cough, and was tired all the time. Tom ordered a pulmonary function test for me in mid-May, which had come out normal. When I went to Virginia for a songwriters' gathering the next week I still felt lousy, but I didn't want to miss the event, which had always been a great time of fellowship, inspiration and creativity for me. Part way through the week in Virginia I started feeling better. I thanked my songwriter buddies for singing me back to health.

By the time I came home at the end of May, I was back to normal. Within days, though, the symptoms returned: cough, fatigue and inflammation in the chest. I went in for a stress test, and again, it came back normal. That night Pete and I were watching TV. My chest felt like it was burning up. I was really tired and just, well, sick. I called my best friend, Nancy Lou, aka "Nurse Nancy," and told her what was going on with me. "Should I go to the emergency room?" I asked. She said that in her experience, if someone is wondering whether they should go to the emergency room, they probably should go to the emergency room. I felt kind of silly–What if it's nothing? I don't want to be a hypochondriac . . . but what if it's a heart attack? I know the symptoms can be different for women. What the hell are they?

I googled:

Chest discomfort or pain–Yes

Upper body pain–Well, yeah, that's where my chest is.

Stomach pain–No

Shortness of breath–Yes, when I'm on the treadmill

Anxiety for no apparent reason–Anxiety yes, but you could say I have reason

Lightheadedness–No

Sweating–Yes, but, hey, I'm post-menopausal. It's a way of life.

Nausea and vomiting–No

Abdominal pain or "heartburn"–Yes, but I have acid reflux. It's a way of life too.

Unusual or unexplained fatigue–Yes

Neck, jaw, shoulder, upper back or abdominal discomfort–No

Pete drove me to the emergency room. My EKG and vitals were normal. The doctor suspected that something was going on with my heart, but all the tests showed nothing out of the ordinary. I went home feeling a little sheepish, but at the same time, I knew something was wrong.

You know, I always thought that spouses should take care of each other when they are sick. So, what happens when both of them are sick? I guess the less sick one takes care of the more sick one as much as possible. For better or worse . . . Things were going to get worse.

❦❦

The day after Father's Day I was fixing lunch when I had a call from my allergist with the results from the CT scan he had ordered. He said that the scan showed "fibrous tissue throughout the lung area." I asked him what that meant, and he said that he couldn't be sure, but it looked like pulmonary fibrosis to him. He suggested that I see a pulmonologist to look into the matter.

I remember standing at the kitchen counter, scrawling "pulmonary fibrosis" on a scrap of paper. What was that? I had a vague memory . . . I went to my computer and googled it. This is what I found on the National Institutes of Health (NIH) site:

Pulmonary fibrosis (PULL-mun-ary fi-BRO-sis) is a condition in which tissue deep in your lungs becomes thick and stiff, or scarred, over time. The development of the scarred tissue is called fibrosis.

As the lung tissue becomes thicker, your lungs lose their ability to move oxygen into your bloodstream. As a result, your brain and other organs don't get the oxygen they need . . .

. . . (Ideopathic Pulmonary Fibrosis) is a serious condition. About 200,000 Americans have it. About 50,000 new cases are diagnosed each year. IPF mostly affects people who are 50 to 75 years of age.

IPF varies from person to person. In some people, the lung tissue quickly becomes thick and stiff. In others, the process is much slower. In some people, the condition stays the same for years.

IPF has no cure yet. Many people live only about 3 to 5 years after diagnosis.

And from the Coalition for Pulmonary Fibrosis site:

Sometimes pulmonary fibrosis can be linked to a particular cause, such as certain environmental exposures, chemotherapy or radiation therapy, residual infection, or autoimmune diseases such as scleroderma or rheumatoid arthritis. However, in many instances, no known cause can be established. When this is the case, it is called idiopathic pulmonary fibrosis or IPF.

All that sank in was "three to five years." *Oh my. Three to five years.* Other sites said the same thing. *Three to five years. There are too many things I still want to do! What about Pete? Who will look after him? Oh Great God in Heaven, three to five years? This can't be. We're just getting started in our life together!*

The thought of being terminally ill was too big for me to wrap my head around. I felt okay except for the fatigue and the inflammation in my chest. Life kept right on happening. The clock kept right on ticking. Nothing had changed–except–everything.

The day after that phone call I had a gig with the South Haven Historical Association. Andru Bemis, Jim Hughey and I shared songs and stories about growing up in South Haven. We had a standing-room-only crowd, and I remember the absolute joy I felt in singing for people. My heart opened and the music flowed out like a beautiful ribbon, as it always does. I was in my zone and loving it. The audience loved it too, but I left wondering, how much longer will I be able to sing? How much longer will I be here?

"On the surface, life can often seem tumultuous and incomprehensible. Yet deep inside, where it truly matters, life is the way you see it and becomes what you choose to make it."
–Ralph Marston

Dear God,

Thank You for this magnificent body temple.

Thank You for its wondrous systems and structures that support my life and allow me to see, hear, breathe, move, touch and feel.

I bless each organ, cell and sinew with loving thoughts and healthy habits.

I bless my entire body and its many interconnected parts.

Thank You for this amazing container that allows me to experience and express life in this realm.

Amen

(Source Unknown)

A word or two or a hundred about death–Ask anyone what is the worst possible outcome in a given grave (no pun intended) situation, and they will often say, "Well, I could die." There is an unspoken agreement in our culture that death is a terrible, tragic thing, the worst thing that could happen to a person. I don't agree with that anymore.

Spiritualists and students of Unity usually avoid using the word "death." Instead, we speak of a person passing, or making his or her transition. We don't really believe in death. We believe that our soul and spirit never die. We just leave our bodies.

Neale Donald Walsch has a beautiful take on this:

> *"On the day you leave your body–what I like to call your Continuation Day–you will be greeted by everyone you have ever loved in any way for any reason . . . and, standing in front of the group, every person who has been so very dear to you. It will be a grand and glorious reunion, with joy and laughter and pure wonderment filling every heart and soul!"*

(From Daily Inspiration Message–See Resources)

Sounds good to me. Still, I'm not in any hurry. Faced with the possibility that I might die within three to five years, I have some thinking to do. If I only have a finite chunk of time (and don't we all?) how do I want to use that time?

I've always wanted to touch people's lives in a positive way. That's why I went into teaching so many years ago. And when people tell me that a song I've written has struck a chord deep within them, I am thrilled. It's part of why I'm here, I think. Or maybe I *want* that to be part of the reason I'm here. And is there a difference?

Pete has always wanted to help people too. We've often talked deep into the night about how we might do that. Although his insurance business does provide a measure of security for his clients, it doesn't fill his pressing drive to serve.

Then I got the call about pulmonary fibrosis, and suddenly there is a much greater urgency. My Canadian friend, Wendy Walsh, had the same thing. Wendy–effervescent, loving, full of laughter and music–she was a dynamo. Eventually she had a lung transplant, but it didn't take. She passed a couple of years ago. I wonder if both Pete and I might check out early too, and if so, what the time we have left will be like. I realize now that I might not have tons of time to do what I want to do, what I am here to do. I'd better get moving.

E-mail, Tuesday, June 24, 2008

Hi Kat and Christine,

Just wanted to update you on what is happening with Pete. Yesterday he was scheduled for a pulmonary function test and some X-rays. When the technician saw the results, he immediately sent Pete across the street to the cardiologist's office. Dr. Abel had him admitted to the hospital on the spot. Pete was coughing a lot, and the fluid in his lungs had increased, rather than decreased since his surgery. He was short of breath and very, very tired.

This morning the doc did another heart catheterization. He says that the heart is weak and very stiff, and that he'd never seen anything like that. He told me that he was going to sock Pete with a heavy-duty IV diuretic to help get rid of the fluid in his lungs quickly, and some other medication to help improve the heart's efficiency. He expects Pete to recover and be able to function well, but said that it may take a while.

In the meantime, I have a possible diagnosis of pulmonary fibrosis. Sometimes it burns when I breathe, and I tire easily. Pete and I are a fine pair!

At any rate, we trust in our bodies' capacities for healing. Thank you for holding us in your prayers, "holding the high watch," as my friend Nancy Lou says. We hope to see you both soon, and do so in magnificent health!

Namaste,

Pam

Return E-mail, Tuesday, June 24, 2008

Hello Pam, and thank you for the update on *both* you and Pete . . . The grace in all of this, of course, is your love for one another and the perspectives and lessons you both are able to bring from your spiritual work.

I've heard it said that those of us walking the Path in a very conscious way are partly working out our own karmic debts and partly taking on (working through vicariously) the negativity in the world around us. The notion is that if we can achieve personal balance and replace fear with faith within ourselves, then the entire web of universal life is stronger for it. Our inner work affects the outer world around us in profound and myriad ways . . .

Blessings, blessings and so much grace to you!

Christine Fiordalis

Without our spiritual grounding, I think Pete and I would have been leaves blowing in the wind. With it, it was still difficult, but there was hope; there was something solid to stand on.

We had already spent a few heart-wrenching days in the hospital when Pete was moved from his room to the ICU. He was having frequent episodes of very high heart beat. One day, Nancy O'Donohue, a dear friend, healer, and prayer chaplain from our church paid a visit. True to her 100% Irish heritage, Nancy has beautiful red hair and flashing green eyes. She studied for years with a Native American medicine man, and is steeped in that tradition, as well as in other healing modalities. She is also a very wise and compassionate woman. I clung to her in a hug that went on for a long time. She prayed with us and we chatted for a while, and then she offered to do some energy work on both of us.

While she was working with Pete, I lay back in a nearby recliner, short of breath and feeling that familiar burning sensation in my chest with each inhalation. My left ankle that I had broken in November was swollen and aching. I needed rest.

After she finished with Pete, Nancy came and did some energy work with me. Without touching, she held her hands a couple of inches away from my body, staying at one spot for a few minutes and then moving on. Her calm, loving presence was soothing and I felt a great sense of peace wash over me. From my own training in therapeutic touch and Reiki, I knew what she was doing, and I welcomed the healing that was taking place. She told me to envision golden roots extending from my feet deep into Mother Earth from whom I could draw strength, and let all pain and worry drain out and sink deep into the soil. I've thought of that image hundreds of times since. My anxiety and fear began to dissolve, minute by minute.

After Nancy left I had another wonderful image. With my eyes closed, I saw two or three dozen tiny angels flying around me, bringing healing and peacefulness. They reminded me of little Tinkerbells, encircling my ankle and flying in close orbits around my entire body.

After a while, though, I started to slip into monkey-mind. *What if I really do have pulmonary fibrosis? Will I not be able to breathe? Will I have to go on oxygen? How will I take care of Pete? Blah. Blah. Blah.*

Suddenly the angelic image in my mind changed. I saw a black cloud approaching the tiny spirits. The little angels stopped what they were doing and said, "*No, no, no! We can't do our work with you here! Shoo! Shoo!*"

It was funny—and perfectly clear. I got it. If I want healing, I have to keep my thoughts focused on healing and wholeness, not disease and fear. It was a powerful image, and I was grateful that it showed up.

I told this story to my dear niece, Wendy, and she sent up to me a little stickpin of Tinkerbell. I wore it every day for months.

❧❧

When I look back on those four days at the hospital in Kalamazoo, it's just a blur. I remember Pete being readmitted on a Monday, and Dr. Abel telling me that he was going to give Pete some strong diuretics. A nurse tried eight times before she could get an IV in. Apparently Pete's veins are very small.

I guess the IV diuretics were strong all right, because before we knew it, Pete was suffering from severe dehydration, and his electrolytes were going crazy. There was a flurry of activity, a change in medications, and then–Zingo!–his lungs filled up again. He was in **congestive heart failure**. They had pulled him off too fast, and he was crashing from the overload. He must have felt like a ping pong ball, going from one extreme to another. His lungs were so congested that he coughed–big hacking coughs nonstop for hours. I kept asking, "Isn't there something we can do?"

Nancy Lou came up to give me moral support. Her take was that Pete's body couldn't handle all that they had put him through. His lungs were not responding well and his labs were off. They simply could not stabilize him. I remember Nancy looking at the nurse on duty, who just looked back, shaking her head as if to say, "Not good. Not good." Nancy finally got Pete sitting up on the side of the bed and draped over forward on the tray table. This opened his lungs a little, and the coughing let up for a while. He was so weak, though, he couldn't sit up for very long.

Dr. Abel came and went; a pulmonologist came and went. They said little and did nothing, as far as I could tell. By Wednesday he was so sick I began preparing myself for the worst. He told me later that he had what seemed to be a near death experience. He felt the presence of his parents and his grandparents, all of whom passed a long time ago. He described a feeling of serenity, comfort, and beauty, but his loved ones told him that he had to go back, that it wasn't his time yet.

Shocked back into this world, he lay in his hospital bed forlorn and fragile. He was having trouble breathing and talking. I held his hand and prayed. It seemed like the doctors had just given up on him

---

Hospital Speak 101

Congestive heart failure occurs when the heart can't pump enough blood to the rest of the body's organs. The heart keeps pumping, but it doesn't work efficiently, making the person short of breath and fatigued.

Pete remembers . . .

They were trying to take the fluid off my lungs with medication. It wasn't working. I remember thinking that if my time is up, my time is up.

I also remember a time when I had this feeling of love and unlimited acceptance. I felt the presence of something–Spirit or something–that was taking care of me, being with me–wouldn't let anything bad happen to me. I was told not to worry, that I had to go through some things.

I felt a bright light surrounding me. I had the feeling of my parents–images of them in the shadows, watching me. I felt loved. My grandparents–they were there. Archangel Michael was there–big wings.

They said, "You will be all right, but you have to go through some things. You may not be taken care of here, but someplace else. You have to stay and recover. It may be a long struggle, but you'll get through it."

I said, "Okay, I'll do what I have to do," and I just went back to sleep.

❧ ❧

There were many phone calls flying back and forth that week. I talked with my brother, Terry, who is a doctor, with Tom and with two other doctors I knew. They all said the same thing–that I should have Pete transferred to the University of Michigan Hospital in Ann Arbor.

I was worried about bringing this up to Dr. Abel because I didn't want to offend him or to imply that we were unhappy with his work, but when he came in yesterday I sucked up my courage and told him what the four doctors had said. His immediate reply was, "I absolutely agree with them. I'll go do the paper work." And he was gone.

It seemed to me that Abel was in over his head, that he had no idea of what to do with Pete. A short time later, a nurse told us that Pete would be airlifted within two hours. That was Thursday afternoon, but, unfavorable weather intervened, making a helicopter flight inadvisable, so we waited. And waited.

Nancy Lou said to the nurse, "What's wrong with his heart?"

The nurse shrugged and whispered, "I gotta tell ya, it's just simply fucked up. I just don't know. They're in over their heads. They aren't giving him a diagnosis. I have to tell you the truth–I'm not sure he's going to get to Ann Arbor if he stays here much longer."

E-mail, Friday, June 27, 2008

To Friends and Family

In a rush—

We're waiting for a chopper ambulance to transport Pete from Kalamazoo to U. of M. Hospital in Ann Arbor. He is extremely ill and fragile. We almost lost him twice. Please send loving energy, prayers, whatever you can. He is worn out from pneumonia and his heart muscle is weak. It's touch and go every moment.

Please—hold us in the light.

Love,

Pam

CHAPTER THREE

Swimming Upstream

*"Life's most difficult moments teach us that we're
stronger than we know. It always
pays to remember that."*
–Ralph Marston

WE WAITED ALL of Thursday afternoon and all that night, because of the weather. Finally, on Friday afternoon we were taken by land ambulance from Kalamazoo to Ann Arbor. There were no sirens, no flashing lights, no speeding, and I was able to ride up front in the ambulance with the driver. Nancy Lou followed the ambulance in my car.

There was a small window behind me that allowed me to catch a glimpse of the back of Pete's head as two emergency technicians hovered over him. Todd, the driver, was very good at small talk, distracting me from the drama of the moment. I was grateful to him and joined in the chat for a few minutes. Then I turned to him and said, "Okay, I'm going to cry now." And I did. I pulled out the cork and let loose. It was about a two hour drive to Ann Arbor, and by the time we got to the hospital, I was pretty much cried out.

Nancy Lou, who had appointed herself my personal nurse, stayed with me for several days, reminding me to rest, to put up my feet, to eat. I was grateful for the gentle, loving care. I felt empty and spent.

E-mail, Saturday, June 28, 2008
Dearest Pam,

I just got home and read both of your e-mails. I am beyond distraught. Of course I will keep both of you in the light and am sending all the energy I can. You are both surrounded by so much love! I await better news and my heart is with you every second.
With deepest love,
Ellen Reinstattler

E-mail, Saturday, June 28, 2008
Oh, Dear Pamela . . .

I just received the news of your and Pete's illnesses. I am so, so sorry and send you uninterrupted prayers and pleadings for healing and good health. Your amazing spirit of strength and faith will see you through this time. I *know* it! May you be strong and resolute, believing that our prayers will be answered!

Pamela, I believe in you and send you my love and prayers with every breath.
Annette Covatta

Monday, June 29, 2008
Journal

It's really strange that Pete and I are both sick now. I wonder if there is something toxic in our house. That would explain a lot. I was awfully sick in May, and then got better when I was in Virginia, only to get sick again when I came home. And Pete was in great shape, or so we thought, before he collapsed. Could it be mold? I know mold can do horrible things, and our basement has always been musty-smelling. We probably should have it tested. And then there is the cat dander. I'm allergic to it, and I suspect that Pete may be as well. We really need to have that cleaned up. Sigh . . .

From the e-blast of Unity Church on the Lakeshore, Monday, June 30, 2008:

Pam Chappell and Pete Wehle are very grateful for the support and prayers you have offered on their behalf. Pete has been transferred to U. of M. Hospital in Ann Arbor; his condition has stabilized but there is still no diagnosis. Last week they asked for good homes for their two cats due to their allergies. One cat has found a home; they still need a home for the other, a wonderful indoor/ outdoor cat, litterbox trained, good with children, and a faithful companion. For more information, please contact Pam. No visitors at this time, please.

E-mail, Tuesday, June 30, 2008

Chica . . .

I researched mold and allergy stuff a bit. I think you should have a mold and pollen count and air monitoring with lab interpretations. There are companies that do this and also the cleaning, etc. I'll attach some phone numbers. Let me know If you want me to make the calls. Possibly your insurance would cover it . . .

Love you,

Mary James

E-mail Reply, Tuesday, July 1, 2008

Mary—

Thanks a million! I'll make some calls this morning. Pete is up and down. Will learn more today. Yesterday was a bit discouraging. Must run.

Love,

Pam

E-mail, Wednesday, July 2, 2008

To Friends and Family—

We've now been here at the U. of M. Hospital for six days. Pete is still very, very sick. The doctors here are amazing, though, and through a zillion tests seem to be zeroing in on what is going on. The current theory is **sarcoidosis**—an inflammation of the heart and/or lungs.

My sister, Connie, and I are staying at a Red Roof Inn nearby, and going in to the hospital for about 12 hours each day. Pete is trying to think positively, but he struggles with that—worries about finances, about the prognosis, etc. We are grateful for every day he is still alive. He's in good hands here.

Thanks for your continued prayers. Each one matters.

Love,

Pam

Hospital Speak 101

Sarcoidosis is a disease that causes one or more organs of the body to become inflamed. After an infection of some sort, some of the immune system cells remain and form lumps called granulomas in the affected organ(s). Sarcoidosis usually starts in the lungs, skin, and/or lymph nodes. It is not very common in the heart, and can become very serious there, affecting the function of the organ.

Some people live many years with sarcoidosis, but in others, it causes organ damage and sometimes, although rarely, death, especially if it affects the heart or brain.

Connie remembers...

I remember the way my dear sister clung to a Mexican shawl, clutching it to her chest. She wasn't well. She couldn't even make it from the parking lot up to Pete's room without stopping to take a rest.

Pam wrote down everything the doctors said in a little spiral notebook. As sick as she was, she was driven to take charge of whatever she could. She called Terry and asked for his opinions. I could tell she took her role as patient advocate very seriously.

Pete was in rough shape. He didn't talk much at all. I looked at his heart monitor at the nurse's station, and it was so erratic, it scared me. I didn't think he was going to make it. He talked to Pam about where his insurance papers were. I remember him staring out the window, tears streaming down his cheeks.

Wednesday, July 2, 2008

Journal

Everyone urges me to take care of myself, but like so many other caregivers, I find it really challenging to do so. The days at the hospital are long and tiring, especially emotionally. My body needs an escape from the stress–but there's fat chance of that, so I try to get adequate rest. When sleep won't come, I just try to relax into the quiet of night. I meditate, but often my mind is so jumbled, I don't feel very successful at it. A friend once told me that when we find it very difficult to meditate, often that is when it is the most beneficial. If that's so, then I should be getting *great* benefits.

I am worried about my lungs. The burning is always there, and it makes me so tired! When Pete sleeps, sometimes I lay down on the recliner in his room and cover myself with an extra blanket. Of course, hospitals are the worst place in the world to try to sleep. There's so much traffic–food trays, vitals checked, housekeeping, rounds, meds, etc.

E-mail, Wednesday, July 2, 2008

Pam,

I am checking in to see how you and your hubby are doing. You continue to be in my thoughts. Happy 4th of July!

Diane Freestone

E-mail Reply, Thursday, July 3, 2008

Thanks so much for your kind words, Diane. We have been here at U. of M. Hospital since Friday. Pete is very weak and fragile. He will probably have his one-month-old pacemaker replaced with a different one today. His heartbeat is very irregular, sometimes dangerously so. He hasn't eaten much of anything in five days.

In short, we continue to need all the prayers we can get. Thank you so much for that. We've had a wonderful outpouring of love and prayers. It's really a comfort. As for me, yesterday was a good day—no pain with breathing. I've kind of put my own health issues on the shelf for now. I can't get in to see a pulmonologist until July 31st anyway. I just try to get enough sleep. My sister is here now. She'll be going home for the 4th.

Thanks for your concern Diane. I know you've been through your own trials and you understand.

Much love,

Pam

E-mail, Thursday, July 3, 2008

Dear Pam,

Just wanted you to know that much love and healing energy is coming your way. Please give Pete our love and let him know that he has many who are supporting him. I'm being told to tell him that it is time for him to "turn his boat around and begin the rest of his journey flowing downstream."

Much love to you both,

Claudia Mierau

Thursday, July 3, 2008

Journal

Claudia Mierau is a dear friend. Through her gentle wisdom and instruction I became a Reiki Master several years ago. In the previous e-mail, she was referring to a discussion we had once about the concept of "upstream/downstream," as taught by Abraham. Abraham is a group of nonphysical entities of great wisdom channeled by Esther Hicks. Abraham's teachings have been shared in workshops around the globe and in many books, CDs and videos.

This is my understanding of what Claudia was referring to when she suggested that Pete flow downstream:

There is a constant stream of well-being for everyone. Source is always there, willing and eager to give to us what we desire. When we feel excited and full of expectation, it is like a powerful river flowing downstream. It seems that if we would just stick our big toe into the water, the current would sweep us up and carry us downstream toward whatever it is that we want.

However, most people take their boats down to the river, point them upstream, and begin paddling very hard, because we have been taught since childhood that good things only come after hard work and struggle. It seems lazy to us to just go with the flow. It's too easy, so it can't be right.

Abraham teaches that nothing we want is upstream, and that everything we want is downstream. When we truly understand this, and that the Source energy within us is down there, tending what we are wanting, we let go of the oars.

So here is the key lesson: Trust the process. Trust the stream. Let go of the oars. Let go of resistance and go with the flow. Not going with the flow of life is what is at the heart of all negative emotions. Make peace with where you are.

Same day, later . . .

Every day I bring to the hospital a beautiful hand-woven shawl that my son Brennan and his wife, Rachel, gave me after a trip they made to Mexico. Lying back in the recliner, I fold the shawl up and hold it against my chest. It hurts less if I keep my chest warm. That's odd. If my lungs are inflamed, why does it feel better when I keep my chest warm? I don't know, but it does. I get very tired when my chest hurts, which is most of the time now.

Even with Pete so sick and me feeling lousy, I realize that I'm stronger than I thought I was. I used to wonder how people got through things like this. Now I know. We draw from deep, deep down inside. We keep moving when we're tired and depleted. We refuse to give up. We lean on the kindness of friends. We sink into the awareness that God is in charge. We keep going. There is no making sense of it. There is no room for wondering why. We just keep going.

Same day, later . . .

It is a miracle, you know—being alive. I think of when Brennan and Phil were babies. Like all parents of little ones, we had to watch them every waking moment to protect them from harm. It seemed that there were so many things that could go wrong, it was a miracle that anybody survived childhood. And somehow they survived, most of them.

When he was a teenager, my younger son, Phil, went through a terrible (as *I* saw it) journey with drugs. He was in and out of juvenile homes and rehab for several years, during which time seven of his close friends died. There were different reasons—car accidents, a drowning, fire, suicide. Those young people were all fragile, and living on the edge. I know in my heart that if I hadn't put Phil into rehab he would have been in one of those deadly cars. But he wasn't. He survived.

And now, here we are, and Pete is hanging on to the edge of life with gritty fingernails. His will to live is ferocious, even though his body is so frail. His own father died when Pete was only 18, and he does not want to do that to his own sons.

I think he really wants to live for me too. I know he does. Our life together has given new meaning to both of us. I hope he means to live for himself, too–for all the loving, generous things he will do, the songs he will sing to delighted faces, the people he will help, and the grandchildren he will hold in his arms.

There is more, of course, on the other side. More love, more joy, more peace–but while we are here, in this incredible physical experience, we might as well squeeze every drop out of it, right? Even the drops of pain, the drops of fatigue and worry. It's all life, here on the earth plane. It's all life.

Looking back, much later–a daily message from Neale Donald Walsch:

On this day of your life, Pamela, I believe God wants you to know . . . that life will resolve itself in the process of life itself. Let the moment play itself out. Try to not push the river.

Life knows what It has in mind. Trust Life. It is on your side.

Do you know how I know? You are still here. How much more proof do you need?

Love, Your Friend . . .

Neale Donald Walsch

(Daily Inspirational Message–See Resources)

Same day, still later . . .

Pete is in a double room. His roommate, a very chatty, morbidly obese young man, is waiting for a hip replacement. Today Pete had just finished eating a little breakfast, and I was there, reading a piece from the newspaper to him. The other fellow in the room was watching CNN on the TV. A middle-aged woman with short brown hair, friendly eyes, and a competent manner came in and introduced herself as Ruth Halben, the social worker who worked with cardiac patients and their families. I liked her right away, and would come enjoy her sense of humor and trust her judgement.

"I'm here to explain the procedures for evaluating patients for heart transplants and to answer any questions you might have." She must have seen our eyes open wide and our jaws drop. "No one has mentioned the possibility of a heart transplant to you?"

"Uh–no." I said.

"I hate it when they do this to me," she sighed, and sat down.

I took a deep breath and asked, "Are they considering a heart transplant for Pete?"

"Yes," she said. "It looks like that is the direction they are heading. They have tried to treat him with medicine, but his heart is too damaged."

Pete lay there, stunned. I felt a little dizzy myself.

Ruth told us that Pete would have to undergo a number of tests to see if he was eligible to be placed on the heart transplant list. If he qualified, then . . .

I don't know how much I absorbed from what she was saying. My mind was racing through all the ramifications, all the concerns. I shook my head in disbelief and tried to keep breathing. I watched Pete as Ruth was talking, and tried to read his response, but his face was blank. I wondered how much he was taking in.

Ruth had us sign some papers and left us with a pile of pamphlets and information sheets. She said we could call her any time if we had questions. After she left, Pete and I looked at each other for a long time without speaking. Then one of us–I forget which one–said, "Wow!"

Pete remembers . . .

I was stunned.

Well, wait a minute–They're thinking about taking my heart out and putting someone else's in? That means . . . someone else has to die in order for me to live.

It felt very sad, but at that point I didn't have a whole lot of control of the situation. I could have said no, but I knew they wouldn't have recommended a heart transplant if it wasn't necessary. The docs told me the prognosis was good–I was relatively young for the procedure and the tests that had come back so far were encouraging.

Still . . .

Same day, much later . . .

I can thank my son Phil for helping me develop coping skills. One of the great lessons that became real to me in the throes of his drug use was to accept what is. I didn't have to like it, endorse it, or ignore it. It didn't mean I wouldn't do what I could to change it. It was simply a matter of acknowledging what was happening, rather than resisting it, with hand clenched, screaming at the heavens.

Pete needs a heart transplant. And so it is.

Same day, still later . . .

When she dropped the bomb about the possibility of a heart transplant, Ruth Halben mentioned that I am now eligible to stay at the Transplant House. Family members of transplant patients, including those being considered for a transplant, can stay at the house, which is supported by the Friends of the Hospital. It's only a few blocks away and it costs a fraction of what I was paying at the Red Roof Inn–a Godsend. I moved in today. The Universe provides.

Years ago in a deep meditation I was given the message that I would never experience severe poverty in this lifetime. I have come to believe that. Sometimes I wonder if the messages I get in meditation are just wishful thinking or the products of my imagination–but then, where do the thoughts of our imaginations come from? All I know is that we needed help and it has shown up. All is well.

Same day, much, much later . . .
Suggestions for Stress Relief:

Imagery
Deep breathing
Relaxation
Meditation
Yoga
Tai Chi
Simplify
Pace myself
Rest

Pray

Trust

E-mail, Friday, July 4, 2008

To Friends and Family

Dear Ones,

My husband, Pete, is now in ICU at the U. of M. Hospital. We've been here a week. Pete's heartbeat is very irregular. There has been talk of a heart transplant, but we are all hoping it won't be necessary. For now, he is resting—and we are on the schedule for a replacement pacemaker and a heart ablation on Thursday. As I understand it, a catheter will be inserted into the heart to provide a sort of electric map, indicating what areas are causing Pete's irregular heart beats. Then those pathways will be disconnected, hopefully resulting in a more steady beat.

We are immensely grateful for the loving thoughts and prayers that have come our way. Please keep 'em coming, and maybe even step 'em up a notch. Thank you!

This is the prayer I am asking folks to pray:

Thank you God for healing Pete's heart and lungs.

We are grateful for Pete's whole and healthy spirit.

Thank you for keeping Pamela healthy and strong.

We affirm that this is already done, and all is well.

And so it is.

Thanks so much for your concern. We are managing.

Love,

Pam

Sunday, July 6, 2008

Journal

It's been a wild ride for more than a month now. I'm glad we are here at this hospital, though. Pete's getting excellent care. I slept last night until a little after three. Suddenly I was wide awake and unable to get back to sleep. So many things to think about . . . so hard to empty the mind.

I'm back at the hospital now, and Pete is sleeping. The nurse brought in an extra tray table so I could work on my computer. Writing gives me something to do. I have Enya playing softly. All is well for the moment. This moment. This precious moment. Sometimes I feel like I'm waiting for the other shoe to drop—but all is well now, for the moment. After all, now is all we have, right?

E-mail, Monday, July 7, 2008

Brennan, (Son in Montana)

Yesterday was tough. Pete's liver function was in trouble and his heart failure was getting worse. The doctor changed his plan of action. An intraaortic balloon pump was put in to help increase the heart's output. The pump will probably be in for a few days. It's a "bridge" to the next therapy—which will most likely be a left ventricular assist device. That's an implant that does the work of the heart until a heart is available for transplant. It looks like we will be here for three more weeks at least.

Whew! We are pretty overwhelmed by the whole situation. Our faith is strong, though, and is sustaining us. Your Uncle Terry was here yesterday. His presence is both informative and comforting. More later—I want to get up to the hospital as soon as I can.

Love you,

Mom

Monday, July 7, 2008

Journal

The news isn't good. He's failing. I watched the heart monitors in the hallway by the nurses' station. All the other patients' monitors showed steady, even patterns, but Pete's was all over the place, irregular as all get out. I've saved some of the strips of paper that print out from the heart monitor and pile up on the floor—strange souvenirs of his heart's erratic rhythm. I clutch them as if they could keep him going. Strips of paper with jagged lines—Pete's heart, working so hard.

Nurses run in every now and then, and yell at him, "Cough! You can do it! Cough!" They mentioned **V-tach**, **ventricular tachycardia**, **Bradycardia** and **atrial fibrilation**. I need to look those up.

We both know this is very serious business. We are caught somewhere between life/existence/now—and the staggering uncertainty of *what if.* Pete asked me to take a letter for him. I got out my notebook and waited. He stared out the window for a long time before beginning.

Monday, July 7, 2008
A Letter Dictated by Pete
To My Loving Sons, Paul and Sean,

I love you both unswervingly, and want you to always be healthy and wise. It's a brand new world out there, and you are part of that world. You can both do so much good for humanity. It is in giving that you will receive all the gifts. Live by the Golden Rule. Never judge anyone too harshly or too quickly, especially yourselves.

There is a loving presence that is always with you, deep down inside your souls. You can call on it anytime for strength and guidance.

You cannot avoid challenges in your lives. Challenges will come. I pray that the way you handle those challenges will be for the better, rather than causing you to become bitter.

I'm so very, very honored and proud to be your father. I'll always be with you on this plane and in all forms, seen or unseen. I'll always be with you. I ask for forgiveness for any harm I may have caused you. I spread my arms around you. Be at peace.
Love,
Dad

Hospital Speak 101

Ventricular tachycardia—a pulse rate of more than 100 beats per minute, with at least three irregular heartbeats in a row. It is a major cause of sudden cardiac death.

Bradycardia—a slow heartbeat, usually at a rate under 60 beats per minute. Normal resting rate is 60-100 beats per minute.

Atrial fibrillation—a problem with the rate or rhythm of the heartbeat, which becomes very fast and irregular. The upper and lower chambers of the heart don't work together. Atrial fibrillation can cause stroke, chest pain or heart failure when the heartbeat is very rapid.

CHAPTER FOUR

Bare Bones

"If you're going through hell, keep going."
–Winston Churchill

Monday, July 7, 2008
Journal

I TALKED WITH ELFI, my dear friend from the Dominican Republic. She said that when her close friend, Greg, was hospitalized with a life-threatening condition, she prayed fervently, over and over again–and that her prayer was simply, "Please." I think about that a lot. I also think that if a person can offer only one prayer, it should be a prayer of gratitude. And so I began singing to myself a little chant:

Please, please, please, please!

Thank you. Thank you. Thank you. Thank you.

Update Monday, July 7, 2008 at 8:31 p.m.

Pete had a balloon pump inserted yesterday to boost his heart function, but it wasn't enough. There was just 15% improvement. He was very weak and tired today as he waited for yet another surgery.

He is now undergoing open heart surgery to be given a temporary cardiac assist device that will pump his heart, since his own heart is in severe failure–**cardiogenic shock**, they call it. The surgery will take six to seven hours. They began around 8:00 o'clock tonight.

Pete will have this device, which is an exterior device, for several weeks. We will be here all that time. The docs will be monitoring him to make sure that his other organs are improving in function and to determine what kind of left ventricular assist device (L-VAD) they will want to put in after that time.

The L-VAD is a battery-operated pump the doctor referred to as a "bridge to transplant." It will be implanted in the abdomen with a tube that connects to the pump's control system in a little fanny pack outside of the body. With the L-VAD, we can go home. Pete will be able to resume much of his normal activity while we wait for a suitable heart to become available for transplant. That could take a year or more. Some people on the L-VAD wind up not getting a transplant at all. Their hearts heal and eventually they don't even need it. That is what we are hoping for with Pete.

Pete and I both are experiencing a profound awareness of Spirit present with us throughout this journey. We expect that our lives will be quite different afterwards–not just because of any physical reasons, but more because we feel called to serve, and expect that this experience will give us unique perspectives and understandings to share.

I plan to update this Care Page daily if I can. Thanks so much for checking in and for holding the high watch. We are blessed.

Namaste.

Pamela

Hospital Speak 101

Cardiogenic shock—a condition in which the heart can't pump enough blood to the rest of the body. It's a medical emergency and can cause organ damage and/or death if not treated.

(I'm so glad I didn't look this up at the time!)

Looking back . . .

I signed a consent form for Pete's surgery on July 7. This would be one of many consent forms I would sign in the next few months. It included consent for the procedure to be done and for blood component transfusions if required. A hospital representative is required to go over the form with the signee, step by step, including all the risks. The risks for this procedure included:

Bleeding

Need for transfusion

Infection

Stroke

Dysrhythmia

Need for new pacemaker

Heart attack

Pulmonary dysfunction

Other organ dysfunction (ex: liver, kidney, etc.)

Device malfunction

Death

Gulp. I signed.

Monday, July 7, 2008 at 8:10 p.m.

Journal

Pete has gone in for surgery to implant a life support device. When I signed the papers for the procedure, I asked Dr. Haft why they were doing Pete's surgery at 8:00 p.m. Why didn't they just wait until morning?

"He won't make it until morning," he said.

He won't make it until morning? Oh my dear, precious God, he won't make it until morning?

> *"When disaster strikes, there are no magic words that will make*
> *everything all right, for if there were, life would necessarily*
> *have to be unbearably empty and shallow in order to*
> *accommodate them. What there is, is the*
> *opportunity and the obligation to love*
> *as you never have before."*
> *–Ralph Marston*

Tuesday, July 8, 2008

Journal

Marty says that when an angel appears in the Bible, the first thing the angel says is, "Be not afraid." Good to know.

Same day, later . . .

I just talked with the surgeon, Dr. Haft. Pete is out of surgery and going into the ICU. The doctor said that the procedure itself was complete by midnight. After that, they dealt with controlling the bleeding, which sometimes happens. I asked if Pete had needed a transfusion, and he said, "Oh, he's had hundreds of them!" Gulp.

The surgeon has not closed Pete's chest in order to prevent an accumulation of blood from collecting there and causing more problems. He may remain that way for two to three days. He'll be kept under sedation until he goes back in to have the chest closed.

Dr. Haft said Pete was stable and he encouraged me to go get some sleep. They will call me if they need to take him back into surgery or if anything of immediate concern occurs.

E-mail, Tuesday, July 8, 2009

To Friends and Family—

It's a little after 5:00 a.m., and I haven't been to sleep yet, so I hope this will be coherent. My dear husband, Pete, had open heart surgery last night. It's a long story—and I'm too beat to tell it all over again, so I've set up a webpage for loved ones. To get the latest update, please go to www.carepages.com. Click on "Visit" and you will be asked to create a user name and password. It's all free. Pete's page is: Petewehle

I will try to update the page each day—or whenever I have new information. You will receive an e-mail notifying you that there is an update. You can opt out of that if you wish. It's been quite a journey—and it's not over yet.

Thank you for all the wonderful messages and prayers. Every one of them is important. We are supported by an army of loved ones and friends—and are very grateful for that. Our faith is strong.

God bless you all.

Namaste.

Pamela

Please note: Here begins a representative sampling of the more than 2,000 precious postings over the next few months:

---

13 Messages Posted Tuesday, July 8, 2008

As I hold you both in sacred space, I see the gentle light of God's powerfully healing Spirit surround you, enfold you, and embrace you in health, wholeness, peace, and grace.

Love,

Joan Van Houten

Please know that many people are praying for you and with you. Remember that God is holding you in the palm of his hand. He definitely has a plan for you!

Love,

Diane Freestone

Your love will transcend all obstacles now and in the future. We pray for a good outcome with the surgery. Pam, your strength and love for my brother is a gift he never expected to find. Thank you from all of the Wehle family for being you.

Bob & Claudia Dutkiewicz

I'm thinking of you from across the pond. My heart goes out to both of you . . . Love to both of you,

Jonathan Howie (England)

We send our love and thanks to you for supporting Pete through this difficult time. He is very blessed to have you in his life. I am hopeful that with all the blessings surrounding him now he will soon get back on his feet and have some great stories and a few jokes to tell about this experience.

Please let him know the boys love him and want him to stay strong with their love and prayers. This is a difficult time for you too; let us know how we can help.

Love,

Mary Dominick, (Mother of Paul and Sean)

I'm reminded of a nurse friend of mine who spoke with a patient who appeared to be unconscious. When he returned to what we call consciousness he had heard every single word she had said. My dad, too, heard me, and he was utterly without distress when in ICU. He heard everyone, observed peacefully. I hold the conviction your Pete is doing the same.

Judy Cassidy

Holding you in the high watch and knowing that you are safely cradled in the arms of Mother/Father God, I pray for strength and healing for both of you. Know that you are loved.

Treasure yourself,

David Sterken

Looking back . . .

Kelvin was a male nurse that took care of Pete often during this time. He had a great sense of humor, and you could tell that his work was more than just a job. On this particular day, he mentioned that Pete's heart incision was still open. I knew that, but the idea kind of freaked me out.

"Do you want to see it?" he asked.

"No, I don't think I so," I said, unable to even imagine looking inside Pete's body. Finally, though, my curiosity got the best of me. I decided that if I could maintain a strictly clinical mindset, I could do it. Doctors do it all the time, I thought. I can do this. After all, the body is a miraculous thing, created by God to be our vehicle for this brief time on the earth plane, right? How could I pass up a chance to witness this miracle from a unique perspective? I told Kelvin I had changed my mind.

Pete was still heavily sedated—out cold. When we drew back his hospital gown, I saw a thin sheet of what looked like Saran Wrap covering Pete's open chest. His organs, deep red and moist, rested neatly inside the open incision where the skin had been pulled back. I marveled. I stared, overcome with awe. This is what we look like inside! It isn't gross or disgusting at all. It's—wonderful. This is life. This is my beloved, inside.

Update Tuesday, July 8, 2008 at 1:40 p.m.

Pete's bleeding has subsided somewhat, so it looks like they will be able to close the chest incision tomorrow. Hooray! At that point, they may bring him out of the anesthesia. The doctor will put feeding tubes in his stomach today so that he will be getting nutrients. I've been with him most of the time, telling him I am here. Somewhere in the deep recesses of his consciousness he will hear.

I had a surprise visit today from Dr. Ken Pituch. Throughout our high school and college summers, Ken and I both worked at Van Buren Youth Camp, a small, non-profit camp in southwest Michigan. He worked the waterfront, and I was the crafts lady. Funny, isn't it, all these years later, he visits as a physician and friend. Ken works with children who have cancer. Bless his kind and loving heart. I guess we've grown up.

I can't call everyone I would like to, so please understand—and check in here for any news. Again—we are grateful beyond measure for all of you.

Love,

Pam

Update Wednesday, July 9, 2008 at 11:22 a.m.

Pete is stable this morning, awaiting surgery to close his chest this afternoon. Amazing. He is awake, but for now only able to communicate with a nod or shake of his head, or by lifting his hand. It must be terribly frustrating, but the nurses and I are doing our best to figure out what he is trying to say to us. He is resting.

Looks like he'll be here for the next two to three weeks.

Love to you all,

Pamela

---

43 Messages Posted Wednesday, July 9, 2008

Thank you for your updates. We are all bonding back here and pulling for you and Pete!

Love,

Donna Leonard

Wednesday, July 9, 2008

Journal

Yesterday I had a visit from my daughter-in-law's mother. Lesley is a gem. I liked her from the moment we met, and it brightened the day just to have a chat with her. She wanted to give me a hug, but she had just visited her niece in the hospital here, and her niece has a staph infection. We can't risk passing a staph infection to Pete, so we pretended to hug by facing each other a few feet apart, and wrapping our arms around ourselves. It was so tender, I almost cried.

There's something very comforting about having time with a woman friend. We're nurturers, comforters. I love being a woman.

Same day, later . . .

For years now we have had problems with the city sewer system periodically backing up into our basement, leaving slightly smelly standing water with little white floaties in it. I have not been able to get any help with the problem from the city.

Each time the water backs up I hire someone to unclog the drains at about $100 a trip. Then I go down and throw out the things that are ruined and clean up with a bucket of bleach water. I suspect that there may some mold lurking down there . . .

Today I made a few calls and found a lab that has rental kits for collecting air samples to be analyzed for mold and swabs for checking bacteria levels. The person who collects the samples has to wear rubber gloves and an M-100 filter mask.

I don't think I can do it. I really don't want to leave Pete, and with my allergies and whatever is going on in my lungs, it's probably the last thing I should be doing. Who can I ask to do this?

Same day, later . . .

Nancy Lou called. She asked Peter Hawkins, a very dear, retired chemist from our church, if he would collect the samples. He said he would be delighted. The Universe provides.

You know, I marvel at how things work out. I can stew and stay up nights worrying, tying myself in knots—and then, out of the blue, things work out. All is well. Everything is all right. It reminds me of a song I wrote a few years ago. I guess I should listen to my own advice . . .

Everything is All Right

Everything is all right.
Take it easy and slow.
Ain't no use in getting so uptight,
Just go with the flow.

In good time we will know what it's all about.
All this fussing and fuming
And dooming and glooming doesn't help us out.

There's a place in the heart that is calm and still.
You can take yourself there,
Settle down, have a chair, if you only will.

Everything is all right.
Take it easy and slow.
Ain't no use in getting so uptight,
Just go with the flow.

©*2001 Pamela Chappell*

Update Wednesday, July 9, 2008 at 8:12 p.m.

Pete was scheduled to have his chest incision closed today, but it was postponed because of some other emergencies at the hospital . . . It was a long day, but the good news is that it was one more day for his kidneys and liver to heal. I guess they've taken a beating.

I'm a bit tired and emotionally weary, but other than that, I am doing well. Thanks for the wonderful messages and prayers. They are such a comfort to us, and we know that every prayer, every loving wish, has it's own powerful energy. We'll take all we can get.

Love to you all,

Pamela

Thursday, July 10, 2008
Journal

It's 5:45 a.m. I woke up at 4:00 and haven't been able to get back to sleep. My mind races so! It occurs to me that this is bare bones living. Pete is living one heartbeat, one breath at a time. A machine, sounding like a washing machine in agitation cycle, beats his heart for him. As for me, I get up, have a bowl of cereal, go to the hospital, come back, check my e-mails and the CarePages, and go to bed. Bare bones. It's simple–simple and big, filled with drama, pain, and a lot of waiting. In its simplicity it is also deep and profound. Each new day is both blessing and nightmare.

I've been reading Eckert Tolle's *A New Earth*, and it really has me thinking. All of our physical challenges are things of matter, of form. What is really happening, though, on a spiritual level, is beautiful and uplifting. For example, the other night during Pete's open heart surgery, I sat in the waiting room, reading, pacing, making phone calls. The room was empty except for me. Finally, at 4:30 in the morning Dr. Haft came out and told me that everything went all right and that I should go home and get some rest. He must have been exhausted. Pete had been in surgery eight and a half hours.

As I trudged down the very long corridor to Parking Lot A, I saw myself as if I were watching a movie . . . that poor woman, dealing with her husband's struggle to live, walking through the empty hospital hallways all alone at 4:30 in the morning. Then I remembered something I learned a long time ago–*We are never really alone.* The moment that thought entered my mind, I sensed a huge Presence with me. It felt like the hallway was full of loving spirits. We were, together, a crowd, an entourage! I was electrified by this Presence, walking with me, supporting me. It was a palpable thing–a holy thing. I understood in a whole new way then, that I was not alone at all. The sensation was so strong, that when a man came up the hallway in my direction, I thought we might all have to move to the side to let him pass!

In the midst of all the hospital machines, the tubes connecting Pete's heart to the artificial heart, the people sleeping in chairs in the ICU waiting room, the shift changes, the monitors, the jigsaw puzzles and the occasional flood of tears–there is always a loving, sustaining Presence.

We are blessed.

E-mail, Thursday, July 10, 2008

To Mary Dominick (Pete's former wife)

Mary,

Paul called me tonight from Colorado. I told him everything I know. Bless his heart—It's a lot to handle. I will e-mail Sean. I don't know how else to reach him in Spain. It will be hard for them both to be far away when their father is so ill. I'm glad you gave them the link to the CarePages, though. They should know what's going on every step of the way. Bless you.

I'm trying to get enough rest and to eat the best I can. Can't do much about the stress, but I work on remaining positive.

Warmly,

Pam

Thursday, July 10, 2008
Journal

Sometimes I teach workshops on self care, so I know how important it is. I get as much sleep as I can, but sometimes that's not easy. I tend to wake up at four in the morning, and the monkey mind *loves* to play at four in the morning. I try to meditate.

I call Pete's nurse to see how he's doing, send an e-mail or two, go to the bathroom. Then I get back in bed and try again. Usually I toss and turn, finally slipping off into strange dreams, waking earlier than I had hoped. Then I give up, get up, and start another day at the hospital.

The most exercise I get is walking, and I do a fair amount of that, because the hospital is huge. I try to eat healthy foods, but I don't have much of an appetite. The cafeteria food is not very exciting day after day.

It's been a major challenge to take care of our bills. I've been paying some of them on line, but I can't do all of them that way, and I still have to figure out how to pay them with the limited money we have. It takes time and phone calls and energy. It's exhausting.

The last few days I've been having fleeting dizziness. It's not enough to make me pass out, but I do feel unsteady and usually have to sit down. I'm guessing it's stress. It does make me a little nervous, though, because dizziness was Pete's first symptom.

"We are all healers who can reach out and offer health,
and we are all patients in constant need of help."
–Henri Nouwen

CHAPTER FIVE

Just Here in Ann Arbor

"The opportunity to be of service may come on any level,
including in areas you don't expect. Be open to the
opportunities to serve, wherever and
however they may appear."
–John-Roger

Thursday, July 10, 2008
Journal

IT'S BEGINNING TO feel way too familiar here at the University of Michigan Hospital. I'm friendly with the guy who mops the floors, the woman who validates my parking ticket and the 4-year-old with wispy, blond hair who is here with his mom and grandmother while his father has heart surgery.

I work at jigsaw puzzles. They're great therapy. I don't have to think about anything except what will fit. Every little piece that I find a home for is a tiny triumph, and that is a welcome thing these days.

I'm generally here at the hospital all day. Mostly I sit with Pete and hold his hand. He can't speak now because he's heavily sedated and has three tubes in his mouth. When he is awake he can respond with a squeeze of the hand or a nod or shake of the head. I find my encouragement in minuscule doses.

Pete's artificial heart reminds me of the old portable dishwasher I had back in the 70's. It is robin's egg blue in color, and the steady, swishing sound is a gentle metronome, marking the minutes, the hours, the days. This incredible machine that is attached by tubes to his heart and abdomen does the work of his heart. Amazing.

Dr. Haft expects Pete to be on the machine for two to three weeks, giving his kidneys and liver time to heal from the recent trauma. Then the doc will have a better idea of which kind of an implanted device will be most effective for Pete.

I've cleared everything off my calendar for July and part of August. It's amazing how easy that was to do–a few phone calls and–pooff!–all of those things that would have required so much time and energy are just gone. People are very understanding when you say the words, "heart transplant."

I wonder if my CarePage buddies have any idea of how immensely important their postings are to me. And the e-mails and cards . . . We are wonderfully blessed by all the people who love us and pray for us. I believe in the power of prayer–big time.

We'll get through this. Somehow.

Update Thursday, July 10, 2008 at 5:53 p.m.

Dr. Haft came by moments ago to tell me that the surgery to close Pete's chest went well and everything looks good. There wasn't too much bleeding, which is great. He is in recovery now. Whew. I can start breathing again. Thanks for the prayers that have surely seen us through and will continue to support us in the days ahead.

The doctor said that they would probably be able to remove Pete's breathing and feeding tubes tomorrow so that he will be able to talk again. That will be wonderful. I'm sure he has a lot bottled up that he will want to talk about. I'll also be able to share with him all the wonderful cards we have received in the past few days. He's been too groggy for that. He will love them. Thank you all so much!

Love,

Pam

---

30 Messages Posted Thursday, July 10, 2008

Thanks for keeping us posted via your web page. We deeply appreciate being able to keep in contact this way because our thoughts and prayers are with you constantly. We have requested that both of you be on the prayer list at Peace Lutheran Church.

Much Love,

Namaste,

Fred & Ella Kauffman (Neighbors)

You were both present at the Healing Service at Unity last night. Much wonderful love and prayers and energy were sent to you both. Please know that you are surrounded. Remember to breathe deeply.

Ruth Tierra

I've been thinking of Pete, picturing him as his energetic, vibrant self. He doesn't shy away from doing things that require hard work, energy and enthusiasm. I also am thinking of his wonderful, terrible, cheesy humor and I laugh to myself. There is no question about the healing power of humor, and we all know Pete is blessed with that in abundance. I'm looking forward to seeing him again, back to his regular life and almost expecting to hear the "ba ba-bump" of percussion after one of his jokes. I bet anyone reading this and thinking about Pete's humor is smiling now!

With much love,

Sue Fischer

E-mail, Friday, July 11, 2008

Linda Beushausen to Fellowship

Hello everyone,

I was grateful for the opportunity to share a very sacred conversation with Pam yesterday afternoon. She is navigating through a myriad of intense and frequently changing emotions, and senses that this is true for Pete as well.

I asked Pam about some of the other . . . more tangible ways we can support them. I sensed that the money for lodging, food, parking, and so forth would be one way to help. Pam affirmed that this is a need and that she is learning to receive the help that has been offered them. We talked about how being a gracious receiver is really also a way of *giving* another person the opportunity to experience the gifts of giving . . .

Pam said that the church she and Pete are a part of, Unity Church on the Lakeshore (in Douglas), has set up a fund for them. If you get the sense that you are to help in this way, you can send a check with a note that the gift is for the Pete Wehle fund to the church.

Pam sends her love and gratitude for everyone. It is wonderful to support the One we are with Love and Trust . . .

Love,

Linda Beushausen

My dear friend, Linda Beushausen, walked this valley herself when her husband passed a few years ago. She shared the following passage with me. I treasure it:

Trust steadily.

Hope unswervingly.

Love extravagantly.

This is what our lives are about these days. It's a sacred journey.

Update Friday, July 11, 2008 at 8:21 p.m.

. . . Today was a long day and a tough one, as Pete didn't get his tubes removed from his mouth, and he's getting discouraged. The doc thinks he needs to be on the ventilator a little longer because he has too much fluid in the lungs. One of the hardest things for him is not being able to communicate his needs. He can point to a chart that has things on it like:

"I'm hot."

"I'm cold."

"I'm thirsty."

"I want to get cleaned up."

But not all communications can be found on a chart. He tries to gesture and the nurse and I try to understand. We do the best we can.

We had three wonderful visits today. Nancy O'Donohue from Unity Church on the Lakeshore came and brought me my guitar (!) along with other much needed things from home. She also came with prayers and energy work for both of us. Just like before, Nancy helped me to become grounded again and to remember my own strength.

Later, I slipped out to attend this month's meeting of the heart transplant support group. There I was encouraged by meeting people who have lived well for years with heart transplants.

When I got back to Pete's room, he was quite agitated, as he had to have the fluid suctioned from his lungs often today, and it's quite painful and distressing for him. I don't think it was an accident that the harpist from Gifts of Art came by then and began to play beautiful, soothing pieces for us. I could just see the tension falling away from him. He applauded with one finger, and then fell into a peaceful sleep.

My brother, Terry, drove up from Ohio and took me out for a scrumptious shrimp and pasta dinner. It was a most welcome respite–a little escape from the trauma–and we had a good time retelling old family stories. Terry's a gem. He is four years older than me, and although we have always loved each other, we have never been particularly close. Now, when Pete and I are struggling with life and death issues, he is here for us, both as a brother and as a doctor who can help me understand what's going on.

When I got to my room at the Transplant House, there on my little twin bed were two packages. It felt like Christmas! One was a delightful gift box of lovely pears, apples and cheeses—a true bonanza for somebody who has been eating like a gypsy for endless days. This came from our precious friends in the All God's Children Community Choir. Thank you, dear ones! I love you too.

Donna Leonard sent a beautiful dream catcher from Sedona with perfect white feathers. She knows that both Sedona and white feathers are very special to me. I love it, Donna. Thank you so much!

You know, we get so many cards every day, it's getting to be a joke with the clerk at the ICU. Thank you all so much for the cards, the prayers, the e-mails and the messages left here. You cannot begin to imagine how wonderful they are to us.

No more news on Pete's condition, except that he is stable, which is good. Now we wait for the healing that is already taking place. Please keep those prayers coming!

Love to you all,

Pam

---

4 Messages Posted Friday, July 11, 2008

. . . You are strong. Keep remembering that you can give all of your troubles to God every night as He is going to be up all night anyway.
Love,
Diane Freestone

Thanks for the update! Tell Pete we are thinking of him and we got all of his business at work taken care of for him today . . . Tell Pete we love him and I miss our daily talks.
Darrell Elkins

Friday, July 11, 2008

Notes from Heart Transplant Support Group Meeting

After the transplant, the first year is the hardest. (The first *two* years, somebody added.)

L-Vads are the way most people make it to transplant.

Variety of pumps to choose from

Avoid swimming where you can't be sure of the water quality.

There are ways to find out who your donor was. (?)

Wait at least three months before you write a letter to the donor family, if you write one at all. They can choose to receive it or not. They can also choose to respond or not.

Should not ever be more than three hours away from hospital while awaiting a heart. If you have to be further away, call hospital. It should not take more than 20 minutes to reach you. If it does, they have to go to the next person on the list. They will *not* leave a message.

Some airlines provide free transport for heart transplant patients.

Prednisone can make some people euphoric, extravagant, grandiose, impulsive, or depressed.

One person told the story of a transplant recipient who went to the supermarket and bought a case of cereal. When he brought it home, his wife was dismayed, as neither of them ate cereal. He said it was for the grandchildren, and besides that, it was on sale. She accepted that, but was floored the next day when he came home with a case of milk! Another fellow went out and bought a sailboat. I was advised to keep any credit cards in *my* possession.

Another person said that people don't always grasp the meaning of a heart transplant. He was in an elevator shortly after his transplant, wearing the required mask. A woman next to him got curious and asked, "Why the mask?"

"Heart transplant," he replied.

"Oh wow!" she said. "Were you the recipient or the donor?"

Friday, July 11, 2008

Journal

We talked about it, and we both agreed I should call Pete's manager and told him that Pete wouldn't be able to do his insurance work anymore. I asked Darrell to shut down Pete's marketing plan, cancel his reservations for the upcoming convention, and asked him to take over Pete's clients. Darrell, understanding, driven, and much more than just Pete's manager, understood and said he would take care of everything.

Pete wants to help people and to sing. Funny thing–that's exactly what I want to do. How that will manifest . . . well, we'll see. I have a hunch that we're being led somewhere, to something, and that Pete's heart has something to do with it.

E-mail, Friday, July 11, 2008

Hi Pam,

I talked with Paul today . . . He is thinking of coming back from Aspen to be with Pete. I told him I could make arrangements for him to fly in and out for a couple day visit, but he seems worried and is thinking that being with his dad is more important than being part of the music program . . . He loves and cares a lot for Pete. I last talked directly to Sean a week and a half ago, to let him know that his dad was back in the hospital, but in good hands at U. of M. I e-mailed him and his American teachers and asked them to keep him informed . . . He's scheduled to return to the U.S. in two weeks, the twenty-fourth of July. Let me know if you think he should come back earlier, and I can make arrangements for that.

Is there any question about whether or not Pete will slowly, but eventually be able to get back to a relatively normal state? You are an angel and I know Pete appreciates all you are doing. God bless you. Take care, and give our best wishes to Pete.

Mary Dominick

Update Saturday, July 12, 2008 at 7:10 a.m.

Just a quick note before I go up to the hospital this morning–Many of you have asked how you can help. We have one thing that continues to be a concern: two beautiful cats that we love very much. Because both of us are immune-deficient now, and allergic to cats, we have to bid them both goodbye. We thought we had homes for them, but that has fallen through. Our wonderful neighbor, Fred Kauffman, has been feeding them for us while we're gone, and they've been living outside–(the cats, not the neighbors) but they're indoor/outdoor cats, and winter will come . . .

Please ask everyone you know (including yourself) if anyone can find it in his/her/your heart to adopt one or both of the cats. They are beautiful, litter-trained, neutered, de-clawed males, and they are both good mousers!

We love these cats dearly, and want to see them in a good home. Thanks so much.

Pam

Update Saturday, July 12, 2008 at 2:42 p.m.

Dr. Haft was in this morning, concerned about some of the blood tests that show that Pete's red blood cells are getting "chewed up," as he put it. They did another echo test and found that one of the tubes that runs from the life support apparatus to Pete's heart has shifted a bit. This sometimes happens when the heart is swollen during surgery and then eventually shrinks back.

In short, the doc had to open Pete up again to move the tube into the proper position so that the blood cells won't be colliding with a brick wall, so to speak. They are also going to switch him to another pump device that Haft thinks will work a little better for him. Pete is in surgery right now. Keep those prayers coming, my friends. That fat lady ain't sung yet.

I'll post again later today after the surgery to let you all know how it went. Thank you for your continuing support and love. We rest in the arms of all of you–and God.

Love,

Pam

---

8 Messages Posted Saturday, July 12, 2008

Wholehearted loving, healing, White Light is surrounding you both as we wish you the best. It hurts us to think that you have to travel this journey, yet we also know from experience that there is always a blessing hidden somewhere. You are blessed to have each other and we stand with you. Angels surround you.

Namaste,

Penny Baker

As you wait, we wait with you. We love you:
Joan Van Houten

Update Saturday, July 12, 2008 at 11:59 p.m.

The surgery went as planned. Pete has a new assist device for his heart, is stable and resting. We should know within a couple of days if this takes care of the red blood cell concern. I'm exhausted, so that's all for now.

Love you all.

Pam

Update Sunday, July 13, 2008 at 4:25 p.m.

Wonderful news! The new device that was hooked up to Pete last night, a CentriMag, seems to be doing very well for him! His blood test results are improved, and he is more at ease. Also, they finally took him off the ventilator, which makes a *huge* difference. He can talk a little–although it's more like a croak now. It was music to my ears to hear him croak out, "I love you." I cried.

He looks much better–and he actually ate a little real food. Who would think that should be such a big deal? One interesting thing about this new machine Pete is on–with the CentriMag, he has no heartbeat. The machine delivers a constant, gentle flow of blood instead of pulsing, like the natural heart does. It is easier on the blood cells–but having no heartbeat sure seems a little weird.

I went to the Unity Church of Ann Arbor this morning and had a warm reception. I may even sing there some Sunday while we are here. Pete and I expect to see our pastor from Douglas, Marty Rienstra, and her husband, John, later today. Our little church means the world to us–such a loving, supportive community!

Thanks again for all the wonderful messages we have been receiving. We are gratified beyond all words. I don't think Pete realized how many people care about him. He's amazed.

Love to you all,

Pam

Update Monday, July 14, 2008 at 7:01 p.m.

Progress. Today Pete sat up in a chair for the first time in three weeks. It took a team of six people to accomplish that, with the tubes and IVs and all. Still, he sat up for a couple of hours and ate a little. That is real progress. The occupational therapist has Pete doing simple movement exercises to keep his muscles working. Tomorrow they plan to get him walking. Stay tuned!

The surgeon will do a heart catheterization and a heart biopsy on Wednesday. Then we may know whether or not sarcoidosis is the cause of Pete's heart failure. He is being monitored very closely and has a nurse that is assigned to him alone, 24/7.

Great news! A dear woman at our church has opened her heart to our two cats and will adopt them both. We are thrilled with this news because we love those friendly felines and couldn't bear to put them down. Thank you, Barb!

We had a wonderful visit from our pastor, Marty Rienstra and her husband, John last night. We had some prayer time together and Marty brought Pete a beautiful, heart-shaped crystal, sparkling and clear, just as we envision Pete's heart. It now hangs on one of the IV poles and the sun streams through, spraying colors on the bland walls.

Looking back . . .

When he looked at Pete, though, I could see in his eyes that John didn't think Pete was going to make it. John is a surgeon. He has seen a lot.

Update continues . . .

This evening we had another visit from Nancy O'Donohue, who again prayed with us and did energy work with both of us. She also engaged us in a sacred Native American ritual and sang an Indian healing song. It was very moving.

We feel so blessed in the way of friends and family! Thank you all. Please forgive me if I don't always respond to every message and e-mail. Know that I read them all and share them with Pete. Sometimes I'm exhausted when I get back to the Transplant House, though, and I just can't make one more phone call or send one more message. Know that we deeply appreciate every single prayer and loving thought!

Love,

Pam

Pete remembers . . .

Nancy's ritual really got to me. I had been having wild, vivid dreams of being an old Indian, a grandfather. Inside my head I heard, "I am Grandfather. I am strong." I started saying that, over and over again like a mantra. Then I started speaking in what sounded like another language. I don't know where it came from—it just poured out from me. Pam wrote down phonetically what I said, but it was lost later when I changed rooms. I am sure I was speaking in a Native American language.

> *"The most beautiful thing we can experience*
> *is the mysterious."–Albert Einstein*

---

30 Messages Posted Sunday, July 14, 2008

I am so thankful that things are looking better for you two. It is great that you are able to keep up with so many of your friends all at once with one update. I am leaving for Amsterdam, but will be sending my prayers from across the Atlantic, and will check in when I return.

Hugs to you both,

Sue Scott

. . . We felt like both of you were with us at All God's Children choir rehearsal on Saturday. We gave the children and their families the Pam and Pete update and they were eager to draw, color, and write wishes of their own. Two of our choir members read the "Pam and Pete prayer" in unison and all of us said the last line together. We hope you felt a wave of love coming your way from Benton Harbor—St. Joe.

With much love,

Sandy and Larry Feldman

Looking back . . .

A few years ago I sang a benefit concert for the Holistic Alliance in St. Joseph, Michigan. During the intermission, a handsome couple approached me and introduced themselves as Sandy and Larry Feldman. Sandy is petite and blond, with sparkling blue eyes and a huge, warm smile. Larry is salt-and-pepper-haired and wears wire-rimmed glasses on his lively, intelligent eyes. They both exuded a warmth and kindness that drew me in immediately. They told me that they were directors of a children's choir called "All God's Children," and that the children had been singing one of my songs, "Joy in my Heart," for some time.

Sandy explained that they had moved to St. Joe recently and became aware of the great social divide between St. Joe and its neighbor across the bridge, Benton Harbor, which was the site of violent demonstrations of pent-up anger and frustration in 1960, 1966, 1990 and 2003.

About 12,000 people live in Benton Harbor on the southwestern Michigan shores of Lake Michigan. Many of the buildings in the city are boarded-up and deteriorating. The Benton Harbor school district is the third poorest in Michigan with ninety percent of its school children living in poverty. The city is predominantly African American.

Just across the bridge, St. Joseph, population 9,000, is quite affluent and is mostly white. That is not to say that all of St. Joseph is wealthy nor all of Benton Harbor poor, but there is a striking economic and social division between the two cities as a whole.

A sense of inequality contributes to the anger and frustration of some of those living in Benton Harbor. During the riots in the late 1960s, one of the bridges between Benton Harbor and St. Joseph was raised to prevent Benton Harbor residents from crossing over to the wealthy areas of St. Joseph. There is mistrust and fear on both sides of the river.

When Sandy and Larry took up residence near St. Joseph they were invited to a meeting of the newly formed Race Relations Council that was seeking ways to bring the two communities into greater harmony. Many ideas were tossed around that day, including a sudden inspiration that struck the Feldmans: Why not form a children's choir and recruit children from both sides of the bridge? We could teach them uplifting songs of understanding, diversity and compassion. We could rehearse and perform in both communities and give the children the opportunity to know each other and move beyond stereotypes and prejudice.

Many people told Larry and Sandy it would never work, that St. Joe parents wouldn't take their kids into Benton Harbor, afraid of muggings and drive-by shootings, and that Benton Harbor parents wouldn't take their kids into St. Joe where they had been snubbed and profiled. They insisted that nobody would come.

But Larry and Sandy Feldman proceeded with their plan, and the All God's Children Community Choir, AGC for short, was formed. With the help of some of the local churches and people in the community, they pulled some children together and taught them lively songs with positive messages. Rehearsals were held in churches, libraries and community centers in both cities. Word got out, and more and more children came. By the time I met the Feldmans, the choir had more than 40 enthusiastic children singing programs all over southwest Michigan, and the choir has doubled its membership since then.

The Feldman's enthusiasm and knack for nurturing spread beyond the children themselves. Parents were very involved with the choir too, and as they got to know each other, they formed significant friendships. The choir became a sort of eclectic family, with everyone looking out for each other. Children from neighboring communities came, and Larry and Sandy never turned anyone away. The children had sleep-overs with new friends they would never have met otherwise. The choir, beaming with pride and singing beautiful music with great enthusiasm, was in large demand for performances.

Sandy told me this story, and I was immediately caught up in her positive energy. It occurred to me that the choir is a microcosm of what our world could be if we all just knew each other's hearts. Then Sandy asked if I might consider being a guest performer at one of their concerts. Of course, I said, "Yes! Yes! Yes!" I began rehearsing with the choir, along my friend, Elfi, who played the piano part for the "Peace Canon," which Sandy and Larry had requested we do with the children.

About three weeks before the concert I had a call from Sandy and Larry. Former President Carter was coming to Benton Harbor to help build enthusiasm for Habitat for Humanity projects there. The choir had been asked to sing for a special program planned for him. Would I like to sing with them?

We performed my "Peace Canon" for President Carter–one of the big thrills of my life. People standing near him said they saw tears well up in his eyes to hear those beautiful children singing, "We must be the change we want to see in the world." At the conclusion, President Carter bowed to the children, hands together in reverence. Then he threw a kiss to Elfi and me. I will never forget that moment.

A year or so later we had the opportunity to sing for Arun Gandhi, Mahatma Gandhi's son, and when I decided to create a children's CD, I asked the choir to sing along with me on five of the songs. What great fun that was! They were absolutely wonderful. I sang with them several other times, too, and Pete and I became part of the All God's Children family. We became good friends with Sandy and Larry as well, and enjoyed dinners out and songfests with them many times.

Along with the fruit basket, the choir has sent a huge stack of precious, crayon-on-construction paper get-well cards. And they prayed for us. Wow. How it lifts my heart!

E-mail, Monday, July 14, 2008

Hello my friend,

What wonderful news about Pete these last couple of days! . . . I love you both and continue to hold you in the Light, remembering that you, Pete, me, and every other being *is* the Light and nothing can separate us . . . nothing.

Linda Beushausen

Update Tuesday, July 15, 2008 at 7:04 p.m.

Pete is steadily getting stronger. He was up twice today and sat in a chair for a while. Tomorrow he is scheduled for a heart catheterization and if "the numbers are right," Pete will be put on the transplant list. He hasn't been on the list until now because he wasn't strong enough. The doc thinks he is doing better now, though.

Then we wait for a heart. Just as you have been praying for Pete, we ask now that you pray for comfort and solace for the individual and the family who will eventually make it possible for Pete to have a new heart. It's sobering to think that someone must make his or her transition in order for Pete to stay alive. What a gift of love from a complete stranger!

And now a special message—Pete dictated the following to me today to send out to all of you, dear friends:

To all my friends, Unitics, dreamers, supporters, nonconformists, and anyone who believes in miracles—

I want to thank all of you for all the love you send out to Pam and me just at the right time—which truly is anytime. And what a time it has been these past several weeks! I won't go into a description of what it is I'm dealing with. People have struggles every day, and we are truly blessed that we are constantly reinforced by the power of prayer and the presence of God working with all of us and showing us the way to be better in what we are, or what we believe we are, as human beings.

We truly are, Pam and I, connected to all of you–loving hands and praying hearts. Thank you for the opportunity to serve you and bless you. You are what we are–the love of God fully present, fully known, fully breathed into our souls forever and ever. Amen.

---

28 Messages Posted Tuesday, July 15, 2008

We are so happy that things have taken a turn for the better! I remember that in the days after my automobile accident, I had this strange sensation of feeling light and lifted up. I didn't realize what it was at the time, but when I became more mobile and started talking to people, I realized how many people were praying for me. I hope that you both feel the same physical, emotional and spiritual uplifting. Your spiritual outlook and connection with God has been a gift to us.

Love,

Jo VandenBerg

Tuesday, July 15, 2008

Journal

I call Pete my Miracle Man. We are *counting* on a miracle. They happen every day. In the meantime, I just put one foot in front of the other, like Pete did today. Surely the grace of God is with us.

Here's another miracle–well, maybe just a mini-miracle, but wonderful just the same. Brennan told me that his father, my former husband, has been checking in daily to see what is happening with Pete and me. I am deeply touched and more than a little surprised. Bless his heart.

"Don't believe in miracles–depend on them."

–Laurence J. Peter

Tuesday, July 15, 2008

The following message was sent to us from a friend who received it from a spiritual medium she knows:

Pete is here to be a great teacher, teaching about Love–Divine Love. There is/was something he needed to see before he could stay in his body and become this great teacher. Before I learned of his open heart surgery, I saw that he would have a "near death experience" while experiencing some sort of crisis involving his heart. I saw him being shown something, the something he needed to see, and could only see at that deep soul level, that place we visit when we have a NDE, while having the NDE. He was given a choice whether to return or not. His great love for Pam, and his great love for humanity caused him to choose to return to this plane. I saw him healing and becoming that great teacher, although he and Pam will need to rely on their great and very powerful love to help Pete heal physically so that he can teach what he now knows in his innermost being. He has a great gift for all of humanity.

All this "came" over the weekend, once I learned that he was in Ann Arbor.

E-mail, Wednesday, July 16, 2008
Pam,

Oh what wonderful news—Pete eating, talking and getting strong enough to be considered for a transplant. Hallelujah! You two have been in my heart and prayers. Throughout the day, I am sending you love and light, envisioning Pete healthy, vibrant, singing with Angels all around him and you . . .

I saw a special on TV where people that received new hearts had some changes in their lives. One example—A woman now has a craving, for Italian foods, which she did not have before the transplant. The donor's family confirmed his love for Italian foods.

Give Pete my best, a hug, and know I love you both!
Jane E. Grady

Update Wednesday, July 16, 2008 at 8:59 p.m.

It was a tough day. I woke up at 5:45 a.m to my cell phone ringing. The nurse sounded frazzled. She told me that Pete was being quite difficult and argumentative. He had even accused her of trying to harm him. She described him as "combative and agitated," and wondered if I could come up and calm him down.

When I arrived, Pete was still angry and keyed-up. He complained about everything–the tubes, the IVs, the food, the bed. He said, "Is this any way to live? I don't want to live like this! They've got tubes in my arms, in my penis, up my butt, in just about every orifice I have! I can't even *move* with all these wires and monitors! I can't get comfortable in this bed, can't sleep on my side. I've been here for *four months* now and nobody even tells me what's wrong with me! I don't want to do this anymore. They're doing another test today. Test after test after test, and they never tell me the results. After this test, I'm done. No more tests! I'm just going home. I'm pulling these tubes out and I'm walking out of here."

And so it went, over and over again. He kept saying the same things, going around in circles. There was no arguing with him, no reasoning, no placating. I told him that he's been here for three weeks, not four months, but that didn't interest him.

This ranting was scary, and very uncharacteristic of Pete. It's as if some demon had burst loose inside of him and was taking over. The Pete I know is an easy-going guy. I wondered if I had lost him altogether to this raging stranger in a green, tie-in-the-back hospital gown.

I did my best to calm him down, but it was a losing battle. As the morning wore on, I grew increasingly distressed myself. Pete was losing it–and was about to take me along with him. I asked the nurse to please page Tommy, one of the hospital chaplains who had been in and had begun to develop at least a surface rapport with Pete.

Tommy strolled in a short time later and talked with Pete a little–"Hi, how you doing?" kind of stuff, keeping it light. Pete dropped the surly bit a little, but within a couple of minutes the ranting kicked back in.

Tommy told Pete that he wanted to talk with "the wife" for a little bit. He took my arm and gently led me down the hall, asking me how I was doing. He could tell I was rattled. He led me to a consultation room off the ICU, and had me sit down. Tommy told me about what they call "ICU psychosis," not a clinical term, but one that accurately describes what Pete was demonstrating. It's a kind of depression and rage that is not unusual in the Cardiovascular ICU, where patients are confronted with some of the greatest emotionally charged issues of their lives and their bodies are being pummeled by heart failure or stroke or surgery–whatever has brought them to this place.

Tommy said that the most important thing for me to do is realize that it's temporary and predictable. He stressed that I need to take care of myself. I was grateful to him. It got me through the rest of the day.

With all Pete has gone through, I guess his rant was understandable. It's also a common side effect of his medications, and the fact that he has had very, very little sleep in quite a few days now. The nurse said they see of lot of it in the ICU. Still, it was hard for me to hear him so unhappy and unsettled, and it went on for hours.

Pete had several procedures in the afternoon, including a heart catheterization and a CT scan. I haven't heard any results yet. The late afternoon was brightened immensely by a visit from Sherry Petro-Surdel and Nancy Plantinga from Unity. Their timing was perfect. They talked with Pete, prayed with us, and later treated me to dinner out at Weber's. When we returned to the hospital, Nancy played beautifully for Pete on her Native American flute. He settled down into the music.

I'm back at the Transplant House now. I just spoke on the phone with Pete's nurse, and she said he is sleeping. Whew! A good night's sleep will do wonders for him. Tomorrow will be better. I hope.

12 Messages Posted July 16-17, 2008

We know how difficult it must be for you to have things going in a good direction one day and then have difficulties the next. It's the old two-steps-forward-and-one-step-back syndrome. Just remember that progress is often in small steps. We haven't met Pete, but he's a lucky guy to have you, and we are sending you the most positive energy we have.
All our love,
Mike Helms & Sue Bensinger

You are both loved so much and held dear by so many. The presence of God within you is your constant source of peace, health, and wholeness. When difficult circumstances make it tough to feel that, we all hold the high watch and affirm it for you.

Love,

Joan Van Houten

Looking back . . .

I talked with my older son, Brennan, on the phone almost every day during this time. He was very supportive, this grown-up child of mine who somehow wound up in Montana. When I was rattled, exhausted, or discouraged, he told me how proud he was of me for being there for Pete, for my strength, courage and devotion. I remember when Brennan fit between my elbow and my fingers. Now my grown-up son was nurturing me, giving me an image–a place to step into. If he sees me strong, courageous, and devoted, then I can be all of that. I can see it in myself. Yes.

CHAPTER SIX

Hamburgers and Milkshakes

*"Masters live in deep appreciation, in peace with
whatever is occurring right now, even if they
can't see its perfection right now."*
–Neale Donald Walsch

Update Thursday, July 17, 2008 at 2:28 p.m.

OH MY FRIENDS, today is *so* much better! Pete actually got some sleep last night and is in a much better frame of mind. We also got some good news on some of the tests that were run yesterday. The CT scan showed no evidence of stroke. What a relief that was! The nurses come into Pete's room with little flashlights every hour or two and go over every inch of the several tubes he is attached to, looking for clots. So far, they haven't found any.

Pete joked some today, and we started creating a new vision for our lives after the transplant. As one of the nurses mentioned this morning, every day is another day closer to walking out the door and going home. We look forward to that so much!

Love to you all,

Pam

---

6 Messages Posted Thursday, July 17, 2008

Isn't it *amazing* how all the prayers are multiplying and intensifying! Ah . . . the miracle of prayer! . . . God bless!

Sandy and Jerry Norland

E-mail, Thursday, July 17, 2008

I just wanted you to know that your beloved cats are great! They are home and well, looking for their spots and loving the inside. Take care. All my prayers are with you.

Love,

Barb Corcoran

E-mail, Thursday, July 17, 2008

To Fred Kauffman (Neighbor Extraordinaire)

Thank you so much, Fred, for all your help with corralling the cats and taking care of them for three solid weeks! You have lightened our load and we're really grateful.

And you know, I haven't worried about the lawn. I just knew somehow it would be taken care of by somebody. So you're the knight in shining armor! Again, we are grateful beyond words. Bless you.

Feel free to help yourself to any raspberries that might be ripe. I'd hate to see them go to waste!

Love to you and Ella,

Pam

Update Thursday, July 17, 2008 at 7:34 p.m.

Dear Friends–

We have wonderful news! We learned today that Pete is now on the heart transplant list! He is in the highest priority category, A-1, which is for people who are hospitalized and currently on life-support equipment–in other words, people who would not survive if they were taken off the machines. Sigh.

The doctors plan to skip the L-VAD (Left Ventricular Assist Device) that I mentioned earlier. The L-VAD won't work because both sides of Pete's heart are not functioning, and the L-VAD is only for the left ventricle. There isn't a similar device for both sides. We're still not sure whether he has sarcoidosis. He has had two biopsies, both of which came back negative, but they tell me that could mean that they just took the wrong chunk of his heart for the testing.

It's scary to learn that both sides of his heart are not working, but the up side is that Pete will get a transplant sooner–and come home sooner. He is now strong enough and his other organs are functioning well enough to make it through the surgery. The doc told the nurse not to order the usual cardiac diet for him, but to give him anything he wants, including hamburgers and milkshakes to help him get stronger yet in the days ahead . . .

We continue to pray for the donor and his or her family. That's the really hard part of this whole thing, but we also realize that people die every day when their work here is done, and that they can leave a huge gift behind in being an organ donor. It reminds me that in truth, we are all connected . . .

Love,

Pam

---

13 Messages Posted Thursday, July 17, 2008 after 7:34 p.m.

Hoorah! Hooray! Just got home to read your tremendous news! This is the window, the blessing, the possibility you/we have all been hoping for. Yes, prayers and thanks for the family who donates. And all love and support to you both and to Team Pete.

XOX,

Sharon Jensen (New York)

> Such "heartening" (pun intended) news! . . . Pam, in sessions with you I have learned that when someone is ready to go, they have completed their mission here on earth, and are very clear about that. It is apparent that Pete has not completed his mission and the donor has - or will. In that sense it is okay. Blessed be that person, whoever it may be, who needs to move on and will allow Pete to fulfill his own mission.
>
> Love to you both,
>
> Donna Leonard

E-mail, Thursday, July 17, 2008

Pam,

I plan on stopping by to see you when I'm in Ann Arbor on Saturday, give you a big hug, and drop off a few treats from Gamma Theta. If there is something special you need or want from over here, just say the word and I'll bring it.

I am grateful that Pete has that good nursing care and that they don't hesitate to call you. I'm sure that helps you sleep. Agitation is a sign of healing. We all continue to keep you in our thoughts.

Tammy Daniels

Thursday, July 17, 2008

Journal

I've learned a lot about heart transplantation. One of the key snippets of information I've gleaned is that there is a specific priority listing for patients on the national transplant list, which is managed by the United Network for Organ Sharing (UNOS). The status categories for listing are 1A, 1B, 2, and 7.

Status 1A includes a patient who is on some sort of mechanical device, such as a ventricular assist device, an intra-aortic balloon pump, an artificial heart or a life support machine such as the CentriMag that Pete is on, or someone who is on continuous IV infusions for seven days or more. It also includes a patient who doesn't meet the specified criteria but is admitted to the hospital with a life expectancy of less than seven days.

Status 1B includes a patient who may be in or out of the hospital and have had a ventricular assist device for more than thirty days, and/or a patient who requires continuous infusion of IV inotropes (to make the heart beat stronger).

Status 2 includes a patient who is outside of the hospital and does not meet the criteria for Status 1A or 1B.

Status 7 includes a patient who is temporarily unsuitable for transplant for one reason or another.

Source: *Preparing for Your Heart Transplant, a Pre-Transplant Guide, University of Michigan Cardiovascular Center*

Pete has been classified 1A. We laughed about that, because 1A is what no one wanted to be during the Viet Nam War. Now it means Pete is at the top of the list for a transplant. One of the doctors said to him, "You're the sickest man in this hospital."

Oh my . . .

E-mail, Friday, July 18, 2008

Hi Mary,

We received a nice, newsy postcard from Sean yesterday. It was all in Spanish, but I was a Spanish teacher once upon a time, so I could translate. He got an A+. Sounds like he's having quite an adventure in Spain.

Haven't heard from Paul about any plans to visit but we're going to call him today. Pete has enough of his voice back to talk now, and I think Paul will be reassured to hear his dad's voice.

I cancelled a flight Pete and I had planned for August. We were going to visit my son, Brennan, and his wife, Rachel, in Montana. We haven't seen their home there yet. Sigh . . .

Thanks again, Mary, for being so gracious and helpful to us. You are wonderful!

Love,

Pam

Friday, July 18, 2008, Morning

Journal

Now that Pete is on the heart transplant list, it's a waiting game. The docs seem to think it won't be long, but you never know . . . when someone is going to die. I don't like to think about that, but it's a reality. Praying for a heart means praying for a death. Well–no, praying for a heart means praying that someone's death will have great meaning in the lives of others, even complete strangers.

I'm not doing too well these days. The inflammation in my chest is back, a constant companion, burning with every breath. I am very tired. I try to get enough rest, but often the sleep won't come, or I fall asleep and then wake up at 4:00 a.m. My mind is swimming in thoughts of Pete, of our uncertain future, of the mold in our house, of how in the world we will make it financially through all of this. I grieve the fact that summer is happening on Lake Michigan, and we are in the hospital, rather than splashing in the waves across the street from our home. I worry about my own health. If I have pulmonary fibrosis–well, my days are numbered. I had always assumed I would live to be quite an old woman. Now I wonder if I will live to make another CD, to hug more grandchildren, to see New Zealand, to enjoy life with this new husband of mine. And what about Pete? Will he . . . be here?

When sleep doesn't come, I meditate, both to calm myself and to try to fall back asleep. They say that 4:00 a.m. is the time when the veil between this world and the next is very thin, and Spirit can get through to us with wisdom and guidance. Nancy Lou says it is when the angels pass by. Oddly enough–or perhaps not–it is almost always around 4:00 a.m. when I wake up. I do a lot of praying, and a lot of listening.

My wee hour meditations often bring comfort and reassurance. Here's what I do: I get as comfortable and relaxed as I can and take some deep breaths, paying attention to the inhalation and the exhalation. I think of the inhalation as bringing in healing energy, and the exhalation as a release of all tension and negativity. I lower my shoulders, releasing the tension there. Then I try to clear my head of all the "monkey mind" talk. Whenever a distracting thought comes into my mind, I gently wave it away, returning again and again to a place of peace, love, and calm. When I finally get to that place for a sustained amount of time–and it isn't always easy–I ask, "What is it I should understand?"

Then I listen . . . deeply. When distracting thoughts pop up, and they inevitably do, I wave them away with love and understanding. *Not now, I'll get back to you later. Peace. Peace.* And I listen.

I remember one night in particular, when I was obsessing over money. I was in near panic about how we would pay our bills, with neither of us working. What were we going to do? Yikes!

So I went into meditation and asked, "What is it I should understand?" I leaned into the silence and listened. Listened. And then, without words, I knew that it would all work out—that we would not lose our house and be on the curb selling pencils. It was as if someone said to me, "Not to worry. We've got you covered!" A gentle breeze of peace washed over me and I relaxed. I fell into a deep sleep, secure in the knowledge that it would work out. Somehow.

Same day, later . . .

My chest hurts almost all the time, and I'm having rather disconcerting dizzy spells. Sometimes I feel lightheaded and have to grab something solid to steady myself. It happens a lot—sometimes several times an hour. I know that stress can do such things to a person, and I certainly have my share of stress, but I'm also troubled with shortness of breath. Not good. This had been going on for some time.

A few days ago I asked one of the docs if there was a walk-in clinic at the hospital where I could have someone check me out, just to be on the safe side. He said, no, but suggested I go down to the emergency room. "Go in the morning," he said. "It's not so busy." All of my friends' admonishments to take care of myself keep ringing in my ears. I know it's important, but I also know that Pete relies on my presence to help him hang in there. He's worried about me too, though, and encouraged me to see a doctor. All was quiet and routine in Pete's room this morning, so I told him I was going to go down to the E.R. to have them check me out and see what they suggest. I kissed him and said that I'd be back in a bit. He seemed to be fine with that.

The emergency room is at least a ten minute walk through corridors, up and down different elevators, over the glass walkway, past the cafeteria. I briefly described my symptoms to the woman behind the front desk, and in a few minutes was led into a large room with beds separated by curtains, just like on the medical television shows. I was tired from the walk and glad to lie down. A nurse gave me a gown, and a tall, rather intense intern with male pattern baldness took my history. A different nurse took my blood pressure, pulse, and temperature; a technician did an EKG. Eventually the intern returned and said that they would like to admit me for observation. I argued that I was all right–just a little dizzy–but I certainly didn't need to be admitted. He gave me one of those well-meant but nevertheless patronizing smiles and said, "I think we'd better be sure there isn't something more serious going on here."

Gulp. I hadn't expected that. Then I thought of Pete alone in his hospital room, wondering where I am, worrying. He's a great worrier. Rounds would have been over by then. I don't like missing rounds. Every day I stand in the circle of white coats, listening and taking notes in my little spiral notebook. I want to be able to tell my brother, Terry, what they have said so he can shed some more light on the situation for me. The doctors are very good about me being there. Sometimes I ask questions. They have grown accustomed to my presence and occasionally ask me about what I have observed with Pete. Is he coughing as much? How is he sleeping? Often I look up their medical jargon on the Internet later to keep on top of things.

I missed rounds. I felt guilty, like I was slacking off on the job. You see, I am Pete's advocate here. I speak for him, ask questions, keep up on all the test results, make sure he's warm enough, alert the nurse when anything goes wrong. Who will do that when I'm in the hospital?

I lay there in the E.R. for a long time, listening to the sounds from other curtained cubicles. At one point a man with a gunshot wound and major attitude was brought in. I think he was on something, because he kept sputtering and yelling about–well, actually it was hard to tell what it was yelling about because he was pretty incoherent. Still, it was an intriguing sideshow until the police arrived and took him somewhere else.

The hands in the clock on the wall kept circling around, and I became anxious about Pete. My cell phone didn't work in there, so I asked a nurse to please call my husband's room and let him know what was going on. I waited, tried to sleep. Nurses came and went. They said I would be moved to a room when one became available. About 4 o'clock I asked for something to eat. I'd been there seven hours. I finally got into my hospital room about 7 p.m.

Saturday, July 19, 2008
Journal

These days in the hospital are frustrating and restful, an awkward combination. My meals arrive on a tray, saltless and tasteless, but I have a stash of contraband salt packets in my purse, so that helps. My medications arrive at the appropriate intervals. I am whisked off on occasion to have various tests taken. I watch television, read. The older woman in the bed next to me leaves the TV on all night, so flashing lights dance across the walls and I have trouble falling asleep. Sometimes I ask for something to help me zone out. I am gaining a new perspective on hospital life. Being the patient is a lot different than being "the wife."

At first the nurses wouldn't even let me walk to the bathroom alone. There is a sign outside on the door: FALL PRECAUTIONS. Oh yeah, I thought, I've been dizzy. Anyway, I did a test walk down the hall with a wheeled walker and one of the nurses. When I didn't collapse in a pool on the floor, they decided to let me walk the ten paces to the bathroom on my own.

I am in the University Hospital, which is connected by a glass walkway to the Cardiovascular Center (CVC) where Pete is. It's a fair walk to get there, so I have to be content with calling him. I let him know what had happened and that I am all right, not to worry. I call him several times a day. Unfortunately, he is on some serious meds, and after I hang up I suspect he quickly forgets that I've called.

Looking back . . .

Months later Pete told me that he thought I had died, as I would certainly be there with him otherwise. Oh my.

Same day, later . . .

One thing I have learned over the years is that when we ask for something in prayer, it is best to add at the end, "This or something better for the highest good of all involved." I do that when I pray for Pete's complete recovery and my own. This or something better . . . What could be better?

E-mail, Saturday, July 19, 2008

Hi Pam,

How is everything going? . . . I am so happy that you are there with my dad right now, helping him through all of this. It has to be very exhausting. Thank you.

I am planning to come visit if that is okay . . . I have been thinking about my dad a lot. I just want him to get better. It is very hard being so far away while all this is going on—almost like a dream. It doesn't seem as if something like this could happen to my dad, but it sounds like he is fighting hard and being taken care of very well. I know that he is going to make it out of this. If you could tell him that I love him very much and thank him for believing in me, that would great. See you soon.

Love,

Paul

Update Saturday, July 19, 2008 at 10:06 a.m.

This is Pam's son, Brennan, with today's update, which is actually yesterday's update. I thought I hit the right button, but I suppose not. Yesterday's update follows directly:

Mom was having dizzy spells and, while it's most likely stress, on a doctor's recommendation she went to the E.R. to be checked out. They surprised her and admitted her for overnight observation. She's feeling all right, and says there's no need to worry. Pete's doing well, resting and waiting. Send love and prayers their way. Check back tomorrow for another update.

Love,

Brennan

---

23 Messages Posted July 19-21, 2008

Thanks Brennan, for letting us know about Pam. Hope she is okay. I know she was having some lung problems too, and of course all the stress of this and emotional trauma. They are both in our hearts!

Donna Leonard

Pam . . . thank you for setting the example for all of us that we need to take care of ourselves so we can continue to take care of those who need our care . . . Pete, we now affirm that the new heart that is coming to you soon is a perfect match for you and that your body gratefully accepts it. Know that this journey, as tough as it has been at times, has brought many people together as one family, in Unity . . . Thank you. I know we'll be seeing you soon!

Nancy Plantinga

. . . Once again we are reminded how fragile life is and that we need to be grateful for each day . . .

Wishing you peace and much love,

Chuck Doebler

Pete, all the ex-Bruins are thinking about you and praying for you to get well soon. You were the best left fielder the Bruins ever had.

Hang in there Buddy,

Bill Mennella

. . . My wife's older brother had a heart transplant six years ago and he is doing just great now . . . You would never know he had the transplant by how active he is these days. One day this will all be behind you and when you come to the next Bruins' reunion, it will be just another story we can talk about. Stay well friend, our prayers are with you.

Mike Sullivan (Sully)

We will be in Michigan this Friday night. Pam, thank you for the strength you give to all of us.

Love you both,

Bob & Claudia (Pete's sister and brother-in-law)

Aunt Pam, we are all thinking of you and praying for you both in this very difficult time.

Love from Kansas,

Jenny Chappell Deckert

Monday, July 21, 2008

A card came in today's mail from Bill Gesser of the Omega Survivors Group:

Pam and Pete–

> *Perhaps this past week you felt a burst of hope, love, and happiness.*
> *Maybe some star twinkled especially for you . . . you could feel it.*
> *That was us . . . sending love.*
> *Your "Omega Family" is thinking of you . . .*
> *Praying for you . . .*
> *Loving you.*
> *–Bill*
> *Let me know if there is anything I can do.*

Monday, July 21, 2008
Journal

The saga continues. Connie is here, spending half of her time with Pete and half of her time with me. I don't know what I'd do without her. The docs are trying to determine why I'm having dizzy spells. So far all the heart-related tests have turned out normal, thank God. This afternoon I had a CT scan of my lungs and legs to check for blood clots. No results yet.

My brother, Terry, came yesterday and took me over in a wheelchair to visit Pete. I hadn't seen him since Friday morning when I became a patient myself. He had two procedures done Saturday to check for stroke activity, because he had some dizziness, blurred vision, and confusion. Both tests came back normal–again, thanks to God–no sign of stroke. He has a tube in his mouth and is hooked up to a ventilator again, though. It's very uncomfortable for him and it makes speaking impossible, and coughing painful.

Today I had a visit from Ernestine, the U. of M. campus minister for Unity. She was a great comfort to me, and showed up just at the right time. She wheeled me over to visit Pete, who was having a scary episode with fluid in his lungs. He was coughing and gurgling and in great distress. He seemed to be drowning. Can you even imagine how hard that was to watch? I held his hand and tried to reassure him as about ten doctors and nurses in the hallway consulted with each other, reviewed the test results, and looked worried.

They gave him a diuretic just as I had a call that I had to return to the other side of the hospital for my own CT scan. I was reluctant to leave him, but the white coats were about to kick me out anyway. As I was wheeled back to my room with tears flowing, I went inside and asked for comfort and guidance. Within moments, that Still, Small Voice whispered gently, "We've got everything under control." I took a deep breath, let it out, and felt myself relax.

About a half hour later I called and was told that the diuretic had successfully helped Pete to eliminate enough fluid to settle down, breathe more or less normally, and fall asleep. One more crisis averted.

I'm so tired.

Pete remembers . . .

I felt so helpless. I couldn't talk. I couldn't move. I couldn't do anything about my condition. That was frustrating. I was in pain. I thought if I had to live like that I didn't want to live, because I would be just a shell of my former self. I didn't want to be a burden on anybody. But I believed that I would get better. That's what kept me hanging on—that and Pam's love and the other people who cared about me. I wanted to express that, but I couldn't. I was a long way from expressing it.

I realized that I had a lot of work to do if I was going to recover and I didn't know if I was up to it. I sat in that hospital bed and people came to me and gave me food, etc., and I was just laying there. To some people, that would be okay, but to me it wasn't good enough.

Some things are hard to accept.

Tuesday, July 22, 2008
Journal

The mold testing results came in today. Wondermakers faxed the report to the nurses' station for me. I'm stunned. Here is what they found:

- *One fungal type was recovered at higher concentrations indoors than out-of-doors.*
- *Four fungal types were recovered indoors that were not detected in the out-of-doors sample, suggesting a possible indoor source.*

- *Aspergillus/Penicillium-like spores were recovered at elevated levels on all three indoor samples submitted. The presence of Aspergillus/Penicillium-like spores indoors at the levels indicated will produce allergic reactions and/or more serious health effects in most people, with young children and elderly being especially susceptible.*

- *Stachybotrys, a type of mold that can produce potent mycotoxins and is often associated with significant health symptoms, was detected on the ground floor and basement samples. This fungal type requires high moisture and thrives on water-damaged cellulose rich materials such as wallboard, ceiling tiles, and paper products. These particular spores are not easily aerosolized; as such, most industry experts agree that any airborne Stachybotrys spores indoors should trigger investigative action and thorough remediation of the mold source.*

- *Chaetomium was observed on all three indoor samples. Reports about this target fungal type note that it is allergenic, can produce various types of mycotoxins, and has been implicated in skin and nail infections, as well as opportunistic infections in immune compromised individuals. This organism requires chronically moist conditions and is most often found growing on cellulose materials. Since it requires similar environmental conditions for growth, Chaetomium is often found in conjunction with Stachysbotrys.*

- *Arthrinium was observed on the ground floor and basement samples. This fungal type has been reported to be allergenic, especially in sensitive individuals. It is frequently found in conjunction with Stachybotrys, requiring very wet conditions for growth.*

- *Hyphal fragments are the fungal filaments on which mold spores form. Because hyphae are not as easily aerosolized as spores, the presence of hyphal fragments indoors, especially at higher levels than out-of-doors, is often an indicator that a mold source is at or near the site of the samples.*

- *Ascospores, Alternaria, basidiospores, Cladosporium, Epicoccum, myxomycetes, Periconia, Pithomyces, rust, Stemphylium and smut are fungal spores that are typically found out-of-doors, but which can grow indoors under the right conditions–usually water-damaged areas. Exposure to any type of spore at elevated levels (over 500 c/m³) either for prolonged periods or for repeated short periods of time can cause ill-health effects. The possible consequences of exposure to mold spores include developing asthma, allergies, hypersensitivity disease and severe respiratory infections.*

We recommend that the mold source(s) and its extent be identified and corrective action be undertaken to avoid potentially severe symptoms and to reduce exposure to building occupants . . .

There is much more, but you get the picture. No wonder my lungs are inflamed! Our house made me sick. Maybe Pete too.

I'm reasonably sure that my heart is fine, but I am concerned about my lungs, especially now. Still, with the dizziness, chest pain, and the shortness of breath, the doctor's main concern is my heart. My doctor is a cardiologist, and he is always flanked by the usual two to four interns, residents, whatever. When you're the patient, you don't get to stand in with the doctors at rounds. I sit in my bed, watching them talk in the corridor.

Every day I have been here I have mentioned that I would like a consult with a pulmonologist, but it hasn't happened yet. Today it was a resident who came by for rounds. In exasperation I said to him, "Listen, I want you to imagine for a moment that I am your mother. Got the picture? Okay. I've been told I might have pulmonary fibrosis. My lungs feel inflamed. We've just learned that our home is contaminated with black mold. Remember now—I'm your mother! Wouldn't you want her to have a consultation with a pulmonologist?"

The pulmonologist arrived this afternoon. He took a thorough history and ordered a high-resolution CT scan, X-rays, and a rather intense pulmonary function test. Long story short—he determined that I don't have pulmonary fibrosis. What a relief! I'm going to live! Wow!

Instead, he thinks it is chronic hypersensitivity pneumonitis, an inflammation of the lungs due to breathing in a foreign substance, usually certain types of dust, fungus or molds. The chronic part indicates that this has been going on for some time. Of course, the first thing I thought of was the mold in our basement at home.

The only way my diagnosis can be confirmed, the doctor told me, is with a lung biopsy and/or bronchoscopy, neither of which are necessary at this time. He told me to see a pulmonologist at home to follow up. The only treatment for this condition is to avoid exposure to the substance that is problematic and to take medication to reduce the inflammation. The chronic form of this disease, which I have, can lead to pulmonary fibrosis. Don't want to go there.

It's quite possible that Pete's condition, if it is indeed sarcoidosis, is also rooted in the mold issue. Nobody knows for sure what causes sarcoidosis, but a leading theory is that it results from environmental toxins. Looks like we are quickly becoming the poster children for the dangers of mold contamination.

Same day, later . . .

When I learned that I didn't have pulmonary fibrosis, I was elated, thrilled, euphoric, even given the sobering news of mold in our house. For weeks, the notion that I would die within five or six years had loomed over me, a cloud of fear and resignation. I didn't feel like I was "done" with life yet . . . Does anyone? With the doctor's new diagnosis, all of that lifted. I was back in the game!

Immediately I called Pete's room to tell him the good news. I was so happy! Pete's nurse answered the phone. "How's he doing today?" I asked, barely able to contain myself.

She hesitated. "Uh–Well . . ." Pause. " . . . it appears that Pete had a stroke sometime over the weekend."

My heart plummeted. Oh no! What does that mean? Is it life threatening? Is he all right? Is there any paralysis? Will he be able to speak? Will they take him off the transplant list? Will he recover?

There I was, stuck in that hospital bed. I knew Pete would be frightened and confused. He would need me. I called my sister, Connie, who had gone back home. "Connie, I need you. Please come." I could barely get the words out.

"I'll pack a bag and come right away," she said. I leaned back on the pillow and sobbed. The nurses were concerned and asked me if I wanted a sedative. "No," I said, "I want to be composed and alert." I took some deep breaths and called on all the courage and inner peace I could access.

Connie got there in record time. Her presence was comforting. We both learned about caregiving years ago from our mother's example, and we are good at it. She pushed my wheelchair along at a pretty good clip. When we got to the fourth floor of the CVC, there was a group of white coats outside of Pete's room, deep in discussion. I asked Connie to wheel me right up to them. When I got there, I said, "I understand he's had a stroke. What's happening?"

The doctor in charge explained that sometime over the weekend–they weren't sure when–Pete suffered two small stokes in the thalamic region of the brain. It seems that the life support machine had "thrown a couple of clots." The doctor said that Pete was doing okay, and that the strokes were not life-threatening. I took one more deep breath as Connie rolled me into his room.

Nothing could have prepared me for what I saw. Pete lay there, his eyes wide open, a deer in the headlights. Every few seconds his upper lip twitched on one side. His face showed no emotion whatsoever. I knew he would be glad to see me, but there was no sign of it on his face. He couldn't speak intelligibly. His right leg trembled intermittently, like that of a child who has to pee. He looked awful–like he had been beaten up and given a lobotomy. He reminded me of Jack Nicholson in "One Flew Over the Cuckoo's Nest."

What could I do but reassure him that everything was all right? I held his hand, talked to him and kissed his cheek. I told him the good news about my diagnosis. I kept up a good front, I think, or at least the best I could manage. After a little while, Connie wheeled me back to my room, both of us in stunned silence.

Looking back . . .

Connie told me later that she didn't think Pete would make it. He looked awful–all skin and bones . . . She thought, if he survives, what is he going to be like?

Update Tuesday, July 22, 2008 at 9:06 p.m.

From Brennan, Pam's son

Good news and bad news today: While Pam is still in the hospital, the pulmonologist is convinced that she does not have pulmonary fibrosis, but a less serious allergic condition in her lungs. Bad news: Pete had a stroke sometime over the weekend. They don't know quite yet what his prognosis will be. We'll try to keep you posted as we learn more. My mom sends love to all of you. Please send love and prayers their way.

Love,

Brennan

12 Messages Posted July 22-23, 2008

God, the Good, is watching over you. I am sure of that. Rest peacefully.
Jane Walsh

Drums beat for you as the sun set on Lake Michigan today!
Thinking of you with love and seeing you both full of life and laughter,
Kerry Lytle

Brennan, thank you for keeping us posted. I can hardly wrap my mind around what is happening to them! This is a time for me to not understand how this could be God's plan for them. They are such wonderful people, who at this time last year were saying their loving vows for a future in marriage together.

I see Pete vibrant and singing and wholly alive and smiling. And I see Pam as her steadfast, grounded, smiling self, thoughtful and sure. The pictures in my mind are positive.
Bless you and keep you all,
Donna Leonard

E-mail, Tuesday, July 22, 2008
To Fellowship Group
Hello Everyone,

I talked with Pam tonight and thought I would share with this particular group of loving beings the essence of our conversation . . . so that we can hold Pam and Pete in Peace, Love, and Trust . . .

Pam is still an inpatient and was taken by wheelchair today to see Pete. She was not told until just before the visit that Pete had a stroke. Although he is responsive and was even able to sit up in a chair today, she described his eyes as having a vacant stare, like deer in headlights. His eyes and upper lip and other parts of his face are twitching . . .

Pam had an adverse physical response that included extreme dizziness and lightheadedness at the shock of receiving this news and seeing Pete this way. Although this was not a pleasant experience, it did affirm for her and for the doctors that have been seeking to find the cause of her dizziness and lightheadedness, that the symptoms are due to a significant stress response in her body that is causing a temporary imbalance between the sympathetic and parasympathetic nervous symptoms. Knowing this provides a healing visualization for all of us: Begin to visualize that Pam's body (and each of our bodies) . . . particularly the nervous system and adrenal glands . . . are filled with Light and healing, as her body is supported miraculously while her emotions are intense and her whole being navigates through these rough waters. Visualize the stress hormones in her body (cortisol in particular) feeling the Love and Light so that they can relax and slow down their production.

As Pam was wheeled back to her room after visiting with Pete, she took some time to call on Spirit to help her get to a place of feeling more contented. She told me that several things happened. She said she remembered a verse that was shared with her a couple of weeks ago that goes something like this: "Right now I don't understand what's happening. Life is a mystery and I do not know how things will unfold. I can't see clearly at all, but I know that someday I will. Until that time there are three things I can do . . . Trust steadily, hope unswervingly, and love extravagantly."

And so . . . we can do the same. We can visualize Pam and Pete (and the One that we are) embraced by Trust, surrounded with Hope, and connected in Love. The other thing Pam shared is that she heard Pete talking to her psychically and his message to her was . . . "If you really love me, let me go." Whatever "Let me go" may mean, we can hold the energy for them both as they seek clarity and "let go" of that which is calling for release and healing . . .

Pam . . . feels the support and love mightily from all of us and returns that love from the depths of her being. This is a profound time for both Pam and Pete and they know that the deepest, darkest, most profoundly difficult times are unfolding into the most profound healing and transformation. Together we witness the sacred unfolding . . .

Love,

Linda Beushausen

Tuesday, July 22, 2008

Journal

"If you love me, let me go." What does that mean? Is he asking me to let him die? Is he just holding on because I won't let him go? Would it be better for him if he could just . . . slip away?

I can't . . . I . . .

I've been sitting here on my single bed at the Transplant House, pondering this message. I know it came from Pete. It was as clear as can be . . . but I can't imagine giving up. I meditated for a long time. What came to me was that I need to hand over his care, his fate, and his life to the Powerful, Benevolent Presence, God, the Beloved. I need to release and be at peace with whatever is to come.

He doesn't need me to give up; he needs me to give him over–to God.

CHAPTER SEVEN

Stand By for a Miracle

Love is what breathes us.
It is what we are.
–John Morton

Wednesday, July 23, 2008
Looking back . . .

*P*AUL AND MARY *got to the
hospital just before I was discharged
that Wednesday. Not good. It was such a shock to me when I saw Pete after his stroke,
I wanted to be able to prepare Paul. By the time Connie rolled me over in my hospital
wheelchair, freshly discharged from my hospital bed, Paul and Mary were already in
Pete's ICU room, standing around awkwardly, taking it all in.*

*I hugged them both, and, with some difficulty because of all the tubes and wires,
kissed Pete. What do you say? What is there to say? Mary, an attractive, petite woman,
younger than I, with long brown hair and Paul's beautiful eyes, was very gracious in
those difficult days. There we were, Pete's ex-wife, his son, and his current wife, gathered*

around his hospital bed while Pete was lying there, clinging to life. At one point I took Mary aside and told her how much Pete regretted what happened when their marriage fell apart, and how it haunted him that he wasn't there in the home when the boys were growing up. He spoke of it often, late at night, with tears in his eyes, but hadn't been able to bring himself to talk with Mary about it. She said, "That was a long time ago. It doesn't matter anymore." She has a generous spirit. We became friends.

I watched Paul, who was quiet and steady. I'm sure the whole scene freaked him out, but he didn't show it. He told me later that the ICU, in its antiseptic newness seemed surreal to him. He had been in Colorado when I called to tell him how serious Pete's condition was. Leaving his summer job as a concert bassist before the end of the season with the Aspen Music Festival, he took a bus to Denver, a plane to Chicago, the "L" to a friend's house in Chicago, Amtrak from Chicago . . .

Paul is slender, tall, and handsome. He just graduated from Indiana University Bloomington. He moves with the grace of an athlete, and is very, very bright. He reminds me of Brennan in that way. Now, standing by Pete's bedside, Paul didn't know if his dad even knew he was there. Pete's eyes were unfocused, his face expressionless. Paul took his hand, then, and was comforted to feel a strong squeeze. Pete knew.

Update Wednesday, July 23, 2008 at 8:40 p.m.

Hello Everyone,

I have been discharged from the hospital after a six-day stay. They took good care of me, but I'm really glad to be out. We had a visit today from Paul, Pete's older son, and Paul's mother, Mary. Paul will be staying here at the Transplant House for a while. Pete's younger son, Sean, flies back home tomorrow and will come here Friday. He's been in Spain this summer with a foreign exchange student program.

Everyone has come at once. My younger son, Phil, his girlfriend, Katlyn, and my granddaughter McKenzie arrived for an overnight visit this afternoon. We are very rich in family.

My diagnosis is chronic hypersensitivity pneumonitis, a kind of pneumonia that is caused by long-term exposure to something I am allergic to—such as mold, cat dander, and dust. It's less severe than pulmonary fibrosis, for which I am very, very grateful. I will still need to pace myself, though, and I still have the inflammation in my chest.

Pete has suffered two small strokes primarily impacting on the the thalamus. He has some symptoms effecting his vision, speech, and ability to swallow. Hopefully these are temporary. The doctor said that the strokes have not compromised his standing on the heart transplant list, which is *very* good news . . . We continue to wait, pray and hope that the issues he's dealing with now are temporary. Healing comes in many different ways. We ask for miracles, and expect to see them. Much love to all of you who have given us such wonderful support. Please know how much we appreciate it!

Love,

Pam

Wednesday, July 23, 2008

Journal

There is a thalamus on each side of the brain. In Pete's case, both sides were affected by the strokes. Apparently two clots formed in the tubing and reached his brain. Blood isn't meant to hang out in tubes, so it sometimes forms clots in there.

The thalamus (I learned now, instead of in eighth grade science when I was overly preoccupied with boys) is like a relay station, receiving and processing information from all the senses except smell. The thalamus also regulates consciousness, sleep and alertness. Severe thalamic stroke can cause paralysis and/or coma, so Pete is very lucky. No—in truth, he is very *blessed*.

As for my diagnosis, I had never heard of hypersensitivity pneumonitis. The chronic form, which they think I have, may lead to pulmonary fibrosis. I hope I don't have to deal with that. Enough is enough.

I'm told that the cause of sarcoidosis is unknown, but many physicians and researchers suspect that it is caused by something the patient breathes in, such as a virus, bacteria, or an environmental toxin. One study I read showed a strong positive correlation between sarcoidosis and occupational exposure to moldy and musty environments. One report considered the strong possibility that some people have a genetic predisposition to the sarcoidosis, so that when they are exposed to an environmental trigger, they develop the disease.

Did our home poison both of us? Sure looks like it.

Same day, later . . .

Paul has a friend, Luisa, from Brazil. They hadn't been in touch for several months, but when Paul was on his way to see Pete, she sent him an e-mail. She said that she'd had a dream about Paul and he was crying. Was he all right?

Same day, later . . .

Last night on the phone Nancy Lou said, "How much can his poor body take?" Just a few weeks ago I would have said that Pete was in excellent shape. He doesn't smoke and he drinks very little. He isn't alcoholic as he suspected years ago, and he isn't overweight. He was working out at the gym six days a week. He's always been high-energy, athletic and strong.

Now it takes six people to get him from the hospital bed to the recliner, three feet away. There are four 3/4-inch tubes connecting him to the life support apparatus, feeding tubes and draining tubes, a catheter to his penis, a picc line for IVs, and whatever else he may have been hooked up to today.

I'm told the speech pathologist was in, and that Pete responded appropriately to questions like, "Do you know what day it is? Do you know where you are?" But when I talked with him later, his response was either unclear or silent. He did grasp my hand firmly though, and I heard him say, "I love you."

When it was time for me to leave, I kissed him and told him I loved him. He said something I couldn't make out, so I leaned in closer. "Twenty-thirty," he said.

Pete remembers . . .

I remember a doctor telling me that I was the sickest guy in the hospital, and thinking the sickest guy in the hospital probably deserves first class treatment. I thought back on my own past and tried to think of what I could have done to prevent the heart failure, to acknowledge my own responsibility. I knew that what the doctors decided on was the best course of action for me, so here I am.

Thursday, July 24, 2008
Notes from Morning Rounds:
   Kidney function okay
   Coughing very important

Some infection in one lung
Pumping socks to avoid clots
Feet look "dusky"–dark and purple
Massage his feet

Update Thursday, July 24, 2008 at 8:00 p.m.

Pete seems stronger today. He gripped my hand so hard it hurt. I know he is comforted to have Paul here. We had several visitors and Pete was quite tired by late afternoon. He coughs a lot, but the docs say that's good, as it gets up some of the fluid in his lungs. Every so often the nurse has to suction him–not a pleasant thing to watch, and probably horrible to experience. They put a long tube down his throat to get the fluid out, causing him to gag and turn bright red. Still, he seems to be a lot more comfortable after the suctioning. I can't watch it anymore, so I step out into the hall. I hope this is one of those things he won't remember.

If you are one who prays, the key prayer now is for just the right heart to become available for transplant. The timing is urgent. Our love and compassion go out to whomever might make that incredible gift.

Thanks and love to you all. Paul says, "Hi" too!

Love,

Pam

10 Messages Posted Thursday, July 24, 2008

. . . Your diagnosis is a blessing and a warning. With all of the love and support you have from family, please make sure to get some good rest, as that will be your best medicine. Pete continues to be in our good thoughts and prayers. Miracles do happen!

Love,

Diane Freestone

Dearest Pam, reading your words this morning was such a gift! I am so very glad that you are strong enough and wise enough to heal and take the time that your body needs for full recovery. You and Pete are in my thoughts . . . With every breath I send strength to you both.

Love, and more love—

Tracey Davis

I bring you prayers and greetings from the Alpha Iota Sisters here in Chicago at the Delta Kappa Gamma International convention. So many have asked about you both! We are rejoicing to hear you are out of the hospital, Pam! *Take it easy!* And, Pete . . . Prayers are coming your way en masse!

Sandy Norland

Update Friday, July 25, 2008 4:04 a.m.

Dear Ones—

Yesterday we had a visit from our good friends, Emmy Highley and Nancy O'Donohue. Nancy said a tender prayer with all of us and then did some energy work again on Pete and then on me. I seem to get some powerful insights when Nancy does this, and I feel moved to share with you what came to me:

It is a sacred journey that I walk with Pete, and I feel privileged to be at his side and in his heart as he walks this valley. That might sound strange, like I think I'm a saint or something, but the truth is I don't feel that way at all. I fumble along, just trying to do the best I can with each moment, knowing my shortcomings and discovering my strengths in new ways each day.

You see, I'm on a mission. Every day is filled with purpose and drive. Everything else is on the shelf for the time being. I am here to support Pete, to make sure he knows that he is surrounded by love, to give him hope when his own slips away, and to make him as comfortable as possible. "Trust steadily. Hope unswervingly. Love extravagantly." That's what my life is about in this place and time. Of course, I know I have to take care of myself in order to take care of him, and I am doing so with the very important support of all of you and the great unseen forces that I can feel all around us.

Please, dear ones, pray for a heart.

We love you.

Pam

7 Messages Posted Friday, July 25, 2008

Chica, when I read your quote in today's update—
"Trust steadily.
Hope unswervingly.
Love extravagantly."
. . . I thought . . . this quote embodies my friend, Chica! It is what she and Pete do that inspires others around them . . . even before the current situation. I hold you in the light and in my heart. Thanks . . .
Mary James

Pam, thank you for letting us in to the beauty and severe truth of your journey in the Now, which is both fully present and fundamentally unknown. I hope for all blessings and good things for Pete and you, and the best possible outcome. I didn't hear your new songs this summer, but the song of your life's journey comes through strong and crystalline here.
Love & best waveforms,
Jeep Rosenberg

Friday, July 25, 2008
Journal

Sean arrived today, fresh from Spain, looking very handsome and sophisticated with his new beard. He is between his junior and senior year of high school, a voracious reader, and a very intelligent young man. He is tall–about six foot two, I believe, with lots of thick, brown hair. He looks different, as if the summer in Spain pushed him from gangly adolescence to the confident young man here now. His Spanish is getting quite good. We were amused to find that we are both reading the same book, *In the Time of the Butterflies*, a novel by Julia Alvarez, his edition in Spanish and mine in English.

He came by train from South Bend, and Paul met him at the station. They will share a room at the Transplant House. When Sean first saw his father, I think he was shocked. He lost his equilibrium for a few seconds, stumbled, and then sat down on the floor. He recovered quickly, though, and blamed it on jet lag.

I am glad to have both of Pete's sons here, but my heart goes out to them. I know all too well how hard it is to see him in this condition. I love both of these young men. When Pete and I were married, I took them aside and told them I felt that I had come into their lives too late to be a stepmother to them, and besides, I didn't like the reputation of stepmothers. I told them that I just wanted to be their friend. They both grinned broadly at that, and we've been friends ever since. It's good to have them here.

Pete remembers . . .

I didn't want to go that way. I was thinking about my kids. I was glad I had life insurance for them, but I didn't want to leave them. I remember Paul and Sean coming into the room. I was glad to see them, but I didn't like them to see me like that.

E-mail, Friday, July 25, 2008
Pam,

Your CarePage update just came through. You describe so beautifully the way that all of us should be living every day—in the moment and with such love that it spills over into everyone that we touch. My love and prayers to you and Pete.

Treasure yourself,
David Sterken

Update Saturday, July 26, 2008 at 2:45 a.m.

Last night my good friend, Nancy Lou, came to Ann Arbor and took me out to dinner. She thought I needed a little sustenance, some quality girl-talk, at least one glass of wine and a healthy dose of non-hospital air. Boy, was she right! The watchman at the hospital recommended Carson's, so off we went.

I'm grateful for the cane she brought me from home, as I am still dizzy from time to time. We sank into a quiet booth and I felt the tension in my shoulders start to let down a little. We had just ordered dinner and taken our first sip of wine when my cell phone rang. It was Dr. Romano at the hospital. "We have a heart for Pete."

They have a heart for Pete!

We made it to the hospital in record time. Now it's a waiting game. The heart is coming from somewhere in Michigan. It may already be here as far as I know. Around 8:15 p.m. they told me that they couldn't harvest the heart until it was determined who would receive the lungs, as both transplant surgeries are done at the same time. We also know that Pete's blood thinner medication has to be stopped three hours before surgery, and the IV is still going now at 2:15 a.m. It will be a long night. The surgery itself could take as long as twelve hours or more. Maybe less.

An incredible thing happened when I got the call from Dr. Romano at the restaurant. I knew that Pete's sister, Claudia, and her husband, Bob, had flown into Detroit from Arizona and were probably driving their rental car from Detroit Metro Airport to Ann Arbor right about then. (Some would call their timing a coincidence. I know better. There are no coincidences.) I called Claudia's cell phone right away to tell her the news, so they could come straight to the hospital, rather than check in at a hotel first.

Claudia and Bob were indeed on their way to Ann Arbor. Claudia had noticed that her cell phone was completely out of charge. She turned it off, annoyed with herself for leaving the charger at home. When I called Claudia, her phone rang–the phone she had just turned off. It *rang*, and I was able to give her the good news.

Pete's younger son, Sean, who has been in Spain all summer, flew back to the states yesterday and joined us here at the hospital today. Pete's older son, Paul, has been here for a few days. My friend Nancy Lou is still here–a rock and a comfort for me. We had a warm reunion when Claudia and Bob got to the hospital. Sean, Paul, Nancy Lou, Claudia, Bob and I sat around, chatting and waiting for hours. My brother, Terry, and his wife, Bobbie stopped by on their way home from their place in the upper peninsula. Claudia and Bob sent out for pizza for all of us. The night dragged on and nothing happened as far as the transplant was concerned.

Now it's almost 3:00 a.m. and I'm camped out in a recliner next to Pete's bedside. The others are getting some sleep at the Transplant House or a motel.

I'm told that Pete is at significantly higher risk than the average heart recipient because of his stroke activity. Still, his chances of survival are much higher with the transplant than without it, and Pete has a very strong will to live. I asked him a few hours ago if he was up to this and he gave me the thumbs up. Scared? Yes, of course, but wondrously courageous at the same time.

The nurses bathed him from head to toe about a half hour ago, and will do so again before surgery. Then he will be swabbed down with iodine. I sit and watch their quiet efficiency with wonder. He is being well taken care of. Compassion, skill, and efficiency run rampant here.

We don't know yet when the actual surgery will take place, so I'm going to see if I can sleep a little in the recliner. Pete is resting comfortably, right next to me. He said something a little while ago, and I moved close to him to hear. He said, "Strong." Yes, indeed, he is strong. Then he said, "Prayer," and we prayed together:

The light of God surrounds us.
The love of God enfolds us.
The power of God protects us.
The presence of God watches over us.
Wherever we are, God is, and all is well.

I reminded him of the hundreds of people who are praying for him all over the country and beyond. Keep those prayers coming. Now we pray for healing, and for Pete's highest good. Thank you all. Our love for you is boundless.
Pam

P.S. The nurse told me that everyone in the ICU thinks of us as "that couple that is so much in love."

---

15 Messages Posted Saturday, July 26, 2008

Once again, your strength and your faith deeply touches my heart. This journey you've been on has inspired so many of us. We are all growing in faith . . . because of you. We are so grateful!

Bless the family, who in their time of grief for their loss, is giving Pete physical life. There truly will be a deep heart connection here . . . Oneness at its physical level . . . Thank you for the energy you have been putting forth to keep all of us informed. We continue to hold you in the Light and affirm that all is well.
Nancy Plantinga

Camp strength
Wishing you both much love and great strength today and beyond.
Karen and Jerry Jennings

Quietly and with a sense of divine assurance, through perfect love, we harmonize with all of life. Concerns, discordant thoughts, fear, or worry have no power over us. We accept health, wholeness, and perfect action now! And all is well . . .
Love,
Deb Lambert, Jaye, Zach, & Josh Mann

Looking back . . .

I remember talking with one of the interns–one of the white coats that was there every morning at rounds. He had warm brown eyes and a kind face, and seemed very approachable. I told him that I was concerned about the transplant in view of Pete's strokes. He smiled and said, "Pete? Ah, with Pete, it's a slam dunk!" He strolled away, giving the thumbs up.

"Hope is the thing with feathers, that perches in the soul, and sings the tune without words, and never stops at all.
–Emily Dickinson

Hospital Speak 101

A *heart transplant* involves removing a person's malfunctioning heart and replacing it with a healthy heart from a deceased donor. Ninety percent of heart transplants are done on patients who have end-stage heart failure, meaning the heart is in such bad condition all treatments, other than heart transplant, have failed.

There are a lot more people waiting for hearts than there are healthy hearts available for transplant. That puts the patient in a delicate position. He or she needs to be sick enough to need a new heart, yet healthy enough to receive it.

About 88 percent of patients survive the first year after transplant surgery, and 72 percent survive for 5 years. The 10-year survival rate is close to 50 percent, and 16 percent of heart transplant patients survive 20 years. Pete will do that. Maybe even more. After the surgery, most heart transplant recipients can resume something close to their normal lifestyles. However, fewer than 40 percent return to work for many different reasons.

Saturday, July 26, 2008

Looking back . . .

What a remarkable 40 hours that was! First there was the call to me at the restaurant, telling me that they had a heart for Pete. I made a few quick calls to family from there while Nancy corralled the young waiter and told him the situation. He said if we could wait ten minutes, he would have our dinners ready and packed up to go. I think he was as excited as we were. I was just finishing my last call when he ran out with a large bag and a big smile, and sent us on our way.

We rushed to the hospital–and then waited. Initially Dr. Romano thought the surgery would be right away, but there was a delay. We waited some more.

We all gathered in the Atrium on the second floor and munched on pizza, then went back up to the surgery floor and waited some more. When it became clear that nothing was going to happen until morning or even later, everyone except me went to get some sleep. I wrapped up in a blanket on the recliner in Pete's room. Finally around 4 a.m. the nurses persuaded me to go back to the Transplant House and get some sleep.

Journal (Undated)

"All is well." This is a familiar truth that is central to my spiritual path. I believe that everything happens for a reason, although sometimes we cannot fathom what that reason might be. I think of the pain I went through with divorce. It was horrible—but now, many years later, I can see how that shift in my life's path made all the difference. At the time, I felt like I was disintegrating in that relationship, losing my soul, my essence. I was dying inside. Leaving brought me home to myself. And all is well.

I lost some friends when my husband and I parted—a heart-wrenching thing—but it moved me to find an entire new group of wonderful friends who have been catalysts in my spiritual awakening. And again, all is well.

When my son, Phil, was using a lot of drugs, I was devastated and desperate for help, which was short in coming. But that entire experience deepened my well of compassion and gave me a whole new perspective on blame and responsibility. After endless soul-searching, I came to the conclusion that I hadn't been a terrible mother. I had done the best I knew how to do. It just happened. After that, I no longer looked at parents of wayward children and judged them for their poor parenting. Sometimes it just happens, regardless of what we do. Phil is on his own path, and will eventually come into his own spiritual awareness, in this lifetime or another. All is well.

Pete is facing what is perhaps the greatest struggle of his life. He is about to undergo heart transplant surgery, which was unthinkable just a generation ago. Will he make it? The doctors seem to think so.

And if he doesn't? I have to believe that if he doesn't make it, still, all is well. That's hard for me to accept, but I know that there is something going on here that I don't understand, that I can't see from my present, limited perspective. It's as if I were looking at the world through a pinhole camera. I can't see the big picture. So I have to remember Pete's words, "If you love me, let me go," and release him to God. Whatever happens . . . truly, all is well.

Homework: Accept what is. Pain and suffering come from resisting what is. Accept what is.

Update Saturday, July 26, 2008 at 9:08 a.m.

Still waiting. I'm not sure what the delay is, but the transplant is still on—we just don't know when. More when we have more information.

Love,

Pam

> 2 Messages Posted Saturday, July 26, 2008 after 9:08 a.m.
>
> Standing firm and steadfast, together with you in the Heart of God. We await with joy and gratitude the healthy heart that will soon be beating in Pete. Thank you, Pam, for sharing those powerful thoughts and insights.
>
> Love,
>
> Carol Johnson

Update Saturday, July 26, 2008 at 11:07 a.m.

I just learned that Pete's heart transplant surgery has been scheduled for 4:15 p.m. today. They will start the final prepping at 2:00 o'clock. The delay was related to finding the right recipients for all the organs of the donor. We have quite a group of folks here, keeping vigil. You are doing that for us too, from afar. It's all the same.

Tons of love,

Pam

> 14 Messages Posted Saturday, July 26, 2008 after 11:07 a.m.
>
> My family had the opportunity to meet you and the love you spread through the All God's Children Choir. We have been watching and praying for Pete's progress. It reminds us of that beautiful song you sang with the kids of southwestern Michigan . . . "Love grows one by one, two by two, and four by four. Love grows 'round like a circle and comes back knocking at your front door." *(Note: "Love Grows One by One" ©1981 Carol Johnson—See Resources)*

> Our prayers belong to you, Pete, the heart donor, and his or her family.
> Sincerely,
> Mark Moreno, Laurie, Mila, Siena, & Oliviana
>
> Waiting with you. I'm with you both all the way.
> All love,
> Sharon Jensen

Update Saturday, July 26, 2008 at 4:14 p.m.

Here we go! Pete is now in surgery. He went in about 20 minutes ago. It's an amazing production to move him with all the tubes, IVs and wires. He was giving us the thumbs up as they wheeled him out of his room and down to the surgery.

We all gathered in the waiting room and formed a circle–Pete's sister and brother-in-law, Pete's two sons, Nancy Lou and me. Nancy led us in a beautiful prayer, and each of us put in our own particular message. It was a very special moment, enveloped in love.

The surgery will be a long one, so I may not update this for a while unless we get any important news in the meantime. Thanks for staying tuned. Knowing that we have an army of friends and family out there supporting us is very, very uplifting.

Love,

Pam

> 9 Messages Posted Saturday, July 26, 2008 after 4:14 p.m.
>
> We're praying for you here in NYC! You are in my heart. Stay strong.
> Love,
> Russ Jennings
>
> We're glad to hear that Pete had his thumbs up. We are praying for him and we love him very much. We feel the surgery is going to be a great success!
> Love,
> Bob (Pete's brother in Florida) & Gisella Wehle

Journal

The surgery, performed by Dr. Pagani and Dr. Romano, had begun. We were the only ones in the waiting room on a Saturday night. When Nancy Lou led us in prayer, the awesome spirit of God was so strong in that room, it was palpable.

I'm glad everyone arrived in time to be here during Pete's surgery. Their company is comforting to both Pete and me, and the six of us have bonded in our love for our dear friend, brother, father, husband. We talked and talked and talked, joking about keeping vigil, and how that made us vigil-antes—Wehle Vigilantes.

It was a long night of waiting. Nancy Lou worked on embroidering a pillow case. Paul and Sean finished a tricky jigsaw puzzle. Then they grabbed a couple of wheelchairs. Paul is good at leaning the chair back and keeping his balance, as if it were a unicycle. He challenged Sean to a race, and the two of them shot down the empty hallway.

Mostly we waited, and waited, and waited. Every time the door to the surgery area opened we all jumped, but there wasn't any news. Hour after hour passed. One of the nurses warned us that Dr. Pagani was not one to give ongoing reports to the families. So we waited.

There were two recliners and several chairs in the waiting room, which we pushed together for makeshift beds. We all tried to sleep, but it wasn't easy. Paul crashed right on the floor, his long legs sprawled every which way. Nancy Lou talked in her sleep. Somewhere around 2 a.m. I fell into severe emotional overload. I didn't want to call attention to myself, so I walked down the long, carpeted hallway to a corner where I could sit and just weep. I tried to be quiet, but Nancy Lou's radar was up, and in a few minutes I saw her coming my way. She held me in her arms and rocked me. A few minutes later Claudia joined us. We were all over-the-top emotionally, and got into the cry-laugh-cry syndrome. I remember we talked about how Pete had needed so many transfusions for his other surgery. *Where do they get all that blood? Do you suppose they go to Sam's Club and buy it by the barrel?*

It was a long night.

Update Sunday, July 27, 2008 at 6:27 a.m.

Well folks, it's 6:25 a.m. Sunday and we have been here in the waiting room since about nine yesterday morning. We learned a few hours ago that the transplant itself was complete and that the new heart is in Pete's body, beating and keeping him alive! The nurse said that there was still much to do, though. He would share no specifics other than that Pete had "required a lot of products." That's probably blood transfusions—maybe other things as well. The nurse said that was not unusual.

We expect to see one of the surgeons any time now. The nurse said that no news is good news, so we are resting in that. We've had coffee and bagels, stories, tears, and laughter.

What a journey! God is here.

Love,

Pam

---

3 Messages Posted Sunday, July 27, 2008 after 6:27 a.m.

Prayers for you and Pete were offered at the Delta Kappa Gamma church services held yesterday afternoon . . . God bless you all today and in the days ahead . . .
Sandy Norland

We are so glad this part of the journey is over! We will be praying for Pete in the days and weeks to come. Tell him we love him and marvel at his strength.
Darrell Elkins

Update Sunday, July 27, 2008 at 9:37 a.m.

Dear Ones, We finally spoke with one of the heart transplant surgeons at 9:00 this morning, fourteen hours after the first incision. The new heart is in place and working well in Pete's precious body. Amazing! Hallelujah!

The surgery went long because of profuse bleeding, but that has slowed down some, and they are bringing Pete back to his room in ICU. We hope to be able to go in and see him within the hour. He will still be sedated for a while, though.

They had to use a pig valve because one of Pete's valves was too big for the new heart. Isn't that mind boggling? The key concern now is whether or not he has had any bleeding in the brain at the sites of the earlier strokes. We can't know that at this point, but we are all hoping for the best.

The six of us who have kept vigil since yesterday morning are beyond exhausted and will get some sleep after we get in to see Pete. It has been a time of great bonding for all of us. After the doctor talked with us this morning we circled up again and sent out a prayer of huge gratitude.

Thanks to all of you for the wonderful prayers and loving thoughts. You are all honorary Wehle Vigilantes now. I know you have contributed to this miracle, and for that we are profoundly grateful!

Love,

Pam

---

10 Messages Posted Sunday, July 27, 2008 after 9:37 a.m.

What wonderful news! We pray that Pete's recovery from surgery goes well and that this amazing gift of a healthy heart will open a new chapter in the loving life that Pete shares with his incredible Pam!

At yesterday's rehearsal, the children, parents, grandparents, and choir directors of All God's Children Choir stopped action (an infrequent occurrence) at 4:15 for a silent moment where we all envisioned a strong, resilient heart being placed in the chest of a strong, resilient and courageous man . . . We love you both and will continue to hold you in our prayers.

Sandy and Larry Feldman

Posted Sunday, July 27, 2008

From Unity on the Lakeshore to Membership,

Pam and Pete have touched so many lives. This is our opportunity to touch their hearts with our love and generosity. Unity Church has set up a fund for their needs during this time. You may send contributions to Unity on the Lakeshore anytime . . .

We are so grateful for the healing that continues to unfold. We are also extremely grateful to have the opportunity to be a part of their journey.

Thank you God for healing Pete's heart, his body. Thank you for the Truth that "All is well." And so it is!

Thank you from our Spirit to Yours,

Pastor Marty, Pastor Sherry, and the Congregation

"If one falls down, his friend can help him up."—Ecclesiastes 4:10

Monday, July 28, 2008

Journal

Courage Through My Lenses

Courage is the capacity to confront challenges and move through them with perseverance and acceptance. It is brought into our awareness by example, and developed through experience. Courage is chosen, not given. Optimism, inner strength and grit all play a part in developing courage, but the bedrock of courage is the deep peace that comes from knowing that we are never alone, that there is a Presence that walks with us through these valleys, and will never desert us.

Sometimes young people take reckless chances with their lives due to inexperience and the sense that they are somehow invincible. That is more ignorance than courage. True courage is in being aware that one *might* fail, one *might* get hurt, one *might* lose something or someone precious, and still doing what must be done, simply because it is the right thing to do.

Fear, the great annihilator of courage, can be what keeps us from doing anything we should, could, or would, or it can be something we move through, fully aware of its presence, yet stronger than *it* can ever be.

Courage is something I have prayed for, and something I have developed in ways I might never have experienced had Pete not become so sick. I own my courage. I choose it. And I acknowledge that it didn't come from me–it came from the Light inside, and the abiding knowledge that truly, God is in charge. Pete's courage–his amazing courage–comes from the same place–God's indwelling Light.

CHAPTER EIGHT

You Gotta Have Heart

"More than 100 people are involved in a transplant operation . . .
and we can't waste time and resources if there is a chance
the caretakers aren't up for an awesome responsibility."
Heart Transplant surgeon and pioneer,
–Dr. Leonard Bailey

HOW TO GET A HEART

I DID A LITTLE Internet research on heart transplantation. The procedure began in the 1960s. The most recent data I could find indicates that about 2,000 hearts are available for transplant in the United States every year. This is in contrast with the 150,000 or more people in the U.S. with advanced heart failure. The average waiting time in the U.S. for a heart is 230 days.

Pete received his heart just ten days after he was put on the list. How was he so lucky? The docs said he was at the top of the list because he was so desperately ill. He couldn't live without the life support machine, he wasn't a candidate for the kind of life support that allows a person to go home and wait for a heart, and he was having strokes from his life support machine. If he had to wait much longer, it would have been too late.

To get on the heart transplant list, Pete had dozens of tests, and had to be evaluated by a cardiologist, an infectious disease physician, a social worker, a dietitian, a dentist, the transplant coordinator, and probably others I don't remember. You see, when a person is waiting for a transplant of any kind, his or her name is placed on a list at the United Network of Organ Sharing (UNOS). When a healthy organ becomes available, the decision of who gets it is based on the patient's blood type, weight, and health status, the donor's blood type and weight, and how many other people are waiting. If the patient lives in the same part of the country as the donor, that is a plus. The heart only survives outside of the body for a few hours.

Recipients are taking on a big commitment, as they will be on immunosuppressive medications for the rest of their lives, and those medications have significant side effects, including a greater vulnerability to infections and diseases. They also have to have follow-up tests and biopsies to check for rejection, and must commit to a healthy lifestyle.

Update Monday, July 28, 2008 at 6:53 p.m.

Dear Friends and Family,

Today was a mixed day. Of course we are thrilled that Pete has a new heart and that it seems to be working well. That is so amazing—so *big*—there are no words for the wonder of it.

The wrinkle—and we all hope that is all it is—is the continuing risk of stroke damage. You may remember that Pete had two small strokes before his heart transplant. His CT scan this morning showed some bleeding in the brain—not a lot, but something to be watched.

Paul and I were in Pete's room in ICU this morning when the neurologist came in to do an assessment. Pete's eyes were open—but for the first time since all this began, he didn't respond when I spoke to him. The neurologist asked Pete to wiggle his fingers, his toes—nothing. He asked him again. Nothing. He asked Pete to wiggle his thumb. Nothing.

Paul and I stood by, frightened and anxious, not knowing if this was to be expected right after a heart transplant or not, and wondering if Pete was still partially under sedation. Maybe that was it . . . or not. The neurologist finally explained that Pete might not be fully awake yet and, sure enough, in another half hour or so, Pete did respond to the commands and moved his fingers and toes. He remained mostly still and silent throughout the day, though, with his eyes wide open. We won't know for a while if the bleeding has damaged the brain.

So—we hold on for another ride on the emotional roller coaster. The doctors don't seem to be too concerned, although they are monitoring him very closely. They have been very clear all along the way about the risks Pete faced. They will do another CT scan tomorrow, so we may know more then.

What I'm finding, in talking with other people here who are playing the waiting game for their loved ones, is that we get used to taking good news in teeny tiny doses—an inch here, an inch there.

"He knew me."

"They had him sit up in a chair for an hour."

"She ate a little."

Things we all take for granted become enormous landmarks . . . What happens, at least with me, is a heightened and deepened gratitude for the simple state of being alive—both for Pete and for me—and for the other people here, living on the edge. We are all both fragile and strong—and gifted with this holy opportunity to let God express through us. Be well, loved ones, and be grateful, as I am for you!

Love,

Pam

P.S. Thank you, Claudia M. and Linda B. for the wonderful, tender visit, and the yummy dinner! Thank you, Nancy Lou for being my rock through so much of this. I don't know what I would have done without you.

9 Messages Posted Monday, July 28, 2008

I need your input re my thoughts on a benefit concert for you and Pete here in South Haven . . . It seems like a wonderful way for your multitude of friends to be supportive . . . Please let me know.
Love, light, & blessings,
Betty Smith

We have been awaiting news, so thank you so much for updating us. I do believe that Pete can hear and understand what you are saying to him . . . .When my mother was in the hospital with cancer she was in a coma for days. We were all camped out, watching the sports games, but she was non-responsive. Someone asked what the score was. She calmly gave us all the score and then was silent again! We were blown away!
Love and Life,
Donna Leonard

You and Pete are on our minds day and night, Pam. I don't know if this will help or not, Pam, but I do know that Pete can hear you. We know he can. When Lin had an aneurysm and blood on the brain, the doctors said that it would have to drain off or they would have to go in and remove it. I asked, "Well, where does it go when it drains off?" (I sure didn't know.) It drains down the back of the neck . . . I kept telling her that we needed to get the fluid off of her brain and to imagine herself in a game of golf. With every stroke (I panicked when I said the word too at first!), she took, she was to see some of the fluid running down the back of her neck. Lo and behold, three days later she was out of ICU and the fluid was way down in the brain. I know Pete likes to play sports, so you may want to try that with him.

I hope this helps in some small way, Pam. We see miracles every day in all things. I truly believe it's the power of the mind that allows all these wonderful things to happen in life.
Lou Ann Ziolkowski

Thanks for all of your updates about Pete. You are doing an exceptional job. I've been reading some about the thalamus and stroke rehabilitation, especially about the positive effects and success of rhythmic auditory stimulation. The research indicates that listening to rhythmic music enhances motor activity and encourages motion in stroke patients. It is more than a coincidence that music flows through both of you, so get your fingers strumming on your guitar and begin singing to your dear Pete! You might have him listen to recordings of his favorite, Frank Sinatra . . .

Peace and love to you both,

Chuck Doebler

Hi Aunt Pam,

I have been following your updates and appreciate them. Your strength is inspiring. We think of you and Pete on a daily basis, and send loving thoughts your way.

I especially wanted to tell you, there is a specific speech therapy technique used by music therapists with patients who cannot produce speech, but can still understand language. It's called Melodic Intonation Therapy. A lot of times, even if folks lose the ability to produce speech, they can still sing. I really think it would be worth looking into. . . I think there's a music therapist there at U. of M. Let me know if I can help.

Best wishes and love,

Katie Chappell-Lakin

Tuesday, July 29, 2008

Notes from morning rounds:

Pete's heart–sarcoid? Being analyzed

Weight 165

3 chest tubes, Left chest tube placed

1st CT scan–**subdural hematoma**

2nd CT scan–no change

Remove vent? Extubate tonight or tomorrow

Area of brain affected by strokes:

Motor areas

Not mental

Not language processing

Speech–too soon to tell

Encouraging that he is moving his body parts

Hospital Speak 101

Subdural hematoma - a collection of blood on the surface of the brain. If the hematoma puts increased pressure on the brain, it can cause dizziness, slurred speech, impaired gait, and sometimes progresses to coma and even death.

Update Tuesday, July 29, 2008 at 10:58 a.m.

Dear Ones,

Things are moving along well here. As usual, I listened in on the doctors' reports when they did rounds this morning. I learned that they are taking Pete off the ventilator. They will reduce the amount of air flow a little at a time and monitor how he does as he breathes on his own more and more. That's a major step.

Today's CT scan showed no additional bleeding in the brain–very good news. The part of the brain that was affected by the strokes will probably not impair his motor and mental capacities and the doc said that he shouldn't have difficulty processing language. It's too soon to tell if he will have trouble with the actual speaking part. He did say that it's encouraging that Pete can move his fingers and toes.

I followed Lou Ann's suggestion to tell Pete to envision himself golfing, and with each stroke to envision the blood in his brain draining down the back of his neck and away. Also, after Chuck's research and suggestions about music with a beat being helpful for stroke patients, I made a CD for him on my computer–Sinatra and other music that should be just great for his healing. I played it for him this morning. The nurses love it!

I take things one day at a time. Hope runs and flows in abundance in my heart. You all help me with that. Thank you for your wonderful messages of love and encouragement. In time I'll be able to share them all with Pete too. He knows that many, many people are praying for him and sending him love and healing.

Love,

Pam

---

17 messages Posted Tuesday, July 29, 2008

Every day we stay close to you in spirit, envisioning Pete singing the old Sinatra stuff with his usual bazzazz, doing everything he loves . . . as well as ever. I do the same for you, Pam. Your strength and courage, faith and optimism—*God in you*—comes shining through so beautifully. May your lungs be strong and healthy, powering your own wonderful music . . .

Love,

Carol Johnson

We are overjoyed that the surgery is done and that things are beginning to heal and fall into place. As has been said by others, your strength, courage, love and presence throughout this has been so inspiring. Your updates are filled with grace, blessings and love. Also the messages you have been getting are so remarkable, filled with healing energy, prayers and love. It is a tribute to you both to have surrounded yourself with so many very caring special people in your lives. I feel blessed to be among them.

Love to you and Pete,

Selma Holme

Tuesday, July 29, 2008

Journal

Everyone has gone home, and I'm back to my normal routine here. Life goes on—Thank God! Now we work each day at getting Pete back to where he was before. I don't know if that will happen—what life will be like by this time next year, but I hold the vision of him strong, whole, and alert. In the meantime, I am gaining a great capacity for patience.

I think I'm addicted to the CarePages. I can't wait to get back to Transplant House at night to see who has posted each day, and what they've had to say. It's like bread and water to the hungry. Sometimes I'm able to get online at the Cardiovascular Center and check there. I crave the support like some people crave cigarettes. Gotta have my fix.

I know that the eternal source of comfort, love, and support is God's presence deep within me–but sometimes I just have to read those postings too. They keep me going–caffeine for the shaky soul.

Brennan's phone calls help immensely too. He tells me how strong I am and what a wonderful job I am doing. With all these supportive comments, telling me what a great person I am and how well I'm handling all of this, what can I do but try to be/do that? It's an amazing thing, really. I am fueled by the support–and I keep going. I really think it is God's way of working through people. They become His/Her voice.

I wonder if Pete can feel all of this love coming to him. He's not able to verbalize anything now, but I hope he can feel it somehow. It's powerful. It's grace.

Wednesday, July 30, 2008

Letter To Our Dear Unity Family,

As Pete and I move through this challenging time, I want you all to know that your support, prayers, and healing thoughts have been very much with us every step of the way. I feel it, and I'm sure Pete does too. We are very blessed to have so many wonderful people holding the high watch for us.

This experience is a profoundly spiritual one. We are down to the very essence of life and death–and in that sacred duality, God's presence is very real. I see the divine in the faces of family members in the waiting room; the young woman who comes down to the cafeteria in her hospital gown, pushing her IV pole in front of her; the surgeon, sitting down with the anxious family; the nurse, hanging up "Get Well" cards where her patient can see them; the two women crying in the hallway, holding each other in comfort and pain–it's everywhere.

Most of the time I am optimistic. I envision Pete and me singing together, walking on the beach hand in hand, enjoying Thanksgiving dinner at Camp Friedenswald with family, playing with the grandchildren yet to come, walking into church again for the first time and being greeted by many, many loving smiles . . .

My awesome niece, Wendy, sent me a precious card that I read every day. On the front is a flock of beautiful doves and the word, "Peace." On the side panel she wrote:

Please don't give up on normal life.
It will come back it will come back it will come back it will come back it will come back . . . in all its ordinary splendor.

When fear and doubt start to play around the edges, I remember Sherry's message of "I Believe; help my disbelief." I also think of Reverend Marty reminding us that we are not our thoughts—that we control them, rather than the other way around.

I am also learning about abundance. When Pete and I decided to tithe a few months ago we weren't really sure it would work. Money wasn't exactly piling up in our bank account—but I had written a song, "Send Out More," a few years ago with the message, "Whatever you send out, comes back to you." We decided to walk the talk.

Fast forward to a couple of weeks ago. My car started chugging and hesitating. I needed the car to get to and from the hospital. The repair bill came to a bit over $500. Gulp. At first I was upset and started fighting off panic, as money is tight right now without either of us working. But within minutes I just *knew* somehow it would all work out. The very next day $500 was deposited in my checking account from money that had been donated to the church for us. The Universe provides, and I am learning how to receive.

We needed someone to adopt our two cats, and Barbara Corcoran stepped up to the plate. We needed to have our house cleaned to get rid of the cat dander before we come home. Some angels at our church chipped in to have it professionally cleaned. We needed to have the air quality at our house tested. Dear Peter Hawkins said he'd be delighted. I might be feeling a bit lonely up here, just going back and forth from the Transplant House and the hospital, day after day. Loving friends show up and pray with us and take me out to dinner. I feel the need for prayer support, and loving prayers issue from our church, our family, and from all over the country and beyond. This is the Universe at work, and I am learning to receive.

You, my dear friends, *are* the Universe. We are connected. We are family. Pete and I are overwhelmed with love and gratitude. Thank you, thank you, thank you!

Love,

Pamela Chappell (and love from Pete too)

> *"Giving connects two people, the giver and the receiver, and this connection*
> *gives birth to a new sense of belonging."*
> *–Deepak Chopra*

Update Wednesday, July 30, 2008 at 6:40 a.m.

Hello out there, dear friends and family–

After a brief visit with Pete this morning, I'll be leaving for an appointment with a pulmonologist in Kalamazoo. Since we came here five weeks ago, I have spent every day with Pete, but I have to keep this appointment. I hope to be back by 4 p.m. or so, and will go straight to the hospital. Please say an extra strong prayer this morning for Pete to be aware that he is constantly surrounded by love and supported by prayers. He has two excellent nurses caring for him, and lovely music to listen to, so hopefully the time will pass quickly and he won't realize how long I've been gone.

He had a good night. The main concerns for the next few days is a bit of infection in one of his lungs and the impact of the strokes he had before the transplant. Time will tell, and we are hoping and envisioning the best possible outcome. He's our Miracle Man!

I'd like to share with you a message from Amy Branham in South Haven:

To Be Happy:
Free your heart from hatred.
Free your mind from worries.

Live simply.
Give more.
Expect less.

Love to you all—and deep, deep gratitude for your wonderful postings.
Love,
Pam

---

5 messages Posted Wednesday, July 30, 2008

Pam, I have been reading your updates and praying fervently for both of you . . . My 55-year-old brother was a heart donor two years ago and someone at U. of M. Hospital got his heart. We received a letter from the recipient a few months later, thanking my brother and the family for the life-giving gift. It was one of the most beautiful things we could have ever done. Please know there is a family somewhere praying for you, hoping and wondering . . . even in their grief . . . God be with you each and every moment.
Jan Yelding

We have a friend that waited eight years for a heart. In those eight years, her condition was miserable, but sometimes better than necessary to be put on the urgent list. She spent years wishing her condition would worsen in order to get the new heart. She received it in 1999 and is living so much more happy a life. It must be a blessing for Pete to be free of that hurdle. And he is so lucky to have you.
Much love,
The Morenos

We heard someone sing "The Impossible Dream" recently and immediately thought of you, Pete, and what a terrific performance you did in "Man of La Mancha." We know that you can live that impossible dream.
Much love and many blessings to both of you,
Gary & Shirley Pressnell

I go to sleep at night thinking of you, holding you both, and I awake with such hope and peace. When I arrive at work I check your news, first thing. Blessings upon blessings are there, like a field full of Queen Anne's Lace . . . fragile looking, but steadfast and persevering. You are enfolded every minute.

Love,

Tracey Davis

Update Wednesday, July 30, 2008 at 7:14 p.m.

I'm so glad to tell you that Pete is making good progress. He looked much better today. His eyes, which have been yellowish and unfocused, are much more clear and focused today. He has been taken off the ventilator and is now breathing on his own again. We are encouraged. He has croaked out a few words, but it will take a little while to get his sweet, strong voice back after having had that tube jammed down his throat for days.

This afternoon he kept pointing to the wall across from his bed. The nurses and I were trying to figure out what he was trying to call to our attention. Finally I realized that he was pointing to the beautiful cards we have received, some of which the nurses have put up on the bulletin board. I read them all to him, and he just shook his head in wonder. There are so many! He is amazed that all those people care about us. I'm not surprised at all. I know how blessed we are!

I saw the pulmonologist in Kalamazoo today. He has prescribed something to help with the inflammation. It seems that the most important thing I can do for my lung condition is to stay away from the things I'm allergic to. It's just common sense. I will have some allergy testing done when things settle down a bit with Pete. Apart from that, there isn't a lot I can do beyond just taking care of myself, especially getting enough rest. I'll see the doctor again after some test results come in. I'm feeling much better.

Love to all of you, and big hugs,

Pam

Posted Wednesday, July 30, 2008 after 7:14 p.m.

Hallelujah! My heart is full of joy, love for both of you, and gratitude for your continuing good news! You are both so precious and so needed in our world. So much more to give and enjoy! Bright blessings!

Ellen Reinstatler

Update Thursday, July 31, 2008 at 8:50 p.m.

Dear Friends and Family,

Pete is getting better every day. The O.T. and the P.T. got him up and into a chair this afternoon. He needed a lot of help, but he made it, and sat up for about an hour. This is progress. He doesn't speak yet—but we expect that to come back soon. The doctor said that he is moving along in the right direction. Everything moves very slowly, particularly when strokes are involved. I am thrilled with every little step along the way.

Last night I spoke with my dear friend, Annette Covatta, who is a retired nun, living in Colorado. She teaches the intensive journaling retreat I have been attending for years. Annette is a very wise, fun, and caring person, and I love her dearly. She has mobilized her entire community of 360 retired nuns to pray for Pete, and as she says, "They really know how to pray!"

Pete's brother, Bob, has arranged for a mass to be celebrated for Pete in Port Charlotte, Florida in a couple of weeks. We have people from just about every religious tradition holding Pete up in prayer. How blessed is that?! Thank you for joining this fabulous group. Our focus now is to restore Pete to excellent health, all systems working in harmony and with efficiency as soon as possible as in keeping with his highest good. Thank you!

Love,

Pam

P.S. Special greetings to my dear sisters-of-the-heart who gather every year at this time to celebrate life, love and friendship in our "Goddess Gathering." Know that it stings not to be with you. I hold you in my heart and will be back with you in the flesh next year!

---

12 messages Posted July 31 - August 2, 2008

Hey Pete, looking good, buddy. Pretty soon you will be back in left field, playing a doubleheader with the boys. Keep fighting the good fight.
Still praying for you—
Sully

Update Friday, August 1, 2008

Another day, and some more progress. Pete sat up again twice today. He seemed more relaxed and stronger. I look forward to hearing him speak again. Today he croaked out, "I love you." One of the nurses said she had to leave because it made her cry.

I went to the monthly Heart Transplant Support Group meeting this morning. I asked about what I can expect in the next few months, and the comments from the heart transplant recipients and their spouses were very helpful. I'm learning a lot. For example, Pete's immune system will be suppressed so he will need to wear a mask when he is out in public for the first few weeks to protect him from any germs that may be lurking about. He also may experience some dramatic mood swings due to the steroids. Of course, everyone is different, so we will take it as it comes. There's more—much more. It was a good crash course in what is yet to come.

I have learned that Pete is Heart Transplant Patient # 702 at the University of Michigan Hospital. Amazing. All is well.

Love,

Pam

"Healing does not mean going back to the way
things were before, but rather allowing what
is now to move us closer to God."

–Ram Dass

E-mail, Friday, August 1, 2008

Pam,

I trust slow movement in healing, so that the delicate, exquisite balance our beings work through can be sustained. Thank you for keeping us in the circle of this great healing.

Love and support, prayer and toning with you.

Judy Cassidy

Update Saturday, August 2, 2008 at 7:03 p.m.

What a day! I am exhausted. It started off well. Pete was sleeping when I arrived at the hospital around 8:30 this morning. One of the docs stopped by and told me that Pete had been removed from the "Critically Ill" list. That is substantial progress. Pete's son, Sean, and Sean's mother, Mary, arrived later for a visit. They drove three hours to get here from South Bend. Pete wasn't very communicative, but he held his son's hand for a while.

Sean put up the rest of the beautiful cards we have received. They now cover most of one entire wall, splashing it with color and love.

Later in the afternoon, after they left, Pete began coughing more. It's an "inside" cough–I don't know how else to describe it, except that it rumbles inside his chest and deep in his throat. This got progressively worse until I became really alarmed. It almost sounded like he was gargling, there was so much fluid in his lungs. He was suctioned several times, but it didn't seem to make much difference.

A concerned nurse practitioner stopped in and listened to his chest with her stethoscope. She said, "Oh my God!" and left the room in haste. Gulp. I did some fervent, heavy-duty praying, sitting there by his side. *What the hell is going on?*

Then an X-ray technician arrived with a mobile X-ray machine. I was amazed–I've never seen such a thing. Finally the doctor in charge decided to give Pete a diuretic. Generally they like to avoid that, because they don't want to overburden the kidneys at this point.

After that commotion, Pete settled down a bit, drifting in and out of sleep. It was one of those nights when I just hated to leave him. He finds my presence comforting. I know he is getting the best possible care–but I just feel uneasy walking out of the ICU. I need rest and respite in order to stay healthy myself, though. Sometimes it's hard to balance my own needs against his.

So, my friends, we especially need your prayers and healing thoughts tonight. Please envision for Pete *crystal clear lungs* and all of his body's systems in perfect alignment and harmony.

Thank you, dear and faithful friends,

Pam

---

21 Messages Posted Saturday, August 2, 2008

You two are my heroes! The courage and strength you have shown is an inspiration. Praying for healing for both of you . . .

Love you,

Diana McMann

Pam, We've got this covered.

Love,

Kat Keasey

You both are in our prayers.

Much love,

Dan & Margie Kivel

We're with you.

Darrell Elkins

One day at a time, one crisis at a time, and patience!

Love,

Diane Freestone

Pete remembers, telling Pam . . .

When you left me at night I would feel bad. I was determined to survive the night until you returned, you know? I do remember feeling somewhat abandoned when you left. I knew you were tired, and I encouraged you to go. I'd say, "I'll be all right," but I really wasn't. Sometimes it wasn't easy, because they'd come in and give me a shot or I'd soil myself, which I didn't like. I'd say, "Leave me alone," and they'd say, "What's wrong, Mr. Wehle?"

Update Sunday, August 3, 2008 at 5:37 a.m.

I've been awake since 4:00 a.m. Couldn't sleep. I'm feeling uneasy, unsettled. I just called the hospital and the nurse said that Pete got some good sleep last night. That's a relief. He needs the rest. Actually, so do I. Thanks for all your prayers. More later.

Love you,

Pam

CHAPTER NINE

Solos and Duets

"Time will solve some problems in and of itself. It can happen
if you are strong and loving enough to get out of the way
and let Spirit work in Its own perfect timing."
—John-Roger

Sunday, August 3, 2008
Journal

L ATELY I FIND myself in a
peculiar flow between treasuring
my solitude and feeling lonely for companionship. Being three hours from home
leaves us a bit isolated here. Visits from friends and family become huge events
in our existence, even if it's just a brief chunk of time. It's good to be able to talk
about what's going on with someone who really cares, and it provides a little
window on the world outside of the hospital. On the other hand, at the end of a
long day at the hospital I often don't want to do anything more than go back to
my room, thaw out something to eat, and retire to my little space.

It may seem strange to feel alone at all with Pete right here, but he is asleep or unconscious much of the time. Even when he is awake, he is not really "here." His mind is muddled by the drugs and the illness. He asks the same questions over and over, forgetting what I have told him. He worries a lot, so I hide my own concerns from him, whether it's about his condition, financial matters, or my own health. It's hard to be the keeper of all of that and pretend that it doesn't exist. It weighs me down. When I realize what my thoughts are doing, I do my best to give it all up to God and trust that things will work out. I work hard at maintaining a positive presence for Pete–and for myself. Sometimes it's exhausting.

One of my greatest concerns has been about money. Being away from home and paying for housing, food, etc., is just part of it. The routine expenses with our home continue, of course, and loan payments, etc. Now that I know we need to have our house remediated from mold, I find myself way out of my financial comfort zone. Of course we will also have a lot to think about in terms of medications after we get home–and most likely, Pete won't be able to work. I probably won't either, as he will need round-the-clock care, at least for a while. I'm working on his disability papers. My head swims in numbers and I feel overwhelmed. Then I pray. I ask for comfort and peace. And then, once again, I receive the assuring message that it will all work out, and I needn't worry. I relax into that, not knowing how–but not needing to know how. I trust. Whew!

With the CarePages I don't feel so alone. Years ago I was taught that the Universe supports me–supports all of us. The CarePages have come to represent the Universe for me at this point in time. Pete is amazed at the postings. He says that he never knew that many people cared about him. Messages come in from everywhere–even people we don't know–sometimes thirty or more a day. The Universe. Wow.

My chest is still bothering me. Sometimes it feels like there is a fire going on in there, with a kind of searing pain each time I inhale. And I'm *so* tired . . . I worry about what will happen if I get really sick and I can't take care of him. What will we do then?

I know that it is really important to hold a positive image, and at my best, I see myself as vibrant and energetic, full of excellent health and optimism, standing by the side of my beloved, who is strong, healthy, and smiling. Sometimes I'm just too emotionally exhausted to conjure up that image, so I remember what Marty, said. "When you're too tired to hold that image, we all will hold it for you. Just rest." That's what we call "holding the high watch."

12 messages Posted Sunday, August 3, 2008

Pam, all is well . . . Pete is gaining strength every day, and is going to start singing again to you. Won't that be a wonderful day? I am so proud of you and love you so much. You are a gift to all of us. Please give Pete a gentle touch from me.
Love,
Jane Walsh

As we were singing the Lord's Prayer at Unity today, I could hear Pete's voice joining in. I could feel his lungs clear and his voice strong. Again. Such a gift you both are! Please know I continue to think of you and pray for healing.
Love,
Ruth Tierra

Looking back . . .

Getting Pete approved for disability with Uncle Sam was a long, drawn-out procedure. Ruth told me that a heart transplant patient is usually automatically approved. That may be so, but it still required a lot of paper work and dozens of phone calls. Pete was finally approved, but we didn't see any money until December.

Update Sunday, August 3, 2008 at 8:44 p.m.

A quiet day today–I think a little bit better than yesterday. There is still a lot of fluid in Pete's chest, though. I read half of a novel today, just sitting by his side as he dozed. We learned that the pathology report on Pete's native heart showed that it was full of sarcoid. Now we know.

This evening our pastor, Marty, and her husband, John, came by again to visit with Pete and take me out to dinner at the Blue Nile. We had a delicious

Ethiopian dinner and what was for me a highlight in a very quiet week. Marty never fails to inspire and uplift me, and John makes me laugh. It feels good to laugh.

Today Pete and I listened to a lot of music–things I have on my computer and the few CDs I had in my car when I came here. I've thought a lot about the healing power of music in the last few weeks–and how blessed Pete and I are to be able to share our music with other people. I long for the day when I can hear his beautiful, strong baritone ring out once again, loud and clear. Let's keep that image present in our minds and hearts in the days ahead.

As always, I am warmed and comforted by your wonderful messages on these pages and in e-mails. They keep me going, believe me.

I love you all.

Pam

---

15 Messages Posted Monday, August 4, 2008

It never crossed my mind that Pete would have anything less than a full recovery. It's just a matter of time. My favorite quote from The Course in Miracles: "Miracles are natural; it's when they do not occur that something has gone wrong." Much love to you both.

Nancy O'Donohue

Pam, I love your strength and peace. It comes through clearly in all of your messages. You and Pete are such a match made in heaven! Gary and I knew Pete from Lauren's choir. While he seemed to be happy-go-lucky, we always felt a sadness about him until . . . Pam came along, and those blue eyes had a brightness to them that we had not seen before. You two are truly a team. We look forward to being at another one of your concerts where the two of you are performing.

Blessings, love and joy to you both,

Gary & Shirley Pressnell

Tuesday, August 4, 2008

Journal

I was standing beside Pete's bed. He reached up and cupped my cheek tenderly with the palm of his hand. He looked deep into my eyes—and there was no need for words.

E-mail, Monday, August 4, 2008

Dear Pam,

Just a cute memory of riding to Unity Village with Pete. He had nonstop comments and I asked him how you dealt with it. He said you tell him to turn the volume down, and when he starts in again later, you tell him you didn't say he could turn it up again. Now, we'd all give our eye teeth for a few of his comments. I say this in jest, but filled with love. That story will bring a smile to his face one day.

All my love & blessings to you both,

Betty Smith

Same day, later . . .

Pete does have a . . . well, an unusual sense of humor—sometimes really goofy, sometimes very clever. He loves to make people laugh. One day last spring we were looking out our dining room window at the lake. It was one of those misty, foggy Michigan mornings when everything outside just melts into gray, and the pier, which is only a couple of blocks away as the crow flies, is invisible. All of a sudden, a bit of the fog lifted.

"I can see the pier," I said.

"Yes, it's appearing," he said.

Another time, we drove by a corn field right in downtown South Bend, and when I pointed it out he said, "Yeah, it's corny." It's not the field that's corny.

Same day, later . . .

The hospital has a therapy dog program; volunteers bring in gentle dogs to visit patients and their families. One day I was in the CVC lobby when a gray-haired, petite woman stepped out of the elevator with a huge, black Newfoundland. Within moments, the dog was surrounded by curious people, petting him and asking questions about him. Ralph, the dog, sat down, panting a bit and slobbering as Newfoundlands tend to do. One of the kids there asked, "What does he do?"

The lady smiled and said, "You're looking at it."

Same day, later . . .

Sometimes I just start crying. Something gets to me and the gates open. It reminds me of the first (and last) time I went downhill skiing. I managed to stand up, sort of, but I couldn't get my balance or the hang of stopping, so I went hurtling down the bunny hill, gaining in momentum, flailing my arms around frantically, trying to keep my balance and ultimately collapsing on my butt to stop. I sprained my ankle that morning, and was on crutches for a long time. I never had the urge to ski downhill again. When I cry, I get that same sort of momentum, and it just grows and grows until it abruptly stops. I sit on my butt.

Mostly, I grieve what we have had. We were married just nine months when Pete collapsed, and we were so incredibly happy! Then, like colliding into a tree in the downhill path, our bliss was rudely interrupted. I won't say that it was taken from us, because I still have hope we will return to normalcy. (It will come back it will come back it will come back it will come back it will come back . . . in all it's ordinary splendor.)

I grieve that normal life–
Our house on the lake
Our big bed where we snuggled in the mornings
Our cats, Bojangles and Smoke
Popcorn in front of the TV, watching an old movie classic
Standing next to each other in church, sharing a hymnal, our arms around each
     other
Listening to Pete singing in the shower
Eating spaghetti at Maria's Restaurant
Sitting on the bench across the street, watching the sunset
Pete's voice on the phone, calling just to tell me he loves me

I miss all of that and more. I also grieve summer. Our entire summer has been—will be—inside a hospital. We love summer on the lake, the sun on our skin, the splash of cool water on those dog days. By the time we get home—if we ever get "home"—it will be fall, I suppose. Fall has its good points, and we will enjoy it, but missing summer in South Haven is *big.* I keep reminding myself that there will be other summers with Pete. Dear God, I hope there will be other summers with Pete.

The other big thing I grieve is our home. I don't know if we'll ever be able to go home. It's toxic. It has poisoned my lungs, and may well have created this whole mess with Pete. Still, if I wanted to get in my car right now and drive home, just to sleep in our own bed for one night, I couldn't. I can't go home.

Home is where I lived from the time I was eleven until I went off to college. Home is where our happy, Norman Rockwellian family enjoyed Christmases and birthdays, Ed Sullivan shows and sleep-overs, piano sing-alongs and prom preparations. Home is where my mother died, in the hospital bed where she could look out the dining room window at the lake. It's where I held her hand as she passed.

I miss home.

Update Monday, August 4, 2008 at 5:38 a.m.

When Reverend Marty and her husband, John, visited yesterday, Pete greeted them with his hands in front of his heart, in prayer position, steeple-fashion. He gave his head a slight nod. His face doesn't register much emotion yet, but I could tell he was really glad to see them. Marty said, "Namaste," to him, and I asked him if he could say it back to her. In a very soft, raspy voice he said, "Namaste." The light within me honors the light within you.

Marty swept her hand toward the many, many beautiful greeting cards of all description that nearly cover one wall of Pete's room. "A lot of people love you," she said. He looked up and pointed at me. "Yes," Marty said, "Pam sure loves you."

A little later, as John and I spoke softly with each other at the foot of the bed, I noticed Marty and Pete were gazing into each other's eyes. Pete and I do that sometimes. It is a deep, loving communication that goes where words do not.

Yesterday I was standing to the left of Pete's bed, dabbing his forehead with a cool wash cloth, when he reached his arm around my waist and held the small of my back with the palm of his hand. This simple, intimate gesture made the tears well up in my eyes. I hadn't felt his touch on me, except for holding hands, in six weeks. It was tender, familiar . . . precious.

I was thinking this morning that friends have told me how great I'm doing, and that this experience has been an inspiration to them, and so on. It's very affirming to be supported in this way, but still, I can't help but think that what I am doing is not extraordinary, but rather what almost anyone would do for someone they love. I show up at the hospital every day to *be* with him. It's that basic. I find little ways to make him more comfortable. I sing to him. I read the cards and messages to him. I bring him heated blankets and sit by his side, holding his hand while he sleeps. I listen in on the doctors' rounds and ask questions. I call when I wake up in the middle of the night to be sure he is all right. Little things.

On the pier in South Haven at several intervals there are ropes for emergency use in case someone falls or is swept off the pier. I know that I am a lifeline for Pete right now. He has fallen off the pier. I would do anything and *will* do anything to hold that line, and pull him, coax him back to safety and solid ground. You would do the same, wouldn't you?

Love to you all who love so well. Know that there is nothing more important. Nothing.

Pam

---

7 Messages Posted Monday, August 4, 2008 Evening

Thank you for mirroring that we would do the same, as I know we would. I pray we would all be as you—with such Grace, Strength, and Great-fullness!

We met a man this weekend, who shared advice from his lung transplant experience. He said, "Remember humor." Humor helped him heal.

Jaye Mann

E-mail, Monday, August 4, 2008

Hi Pam,

Your message this morning shows so clearly that you are living in the real world, the healing power of presence. I am so honored. Please tell Pete that our group will be sharing distant healing with both of you this week and we love you both very much. Namaste,

Debra Basham

"Everything, every moment, every person, every stirring in your heart matters. Let yourself love and value life, and be overjoyed at the positive difference that each of your moments can make."

—Ralph Marston

Update Monday, August 4, 2008 at 8:17 p.m.

Pete was asleep when I arrived this morning, and it was a couple of hours before he opened his eyes. When he did, I said to him, "Oh there are those beautiful blue eyes! It's so good to see those eyes!" He said something that I couldn't hear, so I leaned in close and asked him to repeat it.

"It's good to be seen," he said.

The physical therapist and occupational therapist were in to get Pete into the recliner again today. It's quite a production, as he needs three people to help him sit up on the side of the bed, swing his legs to the floor, and walk about two and a half feet to the chair. Of course, there are dozens of tubes and IV lines that have to move along with him, so it's complicated and slow. Still, he walks, in tiny steps, and he stands up straight. He is tired by the time he gets to the chair to sit down. The whole thing takes about ten minutes.

The O.T. and P.T. both agree that he has made exceptional progress since his strokes, a week and a half ago. They said that the way he is progressing is promising for what we can expect in the weeks ahead. They think he will do very well. Of course no one here can or will promise a full recovery, but I was encouraged by their assessment, and I continue to hold the vision of full recovery in my heart.

I've been asked to sing at the Unity Church of Ann Arbor on August 31. I'm so happy to be able to share some of my music with the people there! At yesterday's service I announced that Pete had a new heart. They all applauded and cheered. Many of them have been praying for Pete since I first visited their church three weeks ago.

Much love to you all,

Pam

> *"Once you choose hope, anything is possible."*
> *–Christopher Reeve*

Tuesday, August 5, 2008
Journal

I requested a consult with the neurologist. He came by Pete's room after I left for the day yesterday, so he called me on my cell phone and we talked for a while. He asked what I wanted to know–and I drew a blank. There are so *many* things I want to know! I realized afterwards that what I really wanted to know is that Pete would be okay–that Pete would be Pete again–and that is something no one can tell me. It's not that he won't tell me. It's that they don't know.

Nancy O. posted a message to me yesterday, saying that she never even considered the possibility that he would experience anything other than a full recovery. Her resolve strengthens me.

Looking back . . .

Why didn't I do Reiki more?

As a Reiki Master and a therapeutic touch practitioner, I have had experience working as a channel for healing many times. Although I did do this a few times for Pete, I didn't do it on a daily, or even weekly basis. I've wondered why, and I think I now know at least part of the reason. I was depleted myself. I was physically ill and emotionally drained. When we do healing work, we know that it is important to be a clear channel so that the healing will come through us. I think, at least at some level, I knew that my body and spirit were in need of healing themselves, and that I needed to rely on the healing energy of others to support both Pete and me at this time, rather than try to do it myself.

Nancy O'Donohue did this directly for us, and others sent healing light and love. I know there are many who consider this sort of thing "tree-hugging hippie shit," but I know it helped us. I know.

Update Tuesday, August 5, 2008 at 6:56 p.m.

This morning when I went into Pete's hospital room and greeted him, he said, "How are you?" It was very soft, almost a whisper, but nevertheless, he spoke.

Progress!

Later this morning I played a recording of him singing "New York, New York." I turned around and there was Pete, snapping his fingers in time to the music! Now, I don't know much about neurology, but finger snapping sounds like a pretty complex function to me. Two of the nurses were amazed to hear Pete's voice. "Wow! He's really good!" one of them said.

In the afternoon, with help from three nurses, he walked from the recliner to the doorway, and then back to his bed, about eight feet each way. These little things are huge for a stroke hero. (We won't call him a stroke victim.) The doctors are very pleased with his progress.

Tomorrow Pete will have his vocal cords checked. Sometimes they are affected by stroke, but they tend to heal well. Pete still coughs a lot and has difficulty swallowing. That should improve with time, I'm told. I spoke today with a music therapist from the Cancer Center here, as my dear niece, Katie, suggested. She gave me some suggestions for working with Pete. I had intuitively been doing some of the right things.

Many of you have asked if there is anything you can do. There is: *music.* We need music. Nancy Plantinga sent us some lovely, relaxing music for going to sleep. In that department we are all set. What we need now is songs with lyrics and a good, strong beat. That will help Pete in processing language and regaining his voice. If you'd like to help, please send us something–show tunes, folk music, blues, jazz, standards, oldies, singer-songwriter, soft rock. *Anything.* MP-3s can be sent in e-mails or you can use snail mail. We will be grateful for anything! I want to be able to play music for him throughout the day. Thank you so much!

Much love to you all,

Pam

> 11 Messages Posted Tuesday, August 5, 2008
>
> Tell Pete that he is doing better than me! I am unable to snap my fingers!
> Diane Freestone

Tuesday, August 5, 2008
Journal
Our flight to Montana would have left today. Sigh. I miss Brennan and Rachel.

E-mail, Monday, August 4, 2008
Becky Allen to Omega Survivors
Hello Gang,

I was just on Pam and Pete's CarePage. Pete is recovering well. It will take time, but he is actually up and getting around a bit. Pam seems to be holding up well too. Her CarePage writings are as beautiful as her songs, so full of love and inspiration and hope. She is truly an angel on earth . . . just wanted to pass along the news to everyone. Please keep them both in your thoughts and prayers.

Love to all!

Becky

Looking back . . .

I don't feel like an angel–unless we are all angels and we just don't know it. Becky's message is an example of the loving support I received during this difficult time. It meant the world to me.

E-mail Reply, Tuesday, August 5, 2008
Becky—

Thanks so much for sending this out. You are a dear. It has been a true blessing to me the way our Survivor gang has stepped up with loving messages, cards, and calls. Bill Nedela and Ellen even came to visit—Bill twice. He brought me a card from Omega with messages from friends there at Jimmy's workshops. It felt like a warm blanket. I feel blessed to have such a supportive community of friends.

This is a journey like none other I have experienced. It's deeply emotional and spiritual at the same time. I bounce between solid hope and meek acceptance. "Blessed are the meek," the Bible says. Never quite understood that—but I think it's becoming more clear. I think it's about being at peace with what is.

Jeep sent me a message with characteristically poetic phrases. My favorite was this: ". . . the beauty and severe truth of your journey in the NOW, which is both fully present and fundamentally unknown." I was so taken by that description of what I'm going through, I had to write it down so I could pull it out and ponder it from time to time.

In the midst of all the hospital stuff, I have a couple of singing things going. This Saturday I will sing a few songs at the heart transplant support group annual picnic and I'll sing at the Ann Arbor Unity Church later this month. It will be good for me to sing again—healing.

Much love to you,

Pam

Update Wednesday, August 6, 2008 at 8:05 p.m.

Dear Ones,

Today I played a recording of Pete singing for the docs when they were making their rounds. They were duly impressed. He *does* have a marvelous voice. For him, music is like breathing.

Yesterday I spoke with the music therapist from the Cancer Center here at the hospital. She suggested that I try to coax Pete to sing with me some simple songs with lyrics he knows very well. This morning I encouraged Pete to sing "You Are My Sunshine" along with me, and he did! His voice is still quite guttural and soft, but he was singing along. I think that is huge! I cried.

Also, this evening the ear, nose, and throat specialist did an assessment and said that he didn't think Pete had any damage to his vocal cords. Apparently, the difficulty he is having with speech now is due to the strokes; with effort and practice, he will regain his voice. God is good. Pete would be devastated if he couldn't sing again.

With these great bits of good news, I must confess that it is still quite an uphill climb. I sense that Pete is getting frustrated. I often wish I knew what was going on between his ears. *What is he thinking?* Other times, I think maybe I'm better off *not* knowing. I just try to stay positive, and be *here*, reminding him of how much he is loved. Your messages help, big time.

We had originally planned to fly to Montana on August 5 to spend a week with my son, Brennan, and his wife, Rachel. It was hard to give that up–but it's worth it if it means Pete and I can have more time together. It's all worth it.

Love,

Pam

Pete remembers having music in his room . . .

The nurses said they loved it. "That's Pete singing? Really? Wow!" It was kind of a shock. That's me? It was really good. I had never really listened to myself that much. I appreciated it more than ever–that I once was able to sing like that. That was me! Overall, it made me want to get better so I could sing again.

---

10 messages Posted August 6-7, 2008

My little issues just fade into nothingness when I think of what you two are going through—and how your Light just keeps shining brighter and brighter! You are our Sunshines! Shine On.

Carol Johnson

I know what you mean about wondering what your husband is thinking. Joe hasn't spoken for four years. Alzheimer's. I just chatter on as if we are having conversations, except I am the only one speaking. We do what we can do and trust that the Universe in charge has greater wisdom in all matters.

Love you both,

Jeanie Frattallone

Keep your mind on the light that is always shining, even when it appears dark. The darkness is just an illusion. We are always protected and loved and we can be sure that there is a plan for us.

Take care of yourself, Pam. It is part of your job to do that. You deserve it . . . Let's not lose sight of the miracle.

Love,

Jane Walsh

Pete's frustration is a great thing. It means that he is healing and ready to get better. In physical therapy we see this in all of our patients who are recovering, but not in those who are not. We pray for you both every night and we love you both.

Jim Stark

Thursday, August 7, 2008

Journal

I don't know what's going on inside his head. Wish I did, but he barely speaks. The night before last, he got really restless and agitated, and even pulled out his rectal tube. The nurse said it's soft and flexible, not that uncomfortable—but very necessary. He can't go on his own yet and he has diarrhea. You can imagine . . .

When he is asleep he looks much like he used to before the strokes, except for the weight loss. When he is awake, he still has a tremor on his upper lip, mostly on the right side. He also has tremors with his right leg, sometimes spreading to his left leg too, and much of his torso. It looks like an exaggerated shiver, and goes on for a long time.

Right after the strokes, when I approached him and tried to get his attention, he turned his head in my direction, but his gaze was about two inches above my head. The physical therapist said that he was able to move his eyes from right to left, but not up and down. If he wanted to see something higher up, he had to move his head. Fortunately, that has improved significantly in the two weeks since his strokes. He can look right into my eyes now, and I know he sees. He sees deep into me. I can tell.

He only speaks a word here or there, and his voice sounds gravelly and soft, a jagged whisper. It reminds me of the way he used to imitate the Godfather: "I made him an offer he couldn't refuse." The speech therapist says he has symptoms of **dysphasia** and **dysarthria**.

I asked him if it hurts to talk, and he said no, so I encourage him to use words rather than just gestures, whenever he can. The speech therapist told me to ask open-ended questions that require more than a one word response.

Sometimes he doesn't respond to questions at all. He just stares. I don't know if he is simply fed up with the stupid questions they ask him– *"Do you know where you are? What town is this? What is your name?"*–or if he just gets tired–or maybe he doesn't always *get* it. Maybe he has some short circuits in there somewhere.

He sleeps about half of the time when I'm there during the day, and I am content to let him rest. When he is awake, I talk to him, play music and try to get him to sing with me. The other day I said to him, "Your voice will come back, Pete. It will come back."

"It better," he said.

Whenever the possibility of Pete not being able to sing again crosses my mind, I catch myself, throw that thought out, and replace it with the image of him singing his heart out (so to speak) for an enthusiastic audience. It will come back. It will come back. It will come back. It will come back. It will come back . . .

The nurses get him up to sit in a chair every day now. It's not an easy thing, but they keep telling me he is very strong. He walks in little, inch-by-inch steps, shuffling in his blue, hospital issue, treaded socks. But still, he walks, and he stands tall in the process. Afterwards, he sleeps, exhausted from the effort.

Today we are going to try getting him into a wheelchair for the first time since his strokes and transplant. We hope to wheel him down to the central plaza of the hospital for an open air concert at noon.

Hospital Speak 101

Dysphasia: A condition characterized by difficulty in swallowing. Swallowing problems can result from a number of things, including stroke.

Dysarthria: A speech disorder sometimes caused by stroke and characterized by slurred speech, difficulty in swallowing, speaking very softly, hoarseness, breathiness, and/or slow rate of speech.

Update Posted August 7, 2008 at 7:01 a.m.

Dear Ones–

This is one of the Daily Motivator messages I get every day. It says it all:

There will be times when you find yourself in extremely difficult circumstances. When those times come, it's important to put things in perspective. Whatever else may be going on, always remember that you have been blessed with life and the ability to live it as you choose. Think of how completely awesome that is.

The idea that you are a victim of any particular circumstance is simply not accurate. For when you look at the big picture, you're not a victim at all. You are a very fortunate beneficiary of the greatest circumstance that you could possibly imagine–being alive and able to direct your own life. All other circumstances pale in comparison.

The transitory ups and downs are merely tiny threads in the overall fabric of your life. Each one ultimately adds to the richness of your experience. The quality of that experience is up to you, and the fact that you're aware and able to think and act confers on you an incalculable wealth. See it, value and appreciate it, and spend each day being truly worthy of the unique, precious life that you have.

–Ralph Marston (See Resources)

Update Thursday, August 7, 2008 Evening

This was a good news day all around. Pete has been moved out of the Cardiovascular Intensive Care Unit and is now on the fourth floor of the main hospital. That means that his doctors in the ICU are satisfied with his progress and believe he will do well with less intense supervision. This is very encouraging!

On the other hand, I have been concerned about the mold and bacteria that were found in the basement of our home, and the mold spores airborne throughout all three floors. There is some really nasty, dangerous stuff there! I wonder whether we can ever go home. In some cases where mold is concerned, the building can't be saved and has to be torn down. You can imagine how tough this is to consider for our beloved home on the big lake. Anyway, today I heard from a mold remediation contractor that they *will* be able to remediate our house. I don't have an estimate yet, but I am thrilled that we will be able to go home–to *our own* home–when Pete recovers enough to be discharged.

A week ago Ruth Halben, social worker here, told me that there was a cap on our insurance, and that we will probably go over the allowable amount, as Pete's bill was already in the $800,000 range. I didn't know what we were going to do. Today she stopped in to say that they discovered that our health insurance has a million dollar rider for catastrophic illness that will cover everything at the hospital. Whew! We will still have to deal with after-care and loss of income, but that will be much less formidable. The Universe provides. All of this brings to mind my favorite quote from Mark Twain: "I've had a lot of troubles in my life, most of which never happened." It also underscores for me the importance of living in the NOW, and not letting F.E.A.R. (Future Expectations Appearing Real) take over.

Pete's new heart is doing just great and he is slowly but steadily improving from the symptoms of stroke. He sang "You Are My Sunshine" with me again and did some simple exercises with the physical therapist. Good stuff. He is still very weak, though. After more than six weeks in bed he will need some time to get his strength back. But it will come back. I just know it!

Much love to you all,

Pam

4 Messages Posted Thursday, August 7, 2008

Pam,

Thank you for allowing us to walk through this experience with you and Pete. Everyday that we read your updates, they touch our spirit, open our hearts, and continue to remind us of the beauty of life and love. We are grateful that God continues to shine through you and Pete. Know that you are loved.

Deb Lambert & Jaye Mann

Friday, August 8, 2008
Journal

My cell phone bill for July arrived—over $500. I'm trying not to panic. All is well. All is well. All is well. All is well. All is well. All is well. All is well.

Update Friday, August 8, 2008 at 7:29 p.m.

Today is not just the opening of the Summer Olympics; it is also the eleven month anniversary of our marriage. We sure never expected this! Life is full of surprises.

We received two CDs of a radio show that Ol' Harv (Harvey Stauffer) did in July on WVPE Radio in Elkhart, Indiana. He dedicated the program to Pete. It's great blues, which Pete loves, and heartfelt choices, too. Pete tapped his foot along, and I saw a tear or two in the corner of his eye . . . Thanks, Harv and Armida!

It wasn't an easy day today. Pete seemed to have retreated inside. It took a lot to coax out a word or two from him, yet he went for a walk in the hallway with a wheeled walker and the help of two nurses. He went the farthest he has gone so far, about 40 feet each way. He is definitely getting stronger.

The non-responsiveness on his part is probably due to the medications he is getting, including some for pain. He either sleeps or stares out into space most of the time. I left the hospital this evening immensely sad. I long to feel that deep connection with him, and today he was just . . . someplace else. I know he will come back; he loves me very much. It's just hard today. I drove back to my room at the Transplant House and cried.

Why am I telling you this? Because I want to be honest with all of you–It's not a straight line, each day a little better than the last. It's wind-y and climb-y and sometimes discouraging. I am really touched by Janet McKenzie's message, "To wait is to love." I'm waiting.

---

16 messages Posted Friday, August 8, 2008

You remain close to my heart . . . Pete—we need your help on the church bowling team—it's just not the same without you. No one else cheers for me when I get gutter balls.
David Sterken

Yesterday we received a letter from our bishop about his experiences at the Lambeth Conference. One point struck me: He wrote about a Japanese bishop who said nothing in their small group meetings all week; then, on the last day, as the group struggled with looking forward, he said, "To wait is to love." Amen!
Janet McKenzie (Neighbor)

Friday, August 8, 2008
Journal

I did a little reading on crying. Recognizing that a little bit of knowledge is dangerous, here is what I found:

First of all, humans are the only animals that cry emotional tears. Further, it seems that the tears we produce when we are emotionally stressed out are different from the tears that result from, say, cutting an onion. Emotional tears have more protein and more leucine enkephalin, a natural pain killer. Tears also contain lysozyme,which bathes your eye. Lysozyme is one of the most effective antibacterial and antiviral agents there is.

So, when we say that it is healing to cry, we're not just whistling "Dixie", and we're not just talking about releasing stress, either. William Frey, a biochemist and research scientist, has conducted tests at St. Paul Ramsey Medical Center in Minnesota from which he concluded that weeping actually removes toxic substances that tend to pile up when we are under stress. Amazing. Wonderful. Think I'll go cry some more.

18 messages Posted Friday, August 8, 2008 Evening

I love "To wait is to love" also. Profound. Here is another that occurred to me as I read your last posting. This is from Swami Kripalu: "Crying is one of the highest devotional songs. One who knows crying knows spiritual practice. If you can cry with a pure heart, nothing else compares to such a prayer."

Know that as you cry, we are all holding you dearly and closely, crying our prayers with you. I am honored to be part of this wonderful group of supporters around you.
Deepest love and all kinds of prayers to you and dear Pete,
Ellen Reinstatler

We are waiting with you.
Kathleen Lord

. . . Use the shoulders of all of us holding you. We'll be your strength when you feel weary.
Sue Fischer

Sorrow is a Sometime Friend

Sorrow is a sometime friend. She draws me in for tea.
She holds my hand, and holds my gaze, and fusses over me.
She creeps into my waking dreams, and colors what I say,
Begs me spend some time with her, then slowly slips away.

Sometimes I curse the way she comes and muddies up my day.
At times I just ignore her, or turn the other way.
But sorrow doesn't take my lead; She dances on her own,
And she would have me for her friend; Together we're alone.

Sorrow doesn't hold her peace–No, she will have her say.
Close your windows, bar the door, she'll get in anyway.
She wears a gown of black and brown so smooth it feels like skin,
Woven of the memories and all that might have been.

But oh, she has a secret for those who choose to hear.
To those who cry and wonder why, with every silent tear–
If they would dare to feel the grief, and somehow still survive,
In husky tones of dreams and bones she whispers, "You're alive!"

Sorrow is a sometime friend. She sits and sips her tea.
She isn't in a hurry to take her leave of me.
Her sister, Joy, will also come if I will let her in–
The two of them, a curious pair–Sweet Sorrow and her twin.

©2001 Pamela Chappell

CHAPTER TEN

Baby Steps

"One of the wonderful things about having adversity, difficulties, and challenges is that they will often show you a deeper love, a deeper strength, something that you did not know existed . . . You have within you what it takes to triumph."
—John Morton

Tuesday, August 9, 2008
Journal

MOVING FROM VICTIM-HOOD to unconditional love and forgiveness. I choose this. What an opportunity!

Same day, later . . .

I often think about my mom and dad. Their love for each other was a rock for me. Still is. Dad was a take-charge kind of guy, very confident and wise. It seemed to me that he could handle just about anything, and handle it well. As he aged, though, Dad had a stroke and two heart attacks. He got a pacemaker in 1976 when he was 66. After the surgery the doctor gave Mom and Dad follow up instructions. He told them he didn't see any reason why they couldn't have a normal sex life. Dad turned to Mom and said, "Well, Polly, it looks like we're going to have to cut back."

That pacemaker bought Dad fifteen more years. The last nine were tough, though. He began a steady decline, and became weaker, thinner, and less communicative with each year. In the last two or three years he barely spoke at all, and his eyes took on a fearful look that seemed to say, "Is anybody in charge here? Who's taking care of things?"

During this long, painful decline, my mother took care of Dad. He was taking about twenty different medications, and she had a list of them posted inside one of the kitchen cupboard doors. She had an electric chairlift installed in the stairway that went up to their bedroom. She waited on Dad, chatting away through those long, silent days, and rarely went anywhere, except to the grocery store or the post office, that kind of thing. Days and months and years . . .

She never complained, always maintaining a positive outlook. Once I asked her how she did it, and she said simply, "I love him—and he's still good company." I grew to understand over time that, while I had always seen Dad as the strong one, she was the one who ultimately demonstrated her strength in ways I would remember and hold on to, inspired by her steadfastness and positivity.

Now I see Pete in his hospital gown, staring out into space, his eyes wide open and blank. I cling to the one word or two he might say, and I cheer him on when he shuffles, one tiny step at a time across the floor, clinging to the walker. I remind me of Mom.

I hope, as much for Pete's sake as my own, that his condition is temporary. I can't bear the thought of him staying this way—not Pete, not my energizer bunny, this font of vigor and physicality. I want him back. I want him back.

I know Pete needs me by his side, and I consider that a sacred trust. I am blessed by the example of a strong, resourceful woman. Mom did this. I can do this. This is where I belong, and this is where I'll stay as long as he needs me.

I can do this. Lord help me, I can do this.

Update Saturday, August 9, 2008 at 8:51 p.m.

Dear Ones,

My mother used to say that things always look better in the morning–and she was usually right. We had a better day today. Pete seemed more "with it." He did some good walking, and coughed a lot less.

Nancy Lou, girlfriend extraordinaire, came up from South Haven late this morning and went with me to the Heart Transplant Support Group Annual Picnic. That might not sound like a barrel of monkeys, but it was really enjoyable. It's encouraging to meet heart transplant patients as much as 20 years out from their surgeries, doing well and enjoying life. The camaraderie was wonderful. We asked questions and told our stories to each other, enjoying great food and a deep common bond. I even sang a few songs for the folks. I'd almost forgotten how good it feels to sing!

Nancy Lou left then and I spent the rest of the afternoon with Pete, watching the Summer Olympics on TV. Except for the lack of popcorn, it was very much like what we probably would have done if we were at home. A touch of normalcy feels good.

I'm learning much about what is important–what matters. So much of the "stuff" I tend to focus on is just that–stuff. What's real, and what matters, is loving each other, and doing that the best way we know how. Not a new idea, but one that has come home and knocked on my door a lot lately.

Thank you for loving us. It matters.

Love,

Pam

---

8 Messages Posted Saturday, August 9, 2008

Such grace you've been given. We're still praying.

George & Jeannine Blake

Update Sunday, August 10, 2008 at 8:33 p.m.

Dear Ones,

We had a visit this morning from Christine and Chip from South Bend. They are wonderful friends, and I know it lifted Pete's spirits to see them. Mine too! Pete walked further today than he has in the past and they removed a chest tube, a picc line and the catheter from him—more positive steps.

You all have been absolute prayer warriors for both of us, and I know it has made a huge difference. Here are our key concerns now, as I see it:

Pete still speaks very little, and in hushed, guttural tones.

He is still very weak, and walks only with assistance, and then, very slowly. He is sometimes understandably depressed.

He still has tremors of his upper lip and leg, although these are getting milder.

So here is the prayer I suggest:

> *"Dear God, thank you for restoring to Pete his strong and beautiful voice, his strength and coordination, his courage, faith, and joyful spirit, and the peace that comes with all of his body systems working in perfect harmony. And so it is. Thank you. Thank you. Thank you. Thank you. Thank you."*

And thanks to all of *you* for your incredibly loving and generous support, which is surely God working through you. Throughout this entire experience it has been *so* much easier for me to remain positive because I haven't had to feel like we were sinking into impossible debt. It has taught me to trust that the Universe will provide for our needs. We are both immensely grateful. May we return your kindness in some way someday—or pass it on to someone else.

Love,

Pam

5 Messages Posted Sunday, August 10, 2008

Dear Pam & Pete,

    The progress is all positive, but then, what else could it be with all of us praying for and with you! . . .We are all envisioning Pete strong and healthy and singing with his fabulous voice and sparkling eyes and smile!
Love,
Donna Leonard

    It takes time for the body to reestablish after so much trauma, let alone the surgeries. Also, anesthesia takes a long time to fade. He was under anesthesia for a very long time. It sounds like he's basically a very strong man to be able to even endure the surgery and failing heart. He is coming along . . .
    Continuing to pray and to think of you and Pete very day,
With Love,
Arlene Tolen

Monday, August 11, 2008
Journal

Cardiovascular Center, ICU Waiting Room

Everybody here is in crisis. I watch the people, sitting in little clusters, waiting. I remember the family I saw last week, standing around awkwardly, encircling the mother. There were at least four sons and daughters with some spouses, and a few restless grandchildren. The mother looked to be in her late 70's or more, silver-haired, plump, plain, and frazzled, Mrs. Santa Claus after a particularly grueling day. One of the doctors came out and explained that they had been massaging her husband's heart for five minutes, but there was no response. Did they want them to keep going or to give up? I saw their stunned faces, and the tall, dark-haired daughter holding fast to her mother's hand.

They all looked at each other, and the pain in their eyes was unspeakable. The nurse called me in to see Pete then, so I didn't hear their response to the doctor, but a while later when I passed by again, I saw the mother weeping, and heard her cry, "I need to be with him. I don't want him to go without having me there." It was such a terrible and loving tableau, this family gathered around, trying to offer what comfort they could, most of them bleeding inside.

Then there was Henry, the lanky, thirty-something man with shoulder-length, straight brown hair and Harry Potter glasses. I saw him several times before we spoke. Finally one day I asked him how he was doing and he opened right up, his story tumbling out like marbles from a jar. Henry was there visiting his mother, who was in heart failure, he told me. We talked for quite a while about what the doctor had told him, what the prognosis was, etc. Every day after that, Henry and I gave each other daily updates on his mother and my husband. I became vested in her recovery too. This dear, young man drove two hours after work every day and trudged up to the hospital. He was distressed and exhausted. My heart went out to him. Then one day he didn't come anymore.

Some people come and go in just a day or two. They put together jigsaw puzzles, look nervous, check their e-mails on one of three computers provided and make cell phone calls.

Susan Mann is the greeter at the ICU. She is lovely and warm, always at hand with a welcoming smile or an understanding nod. When I want to enter the ICU, Susan is the one who calls in to the nurse to see if it's okay. If it is, she goes to the glass door and with a wave of her badge on the sensor, there is a click, and I am allowed to enter the world of ICU.

It's *so* important that she's nice! And she is—gracious, kind and sensitive. She seems genuinely interested in how Pete is doing each day. We chat about our grandchildren, the weather, a sale on funky clothes downtown. She is the one human constant in my day. The nurses are wonderful, but they rotate almost daily, so we don't really have much time to establish relationships with them. The doctors drop by, impart their wisdom, and then go, often different doctors each week. Pete changes from day to day, and sometimes from minute to minute, and often is somewhere else, having some test or an X-ray . . . or he's just "somewhere else" in his mind.

But Susan is there every day. She smiles, gives me a hug if I need it, and is my new "girlfriend." Thank God for her.

So the guests come and go, laugh nervously, sip cold coffee, and read dog-eared magazines. Sometimes I tell them which puzzles are missing some pieces. I'm good at giving directions now, too. This place is pretty much where I live. It can be lonely, but it's clean and safe, and it's where my beloved is.

Update Monday, August 11, 2008 at 5:25 a.m.

Since Pete's strokes, almost three weeks now, his face has shown no expression at all. Except for a wince when he was poked with a needle, or a tear in his eye now and then, his face has registered no emotion whatsoever, his own natural exuberance and warmth hidden deep in the recesses of his consciousness. Often I search his face, wondering where he has gone.

Last night, when it was time for me to leave the hospital, I made him look right into my eyes, and I told him, "You're amazing! I'm so proud of you! You've been through so much, and you are working so hard at getting better! You know something? You're my hero!"

And then he smiled. Great God Almighty, he smiled! More than ever, I believe in miracles.

---

31 Messages Posted August 11-12, 2008

What wonderful news! Some days will be harder than others for you, but hold Pete in your heart and I know he will feel the love pulling him through the tough times ahead. On the other hand, you are the reason he is beginning to recover. I can only understand some of the anguish you are going through at times because of my own husband's close calls. Take care my friend.
Love,
Sue Kruizenga

Pete's smile . . . the face of God.
Love,
Kathleen Lord

The Face of God
By
Karen Drucker

You are the face of God.
I hold you in my heart.
You are a part of me.
You are the face of God.

You are the face of God.
I hold you in my heart.
You are my family.
You are the face of God.

We sang this song to each other and to everyone in attendance at our wedding. It is so beautiful–and so true.

❧❧

Update Monday, August 11, 2008 at 6:57 p.m.

Pete slept most of the day. Guess he needed it. We did, however, have an outing before he drifted off into Dreamland. The Occupational Therapist, Yvonne, and I wheeled Pete outside for a breath of fresh air. It was a beautiful, breezy summer day, and the only slice of summer Pete has experienced in the last seven weeks. We spent a few minutes in the garden, soaking in the sun. I think he really enjoyed it. We hope to be able to take him out to the courtyard Thursday noon for the last concert of the summer. I've gone to three of the Thursday concerts on my own so far, enjoying the music of a blues band, a Celtic band and a rhythm and blues/jazz ensemble. People brought their lunches and sat on the lawn, and children frolicked with wild abandon to the music. They absolutely *frolicked*. It was great.

Pete finally passed the swallow test (applesauce without choking) so his feeding tube will be removed tomorrow–another big step. Then he can enjoy real food. (Well, hospital food, but it has to be better than that brown stuff in a bag hanging on the IV pole next to his bed!)

Sometimes I get tired and I need others to hold that dream of Pete's full recovery for me. Today, however, I'm holding strong. Thanks for everything. My heart has never been so full of gratitude.

Love,

Pam

Update Tuesday, August 12, 2008 at 7:06 p.m.

I watch Peter sleeping. His chest rises and falls, and I am in awe that he is still alive. I know I almost lost him—several times—and yet, here he is, this man of my heart, and his chest rises and falls. Tears come.

He looks a little scruffy because the electric shaver I bought for him yesterday was lousy. You get what you pay for when it comes to shavers, I guess. Even scruffy, he still looks handsome—rather beaten up, but handsome.

He is probably down about 40 pounds. I'll have to get him some new pants to wear when he's ready to go home. He has a zipper-like incision that pokes through the top of his hospital gown, and lower, on his abdomen where the tubes have been, he will have scars looking like little additional belly buttons. His chest hair is starting to grow back. Camouflage.

He doesn't talk much at all. I feel a little thrill when he croaks out one word. Sometimes, when spoken to, he just stares. He does seem to be aware of what is going on around him most of the time, though. How I wish I knew what he is thinking!

Today, when we got him up to walk, I was facing him and he put his arms around me. We stood for a precious moment, as if we were doing a slow dance, arms around each other. It felt so good, I didn't want to move. But move we finally did, and with the help of the P.T., he walked to the far end of the corridor, turned left and walked to the far end of that hall. He used a walker on wheels, but walked on his own steam. He rested on a bench then, and we had to get a wheelchair to bring him back to the room, but still, it was farther than he had walked before. Now he is sleeping, obviously bushed from the exertion. His chest rises and falls. His heart is beating. He is still here.

E-mail, Tuesday, August 12, 2008

Dearest Pam,

. . . Marty said something Sunday that was so important to me . . . When praying and affirming Pete's return to health, she said to think of you and him standing in front of the church, singing with strength and vibrancy as you always do, rather than thinking of Pete lying in the hospital. I realized I'd begun to accept the 'reality' of the hospital almost to the exclusion of holding the vision. I'm sure that's got to be a difficult vision for you to hold sometimes. I'm grateful for Marty's reminder . . .

Love to You Both,

Carol Johnson

Tuesday, August 12, 2008

Journal

Over the years I have heard people speak of lifting someone up in prayer. I always thought it was just a generic phrase for praying. I know differently now.

This has been a long haul for both Pete and me. At times I've been discouraged, wondering what lies ahead. I've longed for a return to the way things used to be. Intellectually I know that living in the past and fearing the future are useless and harmful practices, but sometimes worry just wells up in me, like a deep sea monster, sucking me downward. Usually, it doesn't last for long. I have a deep faith and belief in Pete's capacity to heal and in God's purpose for us. But most importantly, when I'm just sort of emotionally numb, I remember that there are literally hundreds of people out there, praying for us. Hundreds. It's amazing. And I am lifted up–lifted up in a way that is more than symbolic, more than metaphoric. It's such a strong sensation, this being lifted up, that I feel as if I am shedding anchors that have been pulling me down. Gentle arms are providing a soft, safe buoyancy.

I am lifted up.

Same day, later . . .

It was probably a family home once upon a time, this 1960-ish frame house, set back from the street and nestled deep into some trees so that you don't really see it until you're right in front of it. The front door is down a few steps, which makes the house look sunken, but from the living room inside, you can see that it is actually perched on a small hill. The back of the house has a beautiful view of a wooded area and then a street way down below.

There are six bedrooms–five upstairs, one down. Each room has two single beds, except for #3, which has a day bed and a trundle. I was in #2 at first. It had the same easy chair as the other rooms, but one of the legs was missing, so it looked a little drunk. There was a big flood light right outside the window that filled the room with harsh light at night, so I covered the window with a towel. The room was a bit small, but okay.

A few weeks later I was able to move into #4, where I am now. The chair in #4 has all four legs, and there is a huge picture window, looking out on the wooded hillside. I like this room. The trees outside my window are comforting to me when I get back at the end of the day, a bit of nature after all the hospital technology.

The Transplant House is sponsored by the Friends of the University of Michigan Hospital. It is for family members of transplant patients and recipients who return for routine checkups or additional treatment. The rent here is a lot less than what I paid at the Red Roof Inn, and the house is only about ten minutes from the hospital. It's a bit spartan here, but a lot better overall.

Downstairs there is a large kitchen with adequate pots and pans, plates, silverware, etc. Each bedroom has its own shelf in the cupboard, and we stake out spots in the fridge for our food. In the dining room there is a computer that doesn't seem to work and a table that seats ten, although only once have I ever seen anyone eat there. The living room has another big window overlooking the woods, a large table, a TV, sofa, chairs, and a rather exotic, cushy chaise lounge. I usually eat my morning cereal and evening dinner at the table in the living room, watching the news or reading one of the many outdated magazines available.

There is a washer and dryer on the second level, and two bathrooms. Quiet time is from 10:00 p.m. until 6 a.m. That means we don't do laundry during that time, and don't throw wild parties (as if we were in that mode) at any time.

As for the other folks staying at the house, they keep pretty much to themselves. Most of us are at the hospital all day anyway. We exchange a few words from time to time, telling our stories in abbreviated fashion, and wishing each other luck or offering prayers. People come and go–a day or two, a week. I'm the longest term resident here now at 42 days.

> *"If God brings you to it, He will bring you through it."*
> *–Posted on the wall above the washing*
> *machine at the Transplant House*

Update Wednesday, August 13, 2008

Pete had a heart catheterization and biopsy today, which is routine for heart transplant patients. I haven't heard the results yet. He slept most of the rest of the day. Not much news–except that I have taken up knitting. I haven't knit in years. Reverend Marty sent me some beautiful yarn, some needles, and an instruction book. She has encouraged me to knit a prayer shawl. Every stitch is a prayer. She loaned me the book, *Zen and the Art of Knitting, Exploring the Links Between Knitting, Spirituality, and Creativity*, by Bernadette Murphy.

Marty talks about "knitting into the mystery." I think I get it. Knitting can be a spiritual act. I find it very calming. It's slow, wonderfully slow. I like that too. For me, it's more about the process than the product. I just slow down and knit three, purl three, knit three, purl three, and over time–something emerges. Something beautiful. It reminds me of the little steps that Pete is making towards his recovery. Knit three, purl three. Something beautiful.

---

19 Messages Posted Wednesday, August 13, 2008

Your words calm us too, Pam. Knit three, purl three, breathe, knit three, purl three, breathe. You comfort us, and we can only hope we comfort you.
Kathy Muench

Pam, is there somewhere close by where you can go and look up at the stars? Medicine for you . . .
Julie Ludwig

Wednesday, August 13, 2008
Journal

As a stroke patient's brain swelling goes down, he or she typically begins to show improvement. I hadn't known that, but it makes sense. Right now he is far from recovered, whatever that means in his case, but I think he's moving in the right direction. At first I thought that he was not cognitively impaired at all because he seemed to be aware of what was going on around him. He answered with a nod or a turn of the head to yes/no questions, and he said a few words here and there. But the speech therapist said today that it is likely there is some brain damage, based on the apparent disconnect when Pete tries to speak. I wonder if we are dealing with a permanent issue . . . I know the brain is capable of establishing new pathways when old ones have shut down. Will he be able to do that in regards to speech? Or anything else? Will he ever be able to sing again?

Often Pete rubs his eyes with the heels of his hands, and then draws his hands up, onto his forehead as if he had a terrible headache. When I ask him is he has a headache, though, he turns his head from side to side, "No."

For a couple of weeks now he has been grabbing his crotch and rubbing, sometimes quite vigorously. His skin is very red and irritated down there due to a yeast infection. The nurses and I tell him not to scratch, but he does anyway. Unless I hold both of his hands, he can't seem to stop himself, and that makes the itching even worse. The nurses have tried powders and lotions, but nothing seems to give him substantial relief. Occasionally he asks for pain meds. Poor guy . . .

Sometimes Pete stares off into space, unblinking, even when someone speaks to him. I have found that I can get his attention by calling his name and asking him to look at me. Then he responds, but his words are few.

When I play music with a beat he taps his feet or his fingers. I really think music could be crucial to his recovery. I talked last night with another music therapist, Lynn. She suggested that when Pete goes for a walk, I sing to him, so he can walk to the beat of the music. The first song I thought of was "Be Kind to Your Web-footed Friends." (Good grief! I'm old enough to remember Mitch Miller!) Lynn suggested tapping the beat on his shoulder or his arm as we walk. I'll try that.

At this point, I wish I knew what else I should/could do to help him progress. Much of the time he just sleeps, and I sit beside his bed, reading or knitting. I'd be happy to do something to stimulate his mind–read to him, coax him to talk, or whatever might work–but I also know that he needs rest, and rest might be a higher priority right now. Hmmmmm . . . How much to push, how much to let him rest–that is the question. I don't know what to do.

"You do know what to do."
–Louise Hay

Biopsy 8/13/2008: Rejection Level—0R
(No evidence of rejection)

Update Thursday, August 14, 2008 at 7:52 p.m.

My, my–summer is drawing to a close. We lost summer this year. No–actually we captured a little slice of it today. Natalia, the beautiful Indian physical therapist, came up around noon and together we took Pete in his wheelchair down to the courtyard for part of the last open air concert of the summer. He really enjoyed the fresh air and the gentle breeze outside. A jazz trio played, and Pete kept the beat with his fingers. Natalia had him walk a bit there too–50 feet or so.

By the time we returned to his room, Pete was exhausted. Everything requires a tremendous amount of energy from him. In just a few minutes his occupational therapist, Yvonne, another beautiful woman, came by to work with him. He just wanted to sleep, but he did get up again. Yvonne had him go to the sink and brush his teeth. He got there, little step by little step, with the help of the walker. When he looked in the mirror, he stared, his eyes as big as saucers. His hand slowly went up to his twitching lip, and his frightened eyes filled with tears. Now, an hour or so later, he is sleeping, plumb worn out. Bless his heart.

Love to you,

Pam

14 Messages Posted August 14-15, 2008

Sunshine and jazz . . . that sounds like an excellent prescription for healing. A mantra that I have kept close for many years is this: One day at a time, one crisis at a time, and patience. Patience is always the most difficult part!
Love,
Diane Freestone

Your postings do much more than give us information to ease our curiosity. They bring me "closer to home" too—I mean the home of my soul . . . . Everyday is a new message for my own spiritual growth, and I am sure many, many others, also.

Today . . . I will taste my food. Today . . . I will look in the mirror and not be so hard on myself. Today . . . I will use my energy more wisely. Today . . . I will love more freely and hold Deb a moment longer. Today . . . I will let others love me.

Wish so much that you two did not have to go through this, but while you are, God continues to shine through you, as God always does . . .
Love,
Jaye Mann

Wednesday, August 14, 2008
Journal

What I didn't say in today's update is what happened when we were out in the courtyard. It was a festive environment, with lots of people around, including quite a few patients in hospital gowns, in wheelchairs, and some who had their IV poles with them. Hospital staff sat on the grass, eating their lunches, and children ran up and down the gentle slope of the courtyard. Natalia wanted Pete to walk a little, so she got him out of the wheelchair and put the physical therapy belt around his waist. She supported him by holding on to the belt as he took a few tentative steps.

As Pete walked, his incontinence pad (read: adult diaper) began to slip. When I saw it was drooping below his gown, I made my way quickly to the two of them, but it was too late. In a moment, it was around his ankles. I fought a momentary panic, imagining Pete's absolute mortification, or worse yet, a fall, but Natalia quickly reached down, scooped it up, and tossed it in a nearby trash can. I'm not even sure Pete realized what had happened. I brought the wheelchair up to him then, and we rolled him back upstairs with his dignity intact.

Pete remembers . . .

I really enjoyed going out and feeling the sun on my face. I just wanted to be outside. Kids were running on the grass. I thought that it was so beautiful, that they were enjoying themselves. I wanted to run with them, but I couldn't, except in my mind. It seems to me that Natalia walked over to the garbage can and dumped something.

Update Friday, August 15, 2008 at 7:55 p.m.

The Things We Take for Granted: Two Big Milestones Today

Milestone #1: Pete pointed to the urinal before he had to go, and then he used it. This is a first in quite a while. The nurse and I cheered! This is a very big deal. It sounds so simple—being able to know when you need to pee and then being able to do it. We take so much for granted, but he is learning how to do everything all over again.

Milestone #2: Elisa, the physician assistant who asked us to please not call her "Elsie," came in this afternoon and removed the last chest tube—the last major tether. Dana, the speech therapist was in today also. She worked with Pete on volume, among other things. She told me that his husky whisper is due to dysarthria, a speech disorder caused by his strokes. She thinks with work eventually he will be able to speak much more easily. It's good news that he can swallow now. I coax him to say the following affirmation: "I am getting better every day."

The plan is for Pete to move up to the rehab floor on Monday to begin intensive rehabilitation therapy. That will be a milestone too—a huge one. The doctor said, "They work 'em pretty hard up on 6A. Patients have to be able to handle three hours of therapy before they can be admitted. We think you're ready." Pete looked doubtful.

We have been listening to a lot of music lately. People have sent us wonderful CDs. Thank you so much! Pete taps his toes to the music, and we hope he'll be walking to the beat soon. I know he really enjoys listening. The nurses say they love to come into our room, as it's always humming.

Natalia, the P.T. with beautiful brown skin and long black hair, told me today that she especially likes our room because she can tell we have a spiritual focus. She said that it makes a major difference with a patient . . . I told her that I don't know how people get through something like this without a sense that there is something bigger than themselves. For me, knowing that all is in divine order is a rock that I stand on. I know that Pete and I are together for a reason, and that there is much for us to do yet as we walk this journey together. Good things, loving things.

Love and hugs to you all,

Pam

---

15 Messages Posted August 15-16, 2008

Pete couldn't be in better hands.
Kerry Lytle

Friday, August 15, 2008
Journal

Today I asked the nurse for a hand mirror, so that Pete can work on his facial expression. He will have to learn to smile again. Imagine that!

Same day, later . . .

Another challenge: I learned from the contractor that it will cost between $15,000 and $22,000 to clean up the mold in our basement. After I picked my jaw up off the floor, I took a few deep breaths and asked inside, "Okay, God–How are we going to get through this one?" I figure something will work out. I refuse to go into panic zone.

It feels like I'm carrying a huge bolder around–and I can't talk about it with Pete. He's too fragile, and not terribly coherent either. Besides, he needs all of his emotional energy just to get through each day right now. The way will become clear, I'm sure. What is it Annette taught me? "Muddy waters, let stand, become clear."–Lao Tse. I have enormous faith. Pete and I just want to be able to go home when he completes his rehab, which could be as soon as the next two weeks. We want to go home and begin again.

I feel a little like Dorothy–this certainly isn't Kansas–but I don't have any ruby slippers here.

CHAPTER ELEVEN

Believe and Wait

"Don't ask the mountain to move; just
take a pebble each time you visit."
–Haiku by John Paul Lederach

Update Saturday, August 16, 2008 at 8:01 p.m.

SYLVIA DAPLE SENT us a wonderful affirmation from the Daily Word. Here is an excerpt:

Today and every day, I bless my heart as I give thanks for the
wonderful work that it does. I focus my thoughts on the power and
efficiency of my heart. Continuing to beat in perfect rhythm, my
heart supplies my body with the nourishment and oxygen it needs. I
bless my heart and know that it constantly beats with faith and love,
carrying life and energy to every cell of my body.

I love this, and will share it with Pete in the morning. He has a wonderful new heart beating in his body, keeping him alive, and sustaining him as he heals. His new heart seems to like its new home. At this point there is no sign whatsoever of rejection. Monday, if all goes as planned, we will begin a new stage of the journey as Pete is moved up to 6A, the rehab floor. He will have intensive occupational, physical, and speech therapy every day. He's already working hard at recovering, and will be working even more soon.

Thank you for your prayers and loving thoughts. They lift us up. The manager of the Transplant House told me tonight that we get more mail than anyone he's ever had here. We are so blessed in the way of friends and family! THAT'S YOU!

Love,

Pam

Sunday, August 17, 2008

Journal

Pete spoke very little today. He slept a lot and seemed to be very tired. This evening, he was scratching his crotch–it's been very itchy–and then he said something. I leaned in to listen, and he said, "Dynamite." I didn't think I had heard him correctly, so I asked him to repeat it. Again, he said, "Dynamite," this time with a sense of urgency. I asked him, "Do you need to pee?"

He said, "I need to pee."

Oh my.

Terry (my brother) remembers . . .

Prior to the transplant Pete was very, very sick, especially with the congestive heart failure and the heart muscle not being able to function. He looked terrible–pale, weak. I was concerned that he wouldn't make it. It's a blessing that they found a donor so quickly. I don't know how long he could have lasted without that.

(About leaving his chest open) I had never seen where they would do surgery and put in an artificial heart and then leave the chest open because of the blood loss. And then they did it again with the transplant. They really knew what they were doing.

(About his prognosis) They used to say that memory and cognitive ability was impaired after a heart transplant, but now they know that although that happens, patients do recover in time. Pete's strokes, though, were very discouraging.

Update Sunday, August 17, 2008 at 7:45 p.m.

I so love this man who lays in his bed, sleeping for hours and hours throughout the day, who held a cup of coffee and drank from it for the first time today, who said, "Dynamite," when what he really meant was that he needed to use the urinal. He has a lot of healing to do yet.

They tell me that the first four to seven months are the most important ones for stroke recovery. I read about a new study by researchers in Finland that found that listening to music soon after a stroke appeared to improve patients' recovery. I play music for Pete a lot. Hope it helps.

I also feed him his mashed potatoes, custard, and strained meat, which he hates. (They serve strained corn that has been set in a corncob-shaped mold. Incredible.) I read him the postings, e-mails and cards. I help the nurse change the linens. When the physical therapist takes him for a walk, I push a wheelchair behind in case he gets too tired to make the return trip on foot. I fill out his menu choices for the food service. I pray a lot.

And then I go back to the Transplant House and read your postings and e-mails. It's my link back to our other life—the one that awaits us after we leave here. Please understand that you play a very role special in all of this is. You are the wind beneath our wings. Thank you.
Pam

---

21 Messages Posted Sunday, August 17, 2008

. . . I saw a friend last night who worked as an emergency room nurse for twenty years and also as a surgical nurse. She said that as well as playing music, which is highly important, keep talking to him about anything to do with his and your life, like birthday dates, wedding date, any facts about your life and his that you know, over and over again. She said patients can hear everything and it sinks into their brain and helps them recover memory and a sense of their lives.

Love to you both, and blessings to you for the heartfelt lessons and loving you are giving to us.
Donna Leonard

Pete remembers, telling Pam . . .

I wanted to get better. I'd wake up and think, Oh God, I'm still in the hospital. Oh God, they're bringing in some pureed crap–corn in shape of an ear of corn. And peas. I hate peas. Give me a break! The oatmeal was good, though, and I even learned to eat yogurt. They tried to fatten me up with Carnation Instant Breakfast.

I couldn't sleep on my side. I didn't like that. More than once the feeding tube came out of my nose when I was sleeping and they had to put it back in again, shoving it into my nose and down my throat, and having me go through an X-ray all over again to make sure it was placed properly. The nurses kept examining my feet and pricking my thumb to check the blood for diabetes.

The one constant I had was you. I didn't want to make it, but you made me want to make it. I literally thought that every day and every night was a battle, and I fought hard. I said, "Thank you God. I hope Pam gets some rest." Then in the morning I'd wake up and start all over again.

Update Monday, August 18, 2008 at 7:35 p.m.

Today was special. Pete said the longest sentence he has spoken so far. He said to me, "Thank you for taking care of me." Bless that man!

When the physical therapist came in to help Pete exercise and take a walk, I asked her to schedule in a few moments for Pete and I to hug each other, standing up. I've missed that so much! So, with great effort, Pete stood, and leaned into me in a tender, prolonged embrace. One hand worked its way around to the small of my back, in a precious, familiar touch. It was beautifully romantic.

Looking back . . .

What I didn't include in the CarePages: When Pete and I embraced, the nurse and the P.T. noticed that he had had an "accident," and they needed to get him cleaned up. He had very loose stools, and he often didn't know when it was coming. So as he stood, his arms around me, two nurses cleaned him up from behind!

Update continued . . .

He needed to rest for a bit then, so the P.T. had him do some exercises sitting down before his walk. I put on a recording of Pete singing "New York, New York," and before you knew it, the three of us were kicking our feet and waving our arms in the air. It was hilarious, and we all wound up laughing–including Pete. How marvelous to hear his laugh again!

The docs from rehab came by then and told us that they will move Pete up to the rehab floor tomorrow. They were pleased with his progress, and said that, although it is difficult to predict, we can probably expect 2-3 weeks in rehab before going home. After lunch Wendy, the viola player from Gifts of Art, came and played for us "Ashakon Farewell," Jay Unger's haunting melody that was the theme in the PBS series, "The Civil War." It was so gentle and calming it brought tears to my eyes. These wonderful musicians come by every now and then to soothe and uplift, and they do it well. Gifts of Art. Indeed.

So–much love from the love birds in Room 4139. We hope you are all well and appreciating life.

Pam

---

16 Messages Posted August 18-19, 2008

"We need four hugs a day for survival.
We need eight hugs a day for maintenance.
We need twelve hugs a day for growth."—Virginia Satir
Truly . . . love is all there is!
Nancy Green

Your love for each other is a gift to all of us. With each milestone in the healing process we cheer along with the angels!
Love,
Joan Van Houten

Monday, August 18, 2008

Journal

This afternoon Pete said, "I want to go home. It's time." I felt my heart break a little, because I know he isn't ready to go home–and he probably doesn't realize it. He still is incontinent. He is quite congested and needs breathing treatments and chest percussion to break up the secretions in his lungs. He still needs speech, physical, and occupational therapy. He's learning quickly, and getting better day by day, but he's not ready, and neither am I. I'm terrified with the idea of going home too soon. It will be a challenge.

And then there's the matter of "home." Ours is full of poison. I don't know where we are going to go–but it won't be our home. Sigh. I miss home.

Same day, later . . .

I experienced an "Aha!" moment about ten years ago. I'd thought about peace of mind often over the years. It was something I longed for, but it always seemed elusive. Any mother will tell you that there are always more things that need doing than there is time to do them. As my kids grew and became less dependent on me, I had more time to spend in meditation, and occasionally would come close to the feeling of peace, but then something would happen and I would be off and running into the Wonderful World of Stress. My son was in trouble with drugs, my mother was dying, and I was stretched way too thin for comfort. Peace of mind? You gotta be kidding. I was lucky if I could *find* my mind.

I was talking this over with an old friend of mine–85-years old to be precise–when it came to me that I didn't have to be at peace with everything around me. All I had to do was be at peace with that moment. There I was, having coffee with a wise and charming man whom I adored, in a little coffee shop in the small town of Bloomingdale, Michigan. I realized that it would be quite possible–no, it would be *easy* to be at peace with *that* moment. And since all we have is the present moment, *that* constituted peace of mind.

So here we are in *this* moment–Pete is in the hospital recovering from a heart transplant. He is cared for with skill and compassion. I am able to be with him–be *absolutely present* with him. I am at peace with this moment. Mmmmmm . . . It feels good.

Update Tuesday, August 19, 2008 at 8:36 p.m.

Today Pete was moved from the fourth floor to 6A. Doesn't sound like much, but this move is big–very big. Pete is now in rehab. It felt different from the moment I stepped into the hallway. It's peaceful here, like a little oasis in a very big mega-hospital. Pete has his own room, with a view of several rooftops and the crane that is helping to build the new children's hospital.

It's like a separate world in this unit. I don't know how to describe it–but it just feels different. Don't get me wrong–We've been very pleased with the quality of Pete's care every day since we got here. It's an excellent hospital, but 6A is where patients go to get ready to go home. Our first nurse, Lisa, said, "Our job is to get rid of people." The staff gently, lovingly, helps the patient get strong enough and healthy enough to go back into the world outside of the hospital. Being on 6A means *intensive* therapy. Pete will have at least three hours a day of it. This is where the rubber meets the road and he must step up to his own recovery.

Lisa is kind and efficient, seeming to have all the time in the world to settle Pete in, chat with us and explain about the unit. I really like it here–and I think he will too.

I want to say a few words here about Pete's courage. I marvel at him. I think it would be easy for him to just give up. There are so many things that are either extremely difficult for him to do, or simply impossible at this point. Yet, the physical therapist comes in and asks him if he is up to going for a walk, or whatever she has in mind, and he gives the "thumbs up." He speaks very little, walks with a walker and someone beside him for support, and still this brave man is firmly committed to healing and regaining all of his capabilities. Even, or perhaps especially, in his physically compromised state, I find him immensely strong. I am very proud of him. With this attitude and the grace of God, he will heal. Completely.

Love to you,

Pam

---

15 Messages Posted August 19-20, 2008

Healed completely, absolutely.

Love,

Kat Keasey

> There is no doubt he will recover fully. Pete is an awesome, loving leader with the courage of a Lion.
> Darrell Elkins
>
> Don't loose track of the knowledge that your body is just the housing for your great spirit, Pete, even when the changes seem overwhelming . . .
> You have the right tools to get the job done . . . I marvel at you everyday.
> Tracey Davis

Tuesday, August 19, 2008
Journal

When Pete was transferred to 6A he was considered to be discharged from the rest of the hospital. I don't know why they do that, but there you have it. His discharge papers indicate the following (Explanations in parentheses are mine):

Admission date: 6/27/08
Discharge date: 8/19/08

Principal diagnoses:
1. Acute Nonischemic Cardiomyopathy, EF 20%
2. Acute Chronic Systolic Left Ventricular Heart Failure

Secondary diagnoses:
1. Large Pleural effusions (Excess fluid between the two membranes that envelop the lungs)
2. Hypothyroidism

Comorbidities:
1. Mild CAD: 60-70% (Coronary Artery Disease)
2. Atrial fibrillation (Abnormal heart rhythm)
3. Cardiac Sarcoidosis

4. Sustained slow Ventricular Tachycardia (Rapid heartbeat that starts in the ventricles)

5. Hyperlipidemia (Elevation of lipids in the bloodstream, including cholesterol, triglycerides, etc.)

6. HTN (Hypertension)

(There followed a list of 19 "pertinent" procedures Pete had gone through, including CT scans, PET scans, EEGs, etc., and a list of 16 discharge medications. There was also a "Clinical Course," a summary of Pete's medical history since he collapsed in early June. I had to look up half of the terms, but it finally made sense to me.)

Unresolved Issues
Other medical conditions/treatments during hospitalization:

1. Coagulopathy (Blood clotting disorder)

2. Thrombocytopenia (Not enough platelets in blood for clotting)

3. ATN (Acute tubular necrosis, a kidney disorder involving damage to the tubule cells of the kidneys, which can result in acute kidney failure.)

4. VT (Ventricular Tachycardia is a fast heart rate, usually over 100 beats per minute. VT can deteriorate rapidly into Ventricular fibrillation, a life-threatening arrhythmia demanding immediate treatment with either an external defibrillator or an implanted one.

5. Acute mental status changes

6. Ischemic right thalamic CVA (Stroke)

7. Pulmonary edema (An accumulation of fluid in the lungs)

8. Hematuria (Blood in the urine)

9. Right parietal hematoma (A collection of blood in a part of the brain)

10. Left hemothorax (A collection of blood between the chest wall and the lung)

11. Elevated post void residuals (Could be evidence of a voiding dysfunction, problem with urinating or bladder emptying).

Tuesday, August 19, 2008

Journal

I spoke with a mold remediation contractor who has been to our house to get an idea of what would be involved. He gave me an estimate of $20,000, saying it was high because they would have to remove the contents of the basement and clean everything. Our basement has been a dumping ground for years. I shudder to think of what is down there.

They told me that the walls and floors won't be so difficult to clean and treat. They will need to either clean or dispose of everything made of wood or paper. Then they would do Hepa vacuuming, wipe everything down with cloths damp with certain chemicals, then vacuum again. If the basement were empty it would take five to ten working days. With the present contents, two weeks to a month.

Oh my.

Wednesday, August 20, 2008

Journal

They work the patients hard on 6A. Here's an example of one day's schedule:

8:45-9:30 a.m.	Occupational Therapy, bedside	Kara
10:30-11:15 a.m.	Physical Therapy	Adrienne
11:15-12:00 p.m.	Occupational Therapy	Kara
1:30-2:15 p.m.	Cardiac Biopsy	Dr. Dyke
2:30-3:15 p.m.	Physical Therapy	Adrienne

Pete is so tired from all of this that he usually just sleeps when he isn't in therapy. I have to work at him to get him to eat something before he drifts off.

In O.T. there is an apparatus that looks like a two foot tall cross with four or five horizontal bars made of half inch dowels. Pete is working at putting rings on the bars—a simple matter for you and me, but he does it with intense concentration. The goal is for him to do so, standing up, for longer and longer periods of time. Right now he can only do it for about a minute before he has to sit down. The O.T. also works with him on things like brushing his teeth, using the bathroom and shaving. All of these things take huge effort and concentration for him.

Adrienne, the new P.T., explained that in a normal heart, the vagus nerve keeps the heart rate slow when the person is at rest. With activity, the nerve allows the heart to speed up. After a few seconds, the adrenal glands are activated and adrenalin kicks in. However, the vagus nerve is permanently severed in the heart transplant process, so the heart beats at a steady rate of 100 beats per minute. The patient needs to warm up to get the adrenalin going. Adrienne works with Pete at kicking from a sitting position, raising his arms up over his head, shrugging, etc. Standing, he pats a balloon back and forth with the therapist. He does all of this before even attempting to walk. When he walks, Adrienne walks along side of him, holding on to the belt around his waist for support, and, I suppose, to catch him if he falls. He walks around the perimeter of the gym, slowly, stopping to rest when he gets tired. I sit by the wall, watching, willing him to get stronger with every step.

There are a lot of things Pete is going to have to learn to do again. I imagine him casually walking down a sidewalk or tossing a Frisbee, and I wonder if he'll be able to do those basic, simple things. We had a visit from a heart transplant recipient the other day. He seemed energetic, healthy, and full of vitality. It was encouraging. Pete is not your average heart transplant recipient, though. I wonder if the strokes will be more problematic than the heart transplant. We will see.

Wednesday, August 20, 2008
Journal

When I walked into Pete's room this morning, he beckoned me to his side and whispered in my ear, "I didn't tell them anything."

"Didn't tell who?" I asked.

"The Japanese."

Oh my . . .

Update Wednesday, August 20, 2008 at 10:22 p.m.

It's been a long day and I am bone tired–but I want to share with you what happened today. Pete was taken down (in his Wehle chair) to physical therapy this morning, as usual. The P.T. room reminds me of a small elementary school gym. There is a mural that covers one entire wall, showing a beautiful lake with rowboats, swans, and water lilies. There are wooden stairs of two different heights for practicing climbing, balls of all sizes and colors, a treadmill, and about eight padded platforms, each a bit larger than a king size bed. Today the P.T. checked Pete's range of motion, his walking, his moving around on the bed, and his ability to follow simple commands.

After physical therapy, we went right down the hall to Occupational Therapy. The O.T. room is a little smaller, and there is less large equipment, but it is where the important small motor and ADL (Activities of Daily Living) activities are stressed–getting dressed, brushing teeth, eating, etc.

I think Pete did well in both sessions. He was very tired afterwards, but they took him right from there to the lab for another heart catheterization and biopsy. They take biopsies every week for the first month or so after a heart transplant. By the time we got back to his room in the middle of the afternoon he was exhausted, but he managed to stay awake long enough to meet a new social worker, and two of the doctors that will be following him up here. They had a big team meeting with all the doctors, therapists, etc., and set a tentative date for Pete's release–September 9. That's the day after our one year wedding anniversary. We will have much to celebrate!

I left the hospital around 5 o'clock to shop for some sweat pants and t-shirts for Pete's therapy sessions. Then I went back to the Transplant House to eat supper and get some rest. I was just getting ready to chill out for the evening when I had a call from the hospital that Pete was looking for me and that he wanted me to come back. So back I went. He was a little disoriented and agitated from the move and the exertion of the day. "I want to go home," he said over and over. It took a while, but in time I was able to calm him down and get him settled in for the night.

As I sat with him tonight, I kept thinking of the value of being present. I didn't really have to do anything but *be* there tonight. Have I mentioned this before? I don't know. But, for me, this has been one of the greatest lessons in this whole experience. I am learning how to be with Pete in the deepest sense of the word. That is what he truly needs now—and it's so sweet for me to be able to do that for him. Sweet and simple. He's very easy to love.

Love,

Pam

---

10 Messages Posted August 20-21, 2008

Dearest Pam,

Thank you for loving my brother.

Claudia Dutkiewicz

"I finally realized that being grateful to my body
was key to giving more love to myself."
–Oprah Winfrey

Wednesday, August 20, 2008

Journal

Many of the postings urge me to take care of myself. I know that it's really important, but like so many other care givers, I find it challenging to do. The days at the hospital are long and tiring, especially emotionally. My body needs an escape from the stress, but there's fat chance of that, so I try to get enough rest. When sleep won't come, I do my best to relax into the quiet of night. I try to meditate, but often my mind is so jumbled, I don't feel very successful at it. Still, I hang in there. Sonia Choquette says meditation is a drink at the well. I drink every night.

I am worried about my lungs. The inflammation follows me everywhere, making me tired and out of breath, even with mild exertion. I eke out as much rest as I can, and still I'm wiped out by evening.

I leave the hospital with a mix of relief and concern. The relief is like punching out at a job. Now it's someone else's turn. I need a break. The concern is—*Will the nurse be attentive enough? Will he or she understand that when Pete says, "Dynamite," it means "Urinal?" I've told them, but there are shift changes . . . Will he feel abandoned?*

I know he needs me. I am his advocate, his comfort, his anchor. I also need to take care of business—figure out how we will pay our bills, how to negotiate with the insurance company, how to arrange for the house to be remediated from the mold, where we will stay if the house isn't ready before Pete is discharged, going through the application process for disability status for Pete, blah blah blah. It's daunting. All I want to do is take a nap.

Looking back . . .

Pete told me much later that when I left the hospital each evening, he would tell himself that he just had to stay alive until morning when he could see me again. Oh . . .

Biopsy 8/20/2008: Rejection Level—0R
(No evidence of rejection)

Update Thursday, August 21, 2008

Pete had a very busy day—two physical therapy sessions, one occupational therapy session, one recreational therapy session and one speech therapy session. He's sound asleep now, at 6:30 p.m., just plain tuckered out. This is intensive rehab, for sure.

There is a sign in the O.T. room: *Effort + Perseverance = Results*

That's what it's all about—and I would add *Believe*. At our church we sing a little song that goes, "Only believe. Only believe. All things are possible. Only believe." We do that too!

Pete smiles now and then, but apart from that, his face shows little expression. The O.T. said today that it could take 6-12 months for his usual animated expressions to return.

The speech therapist observed that he has dysnomia, meaning he sometimes knows what he wants to say, but he just can't remember the words, even for very familiar things. In a testing session, he looked at some pictures of items and couldn't think of the name for a hammock or a beaver. He did, however, know the names for a tripod, a stethoscope and a sphynx. Go figure.

These things are stroke related. His brain is probably very busy in there, creating new pathways to compensate for the ones that are fried. The brain is amazing that way. It will take some time–but for believers–well, we can wait.

The best news of the day is that Pete is singing along with me some these days. "You are my sunshine. My only sunshine . . ." His voice is still soft and breathy, but once in a while he gets a good clear tone, right on pitch. His wonderful voice is coming back! I could never imagine that God would give him such a precious gift and then take it away. He *will* sing again.

I had a similar situation almost thirty years ago when I had thyroid cancer. After the surgery, I couldn't sing for six months. My voice just wouldn't do what my brain was telling it to do. I got a new appreciation for people who said they couldn't carry a tune. I couldn't–and it was terrifying. Singing had been my best, most treasured capacity all of my life. So I really worked at it–went into training, so to speak, and in time it came back. I believe (There's that word again!) that Pete's powerful voice will come back again too.

We can wait.

Much love to you all,

Pam

Journal entry from the past (December 4, 2005):

Music has a way of entering our souls through its own unique door. It knocks, and if we answer, a great dance of inspiration begins. It is magic!

Update Friday, August 22, 2008 at 8:08 p.m.

Good things today! Pete read a passage in speech therapy, and he did quite well. Also, he wrote for the first time since June. The therapist thought he could use a little handwriting practice, which he does–but then, he always did. Later, in the room, a nurse came by with a document that required his signature, or mine, if he couldn't write. He proudly took the pen and scrawled Peter M. Wehle on the line. Triumph!

These days are very tiring for Pete. Up until now, he was sleeping most of the time. Now he has three to four hours of therapy every day. And for anyone who has been in bed for weeks, or in his case, months, it takes significant effort and time to get the body's strength and stamina back. He gets a little discouraged because it's so slow, but when I remind him of what he can do today that he couldn't do last week, he takes heart.

The longer I am here, the more I am reminded of our interconnectedness as human beings. There is the young black girl, 23 tops, who is learning how to walk again. I don't know what brought her here, but I call her by name, Erica, and wish her well. Her face lights up. I feel like her cheerleader. Today the P.T. had her practice getting in and out of a car, using a wooden pretend vehicle. It took her about ten minutes to get into the front seat, but she did it. She's getting ready to go home.

Then there is the 80-ish woman I met in the elevator. She is in a wheelchair, working on rehab too. In her old world accent (Greek perhaps?) she told me about her husband of 65 years who died last year, just like that! (She snapped her fingers.) She shook her head in disbelief.

Pete is heart transplant #702 here. I met #701 in the hallway one day, a man named Don. After he recovers from his heart transplant, he will go on the list for a kidney transplant. He has a great sweatshirt with dozens of signatures and drawings from friends back home in Saginaw.

Yesterday in the physical therapy room I noticed a huge black guy with a jovial manner, saying goodbye to all the P.T.s. I think he was going home, and I could see the affection the therapists had for him. They were all laughing, patting him on the back and giving him high fives.

So—this is what comes to mind: We are all each other's keepers. We are all vested in each other's success. Mother Theresa said, "If we have no peace, it is because we have forgotten that we belong to one another." I feel that truth so strongly here in the rehab unit, where every patient struggles to do one more thing, to climb one more mountain. I marvel at the therapists, doctors, and nurses who have dedicated their lives to helping these people heal. It's a true inspiration and a source of immeasurable gratitude for me.

Much love,

Pam

8 Messages Posted Friday, August 22, 2008

I know his voice will come back. I can't tell you how much I'm looking forward to hearing him again. I visualize it all the time, and imagine him singing with you, us, others. I do believe that visualization by others will also move the process along.

Love,

Nancy O'Donohue

Update Friday, August 23, 2008 at 8:25 p.m.

Pete went to physical therapy and occupational therapy this morning, but he was too exhausted to go to his afternoon sessions; he just ran out of steam. Some days are like that. He slept most of the rest of the day.

Yesterday Betsy Beckerman came to the room, pulling her guitar, case, and her little stool, all on a small two-wheeled cart. She has played and sung for us several times as part of the hospital's Gifts of Art Program. It was good to see her again. I imagine she has seen quite a change in Pete over the weeks.

She asked me to sing one of my own songs for her. I sang "May We Be Healed" for her and Pete. She sang "Keep on the Sunny Side," "Wild Mountain Thyme," and the more obscure "Thyme, It is a Precious Thing." I knew them all, and it felt great to be able to put on a harmony. Our voices sounded lovely together.

I played a recording of Pete singing for her, and she was very impressed. (Everyone is, of course.) I looked over as the song played and saw a tear on Pete's cheek. I stroked his hand, kissed him, and assured him that his voice was coming back, and that he would be able to sing again. I tried not to let him see my own misty eyes.

Many of you have asked me if there is anything you can do. Yes, there is: Enjoy these last few days of summer. Smell those roses. Eat those blueberries and peaches. Appreciate the fact that you don't have to put on hat, coat, and boots when you go outside. Revel in the extra hours of daylight. Enjoy it for us.

We have missed out on summer this year—but, I'm sure that in doing so, we have all those summers yet ahead of us, together.

Love,

Pam

Saturday, August 23, 2008

Journal

I've been thinking a lot about breathing, one of the challenges for Peter these days. He takes short, shallow breaths, and although his coughing is less persistent and intense than it was, he still coughs up gunk from time to time.

He gets a breathing treatment several times a day. A technician comes in and places over Pete's nose and mouth a clear plastic mask that is connected to an apparatus by a hose. When the machine is on, a medicated mist is generated, and Pete breathes it in for about ten minutes. It seems to help.

The speech therapist said that she really can't work much with Pete's voice until he's able to breath more deeply, from the diaphragm, as trained singers do. She gave him some breathing exercises yesterday. His lungs have taken a beating, and like everything else, will need to heal and regain their strength. I wonder if the sarcoidosis that showed up in his heart is also causing problems in his lungs. There's no way to know at this point. Fluid in the lungs, however, is an issue for everyone who has had open heart surgery. The staff gave Pete a dark blue heart-shaped pillow to press into his chest when he coughs to help with the incision pain. It has a maize U. of M. insignia on it. Go Blue!

My chest still burns. I hope I'll be well enough to take care of Pete when he's discharged. I believe that everything happens for a reason, and I trust in the divine wisdom of the Universe, so as these concerns seep into my brain, I just put them in the wait-and-see box. I know how useless and debilitating worry can be, and I won't allow the fear to bury me alive. I just keep moving forward. Most of the time.

Breath.

Breathe on me, breath of God.

Life is precious.

CHAPTER TWELVE

Roller Coaster

"You can accomplish anything if you do not accept
limitations . . . Whatever you make up
your mind to do, you can do."
–Paramahansa Yogananda

Saturday, August 23, 2008
Journal

NANCY LOU CALLED. "When Pete is released from the hospital you two are coming to live with me for as long as it takes to get your house livable again." And that was that. She said that she had emptied all the drawers and closets in her guest room, and that it was waiting for us. Everything will be on one floor, and the house is close to ours. A good friend, John Grib, is ready to help build a ramp if necessary.

It was settled. In a flash–well, in a phone call–fifty pounds of anxiety was lifted off my already stressed shoulders. We will have a comfortable place to be. We will have Nancy's support and nurse wisdom. All is well.

Looking back . . .

Nancy told me many months later that this was Spirit's idea first. She said that the Quiet Voice came and said, "They need our house. Call Quick. Right now. My Pamela is worried. Help her."

Can you see why I love this friend of mine? She listens. She loves.

Update Sunday, August 24, 2008 at 7:31 p.m.

Pete ate a hearty dinner tonight for the first time since his surgery. Progress. Then we took him out for a little stroll/roll outside where summer still reigns supreme. His older son, Paul, (22) is here visiting. Saturday he leaves for a year in Japan. It's a precious slice of time we share with him before he takes off on his grand adventure. Paul will be playing bass in a symphony orchestra that consists of about 50% Japanese musicians and 50% musicians from other countries. We're so pleased for him—and proud too.

Tonight, as we watch the closing ceremonies of the Summer Olympics, I think of the amazing effort and commitment of the athletes involved. Then I look at Peter, and I see *his* amazing effort and commitment. He struggles and struggles and works and works. Then he is exhausted. He deserves a gold medal himself. Maybe several. I've said it before and I'll say it again—He's my hero.

Love,

Pam

Sunday, August 24, 2008

Journal

I told Pete that Nancy Lou has invited us to stay with her when he is discharged. He nodded. He loves her too.

I will never forget the day I met Nancy. It was about ten years ago. My younger son, Phil, was in rehab for drug abuse. He had been in a facility in the Detroit area for five months. It was a harrowing time.

In March I went to parents' weekend, which was very intense. The leader lectured on aspects of recovery and challenged us both individually and collectively about how we had enabled our sons and daughters. The director told us that she couldn't guarantee that our kids would graduate from the program and remain sober and clean, but she could guarantee that they would be kept safe while they were there, and that might give them some time to grow up and perhaps choose a different path.

Part of the way through the weekend one of the counselors took me aside and said that Phil had been sabotaging someone else's recovery. They hardly ever kicked anybody out of the program, but they said they had no choice–Phil had to go, and because he had been there under court order, he would go straight from rehab to jail.

It was his 17th birthday. No more juvenile homes. Now it was jail. The counselor told me that a police escort would come and take him away. He would be handcuffed and shackled.

I had seen Phil handcuffed and shackled once before. I didn't think I could bear to see that again, so I got in my car and drove home, barely able to see the highway ahead through a sea of tears. After the three hour drive home, I walked into my empty house alone and forlorn. *What had I done that was so wrong? How had I failed? What will happen to him in jail? Oh my dear God . . .* Coming home to an empty house was just one more thing. I felt so alone . . . so devastated.

Within two minutes I heard a knock on the door. I opened it to find a petite, smiling woman with sparkling eyes standing there. "You don't know me," she said, "but I know you from hearing you sing at church. My name is Nancy. We're having some people over for dessert tomorrow night after the soup dinner at church and I was wondering if you would like to join us."

"Uh, yeah," I said. "That would be super." She was all bubbly and kind; how could I not? I knew I needed some bubbly. "Where do you live?"

"We're just down on the same street in the big painted lady–You know, the Victorian house on the right side, just after Elkenburg?" I knew.

"Boy, did you show up at the right time. I had a terrible day." Sigh.

"Are you okay?" she asked.

Before you knew it, I was spilling my heart out to this stranger. I told her about the weekend and Phil going to jail. I cried and she held out her arms to me. She told me that she knew what I was going through, having had some direct experience with an alcoholic in her family. She told me about a happy ending in that case. I was encouraged and comforted. We became instant friends.

I went to her house for dessert the next night. The pastor was there, a jolly fellow who loved to tease. He knew both of us, and his remark was, "Uh oh! Watch out! We can't let those two women get together! That's trouble!" He was kidding. Sort of.

Nancy knew where I lived because she had seen me sitting on the porch several times when she drove by. On the day we met, she was out for a walk and as she passed my house she heard that Still, Small Voice inside say, "Go up to the door."

"I can't go up to the door. I don't even know that woman," she reasoned.

"Go up to the door. Invite her over for dessert."

"She'll think I'm crazy—and besides, I'm having a bad hair day. I look a mess." She kept walking.

"Go up to the door," she heard. Finally Nancy turned around, retraced her steps, came up to the door and knocked.

I know she was sent to me, an angel in jeans.

Over the years since then we have been steady, loyal friends. One year we took a trip to England to visit ancient spiritual sites. We went to Avesbury, Glastonbury, and even had a private entrance, arranged in advance, at Stonehenge. We were there, just us among the stones at dawn on Easter morning, which was also my birthday—a profoundly moving experience.

Now she has invited us to stay with her when we leave the hospital. It will be wonderful, perfect, exactly what we need. I just hope it won't put a strain on our friendship. Being pals is one thing; living with someone is another thing. I treasure our friendship so much, I don't want anything to threaten it.

So it won't. God help us, it won't.

Update Monday, August 25, 2008 at 8:31 p.m.

It's been so great to have Pete's son, Paul here! I think it has boosted Pete's energy and enthusiasm for his therapy. Today he walked without a walker for a while and later got out of bed and stood up without any assistance–both significant steps in his recovery. We managed to get in a tender hug in the process. He's still very much Pete!

The discharge coordinator spoke with us today about aftercare options. It's becoming very real to us that, indeed, we will be back in South Haven soon–about two weeks, if all goes as planned. There will still be a lot of rehab ahead, but the big lake is sure to be an inspiration, and being close to our friends there will be great. We may not be going to our own house at first, but we will still be "home."

We're looking forward to going home.

Love,

Pam

Monday, August 25, 2008

Rehab Schedule

8:00 am-8:45 am	Occupational Therapy–Bedside	Kara
9:00 am-9:45 am	Physical Therapy	Adrienne
11:15 am-12:00 pm	Neuropsych–Bedside	Evans
1:30 pm-2:15 pm	Occupational Therapy	Kara
2:30 pm-3:15 pm	Physical Therapy	Adirenne
3:15 pm-4:00 pm	Speech Therapy	Dana

I understand why it was such a big deal for Pete to be transferred to 6A rehab. It's like boot camp. He is working so hard! Every little thing takes immense effort. He is improving, though . . . and exhausted.

6 Messages Posted August 25-26, 2008

Yes, yes, a thousand times yes!
Michael Bieri

This is great news. Kudos to you and Pete for your devotion and perseverance. I don't know Pete, but your letters to all of us have allowed me a chance to know him through your eyes—the eyes of love. Take care. Hope to see you soon.
Love,
Sue Kruizenga

Update Tuesday, August 26, 2008 at 8:04 a.m.
Urgent Prayer Request
Dear Ones,

I just learned that last night's CT scan showed that Pete has blood clots in both of his legs. To prevent another stroke they are going to do a procedure today involving some sort of filter. I'll keep you posted. In the meantime, please continue to hold Pete in your prayers. I think this is a particularly delicate time for him.

Thank you. I love you all so much.

Pam

We're with you.
Darrell Elkins

Update Tuesday, August 26, 2008

Pete received his new heart a month ago tonight. Amazing. The heart is doing well, with no sign of rejection—a true blessing.

When I was a girl I went to an amusement park with Cookie Wiederhold and her mother. I remember going on a ride that went ridiculously fast and looped around, leaving us both thrilled and terrified. Finally our car began to slow down and approach the gate. I was so relieved! We were almost done! Then, with a jerk, the car sped up and we were off again, even faster than before. I didn't even have time to catch my breath. My knuckles gripped the safety bar, holding on for dear life. I knew that we had made it the first time around, and we would make it the second time, but that did little to quiet my terror.

Today we were back on the roller coaster here at the hospital. When Paul and I came in to Pete's room this morning, we learned about the blood clots in his legs. He is not a candidate for the usual anticoagulant medications because of his strokes, the transplant, and a subdural hematoma in his brain, but something had to be done about the clots to prevent another stroke. The other option was a filter.

A filter? Yes, an inferior vena cava filter. They made a tiny incision in Pete's groin (ouch) and snaked up a wire, eventually implanting a little filter shaped like an upside-down umbrella. It is designed to catch any large clots and prevent them from moving up to the lungs. Pete had the surgery around 3:00 p.m. today. He then was returned to his room, where he dozed the rest of the day and into the night. The docs think he will be fine to go back to his therapy sessions tomorrow.

The roller coaster has slowed down again. We can see the gate ahead. Thanks to those of you who got the message earlier today and held Pete in particularly earnest prayer today. I know that helped.

We love you.

Pam

13 Messages Posted Tuesday, August 26, 2008 Evening

Whew! Some ride!

Love,

Carol Johnson

Roller coasters, valleys and peaks, ups and downs - they all spell "life."
Tough times don't last, but tough people do!

Jeanie Frattallone

Pam, know that you are both centered in and surrounded by prayer and love.

Nancy Green

I'm holding you both in the High Watch.

Sue Fischer

Update Wednesday, August 27, 2008 at 7:47 p.m.

One month ago today Pete's heart transplant was completed. A miracle took place. The heart of a perfect stranger, given without strings or conditions, took up residence in Peter's body, keeping him alive and buying for us more years, more songs, more time to love. Soon we will be home, reveling in the simple tasks of daily life and watching the big blue water in all its autumn glory.

I'm reminded to *live in the present,* not the future. So—what can I say about *today?*

Today my older son, Brennan, is 31 years old. Incredible. He calls almost every day from Montana to see how we are doing.

Today Pete rests after another routine heart catheterization and biopsy.

Today we are grateful for a warm visit with friends, Rich and Kathy Wedemeyer, who brought a handmade medal for Pete, patterned after Olympic medals, with a big "#702" on it. Pete smiled broadly to see them. They took me for lunch at Zingerman's, where the three of us munched our luscious sandwiches outside, cafe style, told stories and laughed. Good medicine.

Today, from Pete's hospital room, we watch Barack Obama being nominated by acclamation to be the Democratic party's candidate for the forty-fourth President of the United States. As the nurse hooks up Pete's night feeding tube, history is made.

Today we focus on the slow and steady steps in healing.

Today we live in a deep state of gratitude. Pete is here, alive and getting better every day.

To quote a song by an obscure singer/songwriter:

May we be healed.
May we be whole and true,
And may the light of love and laughter
Like the sun come shining through.

This prayer is not just for Peter, but for all of us. Believe in miracles. Believe in healing. Like today, that is what is real.

Love to you,

Pam

---

10 Messages Posted August 27-28, 2008

I don't think of that composer as obscure. I'm sure Pete would agree. Your belief in miracles is significant in this. And think of the miracle that Pete is. We look forward to seeing you on the stage together, singing the duets that will surely come from this experience!

Dan Kivel

Pete remembers . . .

When I was in the hospital I had a lot of bad dreams, or maybe they were hallucinations. In one dream, Kelvin, one of my familiar nurses, had a sister. She was a nurse too, and she was taking care of me. I don't know how I did it, but somehow I killed her. I don't know why it happened, but it wasn't intentional.

Kelvin's mother, who talked with a British accent, came to care for me. I was going to tell Kelvin I had killed his sister, but his mother said that all was forgiven, that it was going to be okay. I sure felt bad about her taking care of me after I had killed one of her children, but she was very forgiving and loving. "Don't worry. It will be okay," she said.

In a different dream there was a black guy across the hall from me. He was a crack addict or something. I heard him screaming, "I gotta go. I gotta go." I think he took his own life.

In one dream there was a man with a gun. I saw him in the hallway, hiding behind an older nurse. He took her out the back way and then I heard a shot. He came back in and hid behind his grandmother, who was also a nurse. I was talking with the grandma, who was real gentle and kind. The gunman's father was in my room too. He said, "I gotta take care of this," and pulling out his gun, followed his grandson out back and shot him.

I thought, "Whoa, this is pretty bad."

The father said, "I did what I had to do."

Another time I saw a casket being rolled down the hallway. I figured it was for me.

Looking back . . .

One night Pete called me, whispering, "I've got to get out of here. They're trying to kill me." He sounded genuinely frightened, but I knew he was being well taken care of and that there was nothing going on that would harm him. I pulled on some jeans and came back up to the hospital. It took a while, a sleeping pill and some television-induced distraction, but I was able to calm him down and get him settled down for the night.

There was no way for me to get into his head and figure out what was going on, but it was clear that he was greatly disturbed by these dreams/hallucinations. The dream he had about killing a nurse, Kelvin's sister, must have been particularly vivid, because months later, back in South Haven, when he told Nancy Lou about it, we realized that he still thought it had actually occurred. It took us quite a while to convince him that it had never really happened. "You mean I didn't kill anyone?" he said, astounded and visibly relieved.

Update Thursday, August 28, 2008 at 8:39 p.m.

Pete had a very busy day, and was really tired this evening. He had physical therapy twice, occupational therapy twice, and speech therapy once. He walked about 30 feet today with no walker. It's slow going—but it's great progress!

My brother and sister-in-law stopped by this afternoon on their way up to their vacation place in the Upper Peninsula. I'm sad that we won't be joining them this year for our usual Labor Day weekend on Lake Huron.

I'm pretty tuckered out myself tonight, and trying to ward off a cold, so I'll just snuggle in with a book and a cup of tea and get some rest.

Peace and love to you,

Pam

P.S. Please know how very much your wonderful postings and e-mails are to us—like a wondrous tonic. Thank you so much!

---

16 Messages Posted August 28-29, 2008

A patient in my office yesterday told me about a quote that I want to pass on. Her quote came from an add for donating blood, but it is just as appropriate for those who choose to be organ donors: "Give the gift that will allow someone to walk through the fall leaves one more time."

I know that you both will enjoy the crunch of the fall leaves under your feet this year and for many more to come. You are in our thoughts and prayers daily.

Jack Vanden Berg

Pam, we raised you and Pete up in choir prayer Thursday evening. Elsewhere, someone close to another transplant patient shared with me the insatiable craving of the patient for Reese's Peanut Butter Cups. Turns out the person giving the heart was a PB addict. So be on the lookout for surprises!

Love you,

Martin Gruber

Rest well, dear one, and sweet dreams of those beautiful days to come for you and your beloved, amazing Pete.
Ellen Reinstatler

Update Friday, August 29, 2008 at 7:57 p.m.

Dear Ones, Pete was tired this morning because he didn't sleep well. He was short of breath in the night, and I guess he caused a bit of a flurry at the hospital, but he was doing better in that regard this morning. His O.T. set a goal for the weekend of getting Pete to stand for a total of three minutes while doing a simple activity of arranging large plastic clothespin-like devices on a wooden rack. She explained to me that sometimes standing can be more difficult than walking. Then she timed Pete–and he did it for 3 minutes, 20 seconds. I tell you, that man is motivated!

Later we watched a little of the movie, "Guys and Dolls" on TV with his favorite, Frank Sinatra, and others–including a young Marlon Brando. It was great to see Pete singing along with "Luck Be A Lady" and some of the other songs in the show. He was grinning and clearly enjoying it. His voice is still mostly a whisper, but it is coming along.

After dinner, which comes at 4:30 on 6A, I wheeled Pete downstairs and out into the courtyard so he could enjoy a little bit of fresh air. It was gorgeous outside, and we just sat in silence most of the time, soaking up summer.

Most of the time I just sit with him. I'm content to do that. The rest of the world will still be there, with all its drama and trauma, when we rejoin it. For the time being, our world is the hospital, and our job is healing.

Thank you for your continuing prayers and postings.

Love and blessings to you,

Pam

9 Messages Posted August 29-30, 2008

Pam, I am glad you are so clear on your priorities and that you know the wisdom of just BEING with someone in silence. It's very powerful. Words often just clutter up our communication, don't they . . . . What a gift of love and prayer!
Marty Rienstra

"Where there is purpose, there is energy . . . Purpose gives you a reason to get going each day and strengthens your determination to persist when the going gets tough."
–Ralph Marston

Update Saturday, August 30, 2008

This morning I woke up early and started the day with meditation. I relaxed, quieted my mind, and then asked, "What is it I should understand?" What came to me is a reminder that my purpose now is to take care of Pete, to encourage him, and to love him through all of this. That's it. That's all.

Purpose is a very powerful thing. Knowing my purpose makes everything very simple and clear. Everything else can wait. I am on a mission. In life B.T. (Before Transplant), I seemed to be constantly juggling priorities. I couldn't do everything. There were only so many hours in a day. Sound familiar? Recently I think I'd been starting to get sucked back into that mode again, but this morning's meditation reminded me of what is really important now. I can relax into the simplicity of that and release all tensions into the great "Love Net" you have created for us.

Awesome.

Pete is sound asleep in his hospital bed by my side, totally oblivious to the University of Michigan–Utah football game that everybody else in Ann Arbor seems to be watching today and the fact that his son, Paul is leaving for Japan today. That's okay, because his purpose is to heal–and he's doing that well.

Love to you,

Pam

E-mail, Saturday, August 30, 2008

Pam—

What a ministry yours is right now! While it may seem to be about you and Pete, what came to me is that you are teaching the power of presence to all who are willing to ride the wave . . .

Knit three, pearl three . . . just doing what is before you. What a powerful gift! Thank you for walking your talk. Pete may be your hero, but tonight, you are mine. Love,

Debra Basham

Update Sunday, August 31, 2008 at 8:06 p.m.

I sang at the Unity Church of Ann Arbor this morning. It has become a home-away-from-home (church-away-from-church?) for me. They loved my music. The folks there are very warm and welcoming, which has been a true comfort to me, as I really miss our Unity Church on the Lakeshore.

When I was gone, Pete decided to get up and use the bathroom. I think he pressed the call button and then just gave up and went on his own. Afterwards he mentioned it to his nurse, and she found the evidence. That means he got out of bed on his own and walked about twenty feet without a walker or any assistance. The very fact that he could manage to do that and get back to his bed without any help is amazing. We're just glad he didn't fall! He's getting better every day. Hallelujah!

The days seem to crawl by lately. Pete speaks very little–sometimes three or four words a day, so I live a fairly solitary existence. Going to church helps, but it's just a little chunk of time in a long week. This weekend there is only one other person in the Transplant House, and I haven't seen her at all. I read a lot, watch some TV and knit. It's a good time for me to learn about the wonders of solitude. I think I have a lot to learn.

Knit three, purl three, breathe. Knit three, purl three, breathe.

Love to you,

Pam

11 Messages Posted Sunday, August 31, 2008

I know that walk to the bathroom . . . I have looked at the way the walls stretch out, the effort of balancing all that way, demanding everything . . .

Tell Pete I am glad I know him—know one of the many brothers I have who have walked those steps.

Greg Orr

CHAPTER THIRTEEN

Love with a Capital L

*"God does not call the qualified. God finds
the willing, and qualifies them."*
–Source Unknown

Update Monday, September 1, 2008 at 6:18 a.m.

I WAS FEELING REALLY lonely last night. It crept up on me, like a wily spider, spinning its sticky web. Before I knew it, I was wrapped in its silvery strands, unable to move. I know that feeling sorry for myself is useless and destructive but, well, sometimes I do it anyway. It's a little like eating one potato chip. So I wallowed a bit last night, indulging myself in my own drama.

I'm told that feelings are not good or bad in themselves, they just *are*. On the other hand, I know that our *thoughts* are very powerful. I set about to figure out what thoughts were underneath these feelings of loneliness, and I suddenly realized–Ah, yes–it was that old familiar coward–fear. Fear that Pete would not make a full recovery. I imagined him (Oh, forgive me, Peter!) shuffling his feet, head down, like Grandpa Ladyman. I imagined years and years of monosyllabic conversations. I envisioned our life together as limited to staying at home, taking pills, and seeing doctors. Pete would hate that! I saw myself as the long-term caregiver, sacrificing, sacrificing, sacrificing. I imagined financial devastation–having to sell our house, living in a cockroach-infested apartment somewhere. Oh my, how the imagination loves to boogie!

I know about the law of attraction. I know how important it is to envision what we *wish* to have manifested–and I certainly don't want *that* vision to manifest. So, why do I allow those thoughts into my mind?

I'm reminded of a book I have at home called *You Can't Afford the Luxury of a Negative Thought* by Peter McWilliams. Why would a negative thought be a luxury? Maybe it's because when times are tough it is easier to slip and slide into that abyss than it is to discipline the mind to hold a higher vision–easier, and profoundly destructive.

I can't afford to have anything in my mind but the highest thought for Pete's full recovery and our wonderful life together. I choose to replace that negative image with one of health, joy, and love. I see Pete whole, vital and enthusiastic about life. I see him alert, clever and affectionate, cracking jokes, and singing with all his usual exuberance. I envision abundance, adventure and a deepening love and commitment to each other and our family.

Once I am fully aware of what is going on inside my mind, it's amazing how simple it is to replace the old vision with the new one. Simple. It just takes determination and vigilance. I have those attributes at my fingertips, and with God's grace, I can begin again. Today is a new day.

I share this with you today because maybe you've been there. If so, please know how simple it is to turn it around. Simple. Just choose another image. Choose it, and hold it firmly in your heart and in your mind. Hold it with tenacity and your own innate power. Then relax into the new reality. Today is a new day.

Immense love to you,

Pam

15 Messages Posted Monday, September 1, 2008

You're a perfect demonstration of Marty's sermon yesterday on "Enlightenment and Dog Training." We need to put a "leash" on our minds when they "go off chasing sea gulls" or say to the dog, "Drop it!" when he picks up a dead fish. Thank you for sharing the whole journey, for what you are going through is as important as each shuffled step Pete goes through.
Sue Fischer

I was so touched my this morning's entry . . . Each of us is an extraordinary mixture of humanity and divinity. Our challenge remains delicately balancing them in Truth and Love.
Treasure yourself.
David Sterken

The Law of Attraction Through My Lenses

The Universal Law of Attraction received much attention, especially with the popularity of the film, "The Secret." The concept is not new, though. In the scriptures we read, "Everything you pray for, believe you have it already and it shall be yours." And even Martin Luther said, " . . . all who call on God in true faith, earnestly from the heart, will certainly be heard, and will receive what they have asked and desired." For me, it boils down to belief, gratitude, and faith.

As I understand it, the Law of Attraction tells us that what we focus on manifests, wanted or not. Like attracts like. What we resist persists. This law works in our lives even if we are not aware of it. We attract into our lives experiences, people, jobs, money (or lack of same) by our thoughts about them. Once we understand the Law of Attraction, we can deliberately attract to us what we want.

This is oversimplified, as there is more to it than just *thinking* about what we want. We must ask for what we want, be very clear about what that is, and we must allow it into our lives. That part is often overlooked. To allow what we desire into our lives, we must not only believe that it is possible, but we must believe that it is *already manifesting in our lives.*

Let's say that I decide to focus on abundance in my life. Perhaps my thoughts would go something like this: I'*m focusing on abundance. I have all the money I need and more. I just have to keep focusing on this because I got that really big bill and my bank account is dangerously low. If I don't get some money somewhere, I'm going to be in deep trouble. I'm focusing on abundance.*

Do you see the problem with that way of thinking? While I'm saying that I'm focusing on abundance, the thought behind the thought is that I don't have enough and I'm going to be in trouble. My true thoughts aren't in alignment with my desire. Without meaning to, I am not *allowing* my desire to manifest in my life, but rather, the opposite.

So I watch my thoughts very carefully, and I can rein them in if they go into dangerous neighborhoods. I say inside, "Stop! Rewind!" and replace the offending thoughts with positive ones. It takes some practice, but becomes increasingly automatic with time and a little discipline. In this way I can discard any thoughts that do not serve me—including fear, worry, self-doubt, anger, resentment, and so on, and put in their place images of happiness, love, compassion, excellent health, and rich meaning in life.

Update Monday, September 1, 2008 at 6:40 p.m.

I went to the hospital today, refreshed and renewed. I was determined that today would be a good day—and it was. Pete was alert and cheerful when I got there. We went outside for a bit, enjoying the morning. I sang to him in the empty courtyard. It was beautiful out there, and I just let my voice roll out and flow out, giving a private concert for the man I love.

Later Pete did some walking up on the sixth floor. His vitals are all good and his new heart is doing very well. He is healing.

Several times today he sat up in bed and swung his feet over the edge of the bed. I asked him, "Where are you going?"

He replied, "I don't know." I think he just wanted to be out of that bed. The first time he did this we went for a stroll in his wheelchair. The next time, he sat in a chair for a while, and the next time, we went outside again. I think it's good news that he is restless. It means he's getting better. The doctor has ordered someone to sit with him when I'm not there to make sure he doesn't get up on his own during the night. They don't want to risk him falling, of course.

When I got back to the Transplant House tonight and read the postings, I was particularly moved by the ones that came in today. When I'm struggling to hold a positive vision, it's good to know that so many others are holding that vision for us too. It's that "love net" again. Thank you. Thank you. Thank you.

Love,

Pam

---

10 Messages Posted September 1-2, 2008

You have no idea what being in this "love net" is doing for me—and I'm sure we all feel that awe. So thank you!
Ellen Reinstatler

Update Tuesday, September 2, 2008 at 9:31 p.m.

A long day–and a good one. In physical therapy Pete tried climbing stairs for the first time. The P.T. went through a very detailed explanation of how Pete was to put his stronger leg, the right one, up on the first step and then, if he had the energy, bring the left foot up beside it. She said that if he was tired, he could step back down and sit down to rest. She firmly gripped the safety belt around his waist, and told him to give it a try. He stepped up on the first step, then the second, then the third, then the fourth, without a moment's hesitation. I felt like I was watching him scale a mountain! It was fantastic!

He rested for a few minutes in a chair at the plateau, and then made his way back down the other side. By the end of the session he was tired and triumphant. What a guy!

This afternoon a man named Mike came in to sit with him. That means, of course, that he was to make sure that Pete didn't get up and take off on his own. We chatted quite a bit with Mike, and when Pete told him about his sons, Paul and Sean, it was the most talkative Pete has been yet. Another triumph!

A good day. We are grateful for each tiny step along the way–and exuberant over the big ones, like today.

Love,

Pam

Tuesday, September 2, 2008

Journal

There is an Amish family here. I've seen them in the hallway, walking in a group, nine or so of them, in their plain clothes and somber demeanor. I tried not to stare at the men in their suspenders and broad brimmed straw hats, the women with their long-sleeved dresses and bunned hair, the three children as miniature versions of their parents. One of the younger women returned my smile. The others looked straight ahead or down at the floor as they moved together down the long corridors in their own private procession.

I saw them once in the lower level of the parking structure. They stood there, looking out of place and out of time, and I wondered what they were waiting for–a horse and buggy to pick them up? No, of course not. I know that the Amish can ride in cars. They just don't drive them.

I'm sure it must be something very serious that brings them away from their farms and into this high tech environment. They are probably feeling a mix of bewilderment, alienation, and nervousness just to be here, let alone to be facing the serious health challenge of a loved one. Me too.

I know that we are all alike underneath the clothes and the roles we play. We all move through hope and fear, faith and doubt, love and emptiness. And so I tried to put myself into their shoes. I prayed for their–what? Brother? Father? Sister? Child?–and also for them, these dear people who just want to be left alone and to devote their lives and their work to God.

I'm sure they are wondering the same things I am wondering. *Will he/she get better? What's going to happen? Dear God, what's going to happen? We can't know. All we can do is lean on our community, trust . . . and hope.*

Update September 3, 2008 at 2:41 p.m.

We learned this morning that we are still on target for going back to South Haven on September 9. That's less than a week! I think Pete is really motivated by that news, as he worked very hard in all of his therapy sessions today. He did a stellar job in speech, talking more and with greater volume than he has ever before. He even cracked a joke.

Then it was on to physical therapy, where he walked quite a bit, some of it without a walker. He also lifted some weights. In occupational therapy we worked together to make a doormat with the design of a lighthouse on it. That work involves small motor coordination, and he did some of it standing up, which takes a fair amount of energy for him.

The recreational therapist, Dana, is planning a special event for us for next Monday in celebration of our first wedding anniversary. If we get the doctor's okay, we will go out for dinner. If we need to stay in the hospital, Dana is going to set up a special candlelight Italian dinner for us (Pete's choice). Isn't that fantastic?

Thanks so much for your wonderful prayers, thoughts, and wishes.

We love you,

Pam

E-mail, Thursday, September 4, 2008

Hello Pam and Dad,

It's me, Paul. I've made it to Japan in one piece . . . I've been busy learning how to use public transportation and figuring out what food to eat. I can't figure out what is in the packaging at the supermarket because I can't read Japanese, so I've been eating pretty healthy—fresh fruits and vegetables.

. . . It sounds like Dad is doing very well, recovering strongly. I'm thinking about both of you.

Love,

Paul

Update Thursday, September 4, 2008 at 8:13 p.m.

I went through allergy testing in Kalamazoo today, and by the time I got back to Ann Arbor, Pete was done with his therapy sessions and snoozing. He woke up long enough to eat a little dinner and then fell asleep again—so—no real news today.

I have a scratchy throat, so I may have to wear a mask tomorrow when I'm around Pete. It will help sensitize me to why he hates wearing that thing! I'm going to bed early to chase away whatever this is and get back to feeling fantastic.

It's really amazing how resilient the human body is. I broke my ankle last November, and now I can walk without any problem. People get sick with the flu and then in a few days get better. Pete's heart fails, he gets a new one and he heals. It's our body's natural desire to heal itself—and it happens with a lot of help from Life, with a capital L (which I think is just another name for God).

Love (with a capital L),

Pam

---

9 Messages Posted Friday, September 5, 2008

Pam, your scratchy throat could be the result of your allergy testing, I do believe . . . It's allergy season now. Take care, Pam.

Love,

Betty Smith

E-mail, Friday, September 5, 2008

Hi Pam,

It must be a tender time as you are preparing for your homecoming . . . much in the same way that the caterpillar knows nothing of being a butterfly, what awaits you is yet to be revealed. I am assuming you have plans for where you will be going. I trust you will also let folks know what you might need. I want to remind you that your being used is not just something that will happen in the future, but it is already happening. Over and over I am in awe of the living role models of consciousness we see in you and Pete. It is such a gift . . .

We do not need to preach, to teach. We do not need to die to be born anew. You are way—showers. I was listening to an Eckhart Tolle CD and he said how blessed we are when we have a health crisis because we can do nothing but be in the now, and that is where enlightenment happens. While I am not so sure you would think of the circumstance as a blessing, your enlightened being certainly is a gift.

Sleep well. Angels run their fingers through your hair . . .

Love,

Debra Basham

Update Friday, September 5, 2008 at 8:48 p.m.

It's very quiet at the Transplant House tonight. The place tends to empty out on the weekends. I've been here for 66 days now, and at the Red Roof Inn for a week or so before that. We were at the hospital in Kalamazoo for a week before that. It's been a long road–and now we are preparing to go back to South Haven.

Pete is really excited about going home. I am too, but I'm a little nervous as well. Until now I could leave the hospital when I needed to get some rest, knowing that Pete would be well taken care of. Now Pete will need round-the-clock care, and I'm "It." He sleeps a lot, though, and I know I will find the reserves to do whatever is needed.

I have a low grade cold, so I wore a mask today when I was around Pete. We looked pretty funny in our his-and-her masks.

Today in physical therapy Pete worked at getting in and out of a car. He is also able to stand for longer periods of time, and his memory is definitely improving.

I changed his dressings today as training for going home. I've been watching carefully as the nurses do this twice a day. He has several holes in his belly where the tubes for the life support machines went in. The idea is for the wounds to heal from the inside out, rather than the other way around, so the holes are packed with ribbon-like bandages which have to be changed twice a day. Each day the holes shrink a little. I put on sterile gloves and cut about a 10-inch length of the ribbon, which I douse in a clear liquid–saline?–that comes in a little plastic tube. Then I gently pull the old bandages out with a special kind of tweezers. Next I carefully ease the fresh ribbon into the wound with a Q-tip like device. Finally, I cover the wound with a sterile pad. Pete winced only a little today. I was proud of myself after it was all done. I'm going to be quite the nurse.

We both went to the monthly Heart Transplant Support Group meeting today. It was Pete's first time, and he asked the recipients there about what to expect when he goes home from the hospital. It was very helpful for both of us to hear what they had to say, and good for Pete to meet people anywhere from 4 months to 20 years out from their transplants. They are all functioning well. (Of course, I thought, those who aren't functioning well probably are probably back home or . . .)

As our journey unfolds, I am struck by the depth of this experience. It is rich, in the sense that it is full of surprises, emotion, and life impact . . . We both feel that this experience will lead us to something–some way–that we can make a meaningful contribution. Everything happens for a reason. We'll see. (Of course, it has crossed my mind that there might have been an easier way . . .)

Here's hoping you are feeling happy and loved!

Pam

---

11 Messages Posted September 5-6, 2008

. . . Five years ago, when my son was 19, we spent three weeks at Mayo Clinic/Hospital/Rehab. He had been diagnosed with a tumor within his spinal cord. It was obviously life-threatening, and there were many unknowns, including whether or not he would be able to walk after the surgery.

The good news is that the tumor was removed and, we hope, all the residual cells were removed, too. He was young, so his recovery was quicker. He did have to "re-teach" his brain and spinal cord everything from using the bathroom, to standing, to walking.

Those days by his side were very tender for me. It has hard to be the secondary sufferer. Some of the hardest moments or hours are things he does not remember now. I am grateful for that, but my memory is still tender remembering his vulnerable moments. Yet, I was honored to accompany him on that journey. He stayed positive, and when he couldn't be positive, he let me hold that light for him. I cried saying good-bye to his primary physical therapists; my heart was so full of gratitude for how they encouraged my son and taught him to walk again.

It was a long road of recovery once we returned home. But we were home and he was determined. He did return to college, having missed only one semester. But even then, all his energy was on healing—on just getting himself across campus. He took a photography class that semester, and his photos are certainly the best journal of his healing that I can imagine.

> I just wanted to let you both know that your story, your struggle and your hope are all things I share in my own way.
>
> Much love,
>
> Ruth Tierra
>
> Pam, God is already using you mightily as these last months have unfolded before you, like the tracks of a roller coaster ride . . . There is more that Spirit will do through you because you are willing—a great deal more. Your will to allow God to use your lives to bring hope, joy, and inspiration to others is not something that is a goal for the future but is happening right now . . . today . . . in this very moment . . .
>
> With much love, and blessings beyond measure,
>
> Joan Van Houten

Update Saturday, September 6, 2008 at 7:15 p.m.

Today I went down to the hospital's main entrance to mail something, and on the way back I saw a rather scruffy young man in shorts, t-shirt and flip-flops stroll into the lobby. He had a very full, tattered back pack slung on one shoulder and looked like any one of the thousands of students I've seen on campus. He dropped his bag next to the beautiful Yamaha grand piano, sat down, and opened the keyboard. He paused and took a deep breath, and then his fingers began a slow dance along the keys. His music was at once mournful, graceful, and liquid, like a distant river, and I was swept away, only to realize later that my face was awash in tears. Music does that. It opens up places we sometimes try to keep shut.

As the days grow shorter, so does our time here at the University of Michigan Hospital. It's strange, but I will sort of miss this place. It is an amazing little city all of its own. I know many of the staff and patients here by name now. I love the courtyard, the traveling musicians, the therapy dogs, and watching people in the physical therapy room get stronger each day.

Pete walked with shoes on for the first time in more than two months today. He said that it felt strange–but he did well. He has been bumped up to a Level 4 diet, so I think that means he can eat just about anything–anything the hospital offers anyway. We're hoping they will remove the feeding tube before we go home.

This afternoon we were watching an old John Wayne cowboy movie on TV. Wayne played an old gunslinger who was dying. I heard some sniffling, and when I looked over, I saw that Pete was crying. It was a little too close to home.

I remember when my father had strokes, he cried too–something I'd never seen him do before. I think strokes sometimes break down those barriers we use to hide our emotions and they come very close to the surface. Today I was grateful, because it gave Pete an opportunity to share a tender moment with me and talk about those fears. I'm glad he could let a little of that emotion out.

I assured him that we have many good years ahead of us, and that we have work to do! He asked me what that was, and all I could tell him was that the opportunities will present themselves in good time–but first, he needs to give himself time to heal. He accepted that, and slipped back into slumber.

Later, we had one of our precious standing hugs, and he whispered into my ear, "I never thought this would happen to me."

Do any of us?

I'm still a little under the weather, so I'll close now and go to sleep. Much love to you all. Thanks for understanding that I am unable to respond to all of your postings, but we are very, very grateful for them!

Love,

Pam

---

12 Messages Posted September 6-7, 2008

Take good care of yourself, Pam, just as you would take care of God's beloved . . . because that is what you are.

Love,

Joan Van Houten

E-mail, Saturday, September 6, 2008

Nancy Lou—

It was good to talk with you today. I hope you understand how comforting it will be to go to your home Tuesday. You are giving us a precious gift of hospitality and love. We are immensely grateful to you! I'll stay in touch with you, my friend.

Love,

Pam

Return E-mail, Saturday, September 8, 2008

Pam,

Can't wait to get you into this little house. We will be so cozy! Nancy O'Donohue is bringing food Tuesday night; it was the only time she could make it this week. So Tuesday could get a little exciting. I have asked Mary and Jerry to be at the ready to come and help you into the house and get you settled if I am still at work. They are good, nurturing folks and will take care of you until I come. I am ready. The house is ready. God is excited to have us all in the Hearth Room and I have a cute answering machine message all made up for the phone. Blessings to you both. I love you love you love you!

Nancy Lou

Update Sunday, September 7, 2008 at 8:09 p.m.

Dear Ones,

Pete is looking more like his old self every day, even though he has lost over 40 pounds. His appetite is picking up, and he can feed himself now. He smiles more often. I wheeled Pete out to the courtyard to enjoy the feel of late summer. It was a beautiful afternoon. Later, Greg, the guitar player from "Gifts of Art" came by and played some gentle songs for us. All three of us sang together the old Everly Brothers tune, "Dream." Pete slept for a while then, and I did a little online research on cleaning mold. What an engaging topic!

When Pete woke up, he walked with me (!) down to the day room. I got him on the computer there, where he read the postings on last night's CarePages and an e-mail from his son, Paul, in Japan. As he read, the tears rolled down his cheeks.

Tonight I pressed the new pants and shirt I got for Pete for our special anniversary "date" tomorrow night. It's so exciting, it's almost like going to the Prom!

Tuesday, when Pete is discharged, we will be returning to South Haven where we will stay with our dear friend, Nancy Lou, who lives only two blocks from our own home. We'll be there until we can get our house remediated from mold. If you want to visit, please call ahead. Pete will love seeing friends, but he tires easily, so we need to allow enough rest time between visits. Thanks for understanding.

Many of you have told me to ask for help when I need it. I'm a little shy about doing that, especially since so many of you have already showered us with kindness. I'm told, though, that there are friends who are eager to help if they only knew what they could do. So—yes—there is something. I will probably need some help on occasion with respite care—someone to be with Pete when I need to go to the dentist/doctor/bank/grocery store, etc. If you are willing to be on a call list for this, please let me know. We'll make up a "Pete's Pals" list. I'm guessing we will need this kind of help for the first two months or so, but only once in a while.

Okay. I've asked. Now when I wake up again at 4:00 in the morning I can remind myself that all is well and I can just go back to sleep. You're wonderful! Love,

Pam

---

11 Messages Posted Sunday, September 7-8, 2008

Oh, Pam, how I wish I were closer to you! I have been through the mold thing myself and would caution you to be *so very careful*. It is tricky, dangerous stuff, especially if you are allergic as I am and you, apparently, are. One other note: I got bids from several companies to do the mold remediation and found a *huge* variation in prices, so if you haven't shopped around, it might pay to do so.

And on the positive side—all my love to both of you on your anniversary tomorrow. I'm sure it will be incredibly special. Congratulations!

Ellen Reinstatler

Update Monday, September 8, 2008 at 9:10 p.m.

Dear Ones,

We had a great day for our first anniversary. Pete did a terrific job in his last P.T. session. In the afternoon I went back to the Transplant House to get spiffied up. Then, back to the hospital to help Pete get dressed in his new shirt and pants. (His old ones would have fallen right off.) It took a while, as he needs to be helped with every button, each sock, etc., but we finally got him all dressed and ready to go.

At 5:30 we were picked up by Dana, the recreation therapist, in a wheelchair-outfitted van. We had a yummy dinner of pasta and manicotti at Argieros, a cozy, informal little Italian restaurant. The food was great, and we enjoyed having some time outside in the real world.

Pete was exhausted by the time we got back to the hospital just two hours later. He fell asleep almost immediately.

Tomorrow will be a very big day. We're going home. Dear God in heaven, we're going home!

Much love,

Pam

---

28 Messages Posted September 8-9, 2008

Now a new adventure begins. As with a classic hero's path, it begins with a long journey, and there are battles to be fought on the way (such as killing mold). At the end, a return home, as changed people. Wow!
Dan Kivel

Happy homecoming! I'm sending you the gift of ten thousand angels to bring you safely home, to light and lighten your way as you continue a journey that one year ago you would never have expected. May all future surprises be happy ones.
Love,
Carol Johnson

The One that we are is celebrating today . . . and I hear loud and clear that the heavens are singing with joy. A huge band of angels surrounds you as you journey home. Look for them . . . listen for them . . . and feel the Love and support. I would be blessed to be on your list of people who will provide respite.
Much love,
Linda Beushausen

Count me in!
Connie Klug

Pete's hospital discharge papers indicate the following (Explanations in parentheses are mine):

Admission date: 8/19/08 (from other department in hospital)
Dishcharge date: 9/09/08

Principal diagnoses:
12. Cardiac transplant 7/27/08 for sarcoid CM
13. B/L thalamic infarcts (Strokes on both sides of thalamus)

Secondary diagnoses:
1. Large Pleural effusions (Excess fluid between the two membranes that envelop the lungs)
2. Hypothyroidism
3. Acute Nonischemic Cardiomyopathy (Weakness in the heart muscle)

Comorbidities:
1. Sustained slow Ventricular Tachycardia (Rapid heartbeat that starts in the ventricles)
2. Mild CAD: 60-70% (Coronary Artery Disease)
3. Hyperlipidemia (Elevation of lipids in the bloodstream, including cholesterol, triglycerides, etc.)
4. HTN (Hypertension)

5. Complete heart block–>CPR–>pacemaker 6/2008
6. Cardiac Sarcoidosis
7. Atrial fibrillation (Abnormal heart rhythm)

There followed a list of twenty-two medications–twenty-two! Ruth Halben, our social worker, told us that without insurance the anti-rejection meds could run as high as $5,000 to $8,000 a month. At the Veteran's Administration, it will be about $250 a month. We're so grateful that our insurance has a catastrophic illness rider for $1,000,000! That's what Pete's heart transplant and hospitalization cost–$1,000,000. Wow.

Biopsy 9/09/2008: Rejection Level—1R (Mild Rejection)

CHAPTER FOURTEEN

Stepping Out on the Arms of Faith

"Oh, the comfort, the inexpressible comfort of feeling safe with a person; having neither to weigh thoughts, nor to measure words, but to pour them all out, just as they are, chaff and grain together, knowing that a faithful hand will take and sift them, keep what is worth keeping, and then, with the breath of kindness, blow the rest away."
–George Eliot

Thursday, September 11, 2008
Journal

NANCY LOU IS a remarkable friend. She has welcomed us with open arms, adapting her home, her refuge, to meet our needs, and has done so with apparent delight. I don't know how we will ever thank her enough. When the house was built a few years ago, Nancy insisted that the "hearth room" be television free. It was to be a place for quiet reflection and meditation. There is a lovely fireplace, cozy furniture, and her current spiritual reading stacked on the table near the easy chair. It's a place for tea or a glass of wine and conversation. She knows, though, that Pete likes to watch TV, especially sports, and that he will have difficulty navigating the steps down to the family room where the TV is. So, our dear friend bought a new TV and installed it (Oh my gosh!) in the hearth room, just for Pete. It's a small room, and there's barely enough space for it, but it's there, and it will help pass the time as Pete continues his recovery. Nancy also cleaned out the closet and all the drawers in our new bedroom, sending most of the contents to Goodwill. She's like that—always willing and eager to help out anybody who needs something. It brings her joy. I am comforted by her presence. All is well.

Update Saturday, September 13, 2008
Dear Ones—

Time has lapsed here—but I'm so busy with Pete's care, there doesn't seem to be much time to get online. There are medications to stay on top of, dressings to be changed, laundry to do, food to prepare and so on. I also have been meeting with contractors about having our house remediated.

Pete is doing very well. His appetite has improved and he is starting to make little jokes now and then. His speech is more clear, and he is walking a bit better too. It will all take time, but we are encouraged with his progress.

I am reminded of how it felt to bring a newborn home from the hospital. I slept very lightly, so I could be right there if the baby woke up and needed something. I never left him alone, of course, and I pushed everything else in my life to the side. Taking care of the baby was priority #1 and I had to work at finding time to take care of myself. That's what it's like here now although, of course, Pete is no baby. Still, his healing is priority #1.

We thank you for your continued prayers and best wishes. We are flowing in gratitude. Pete is alive and getting better every day.

Love,

Pam

10 Messages Posted Saturday, September 13-14, 2008

When you love what you're doing, what you're doing becomes love.
Kat Keasey

"Eventually you will come to understand
that love heals everything, and
love is all there is."
−Gary Zukav

Monday, September 15, 2008
Notes to Self:

Sharon's birthday

Pete begins cardiac rehabilitation at the Wellness Center.

Meeting with Jim S., attorney−Kalamazoo−re mold remediation and possible litigation w/ city.

E-mail, Tuesday, September 16, 2008
Dear Ones—

Please know that I would be blessed to assist with any kind of need that you two have. I remember how comforting it was when people came to help after Ian died . . . stacking wood . . . cooking a loving, tasty meal . . . renting a movie and dropping by with it and a couple of microwave popcorn packs. Your journey has been profound and meaningful and I know that you realize how loved you are. Please do not hesitate to say "YES!" to offers, or to ask for anything at all. It is a circle of grace.

Much love,

Tracey Davis

Tuesday, September 16, 2008
Notes to Self:

Pete−blood draw, South Haven Hospital−Wheelchair

Must be taken between 11 and 12 hours after last dose of Tacro

E-mail, September 16, 2008

Pam,

We are all so happy that Pete is finally out of the hospital and I am glad that my wonderfully cheesy, funny uncle still has his sense of humor. Please give a big hug and a kiss to him from me and everyone here. Also tell him that I always wished he lived closer to us, because people like us that are addicted to show tunes always have a certain sense of camaraderie that no one else gets.

Much love to you both,

Bernie Wehle (Pete's niece)

Update Tuesday, September 16, 2008 at 3:35 a.m.

Sunday night Nancy Lou, Pete, and I had pizza and watched a video of "The Blues Brothers." This involved Pete navigating a flight of stairs each way, which he did slowly and well. We stretched out and relaxed on the sofa and love seat in Nancy's family room in the lower level. Pete kept calling out the names of the actors and musicians in the movie whenever they appeared, including Pine Top Perkins, an old blues acquaintance of his. We laughed and joked–and it felt like a normal piece of life. Wonderful.

Pete seems more like his old self each day. He still requires a walker, but I don't think he'll need it inside much longer. Monday he will have his orientation to cardiac rehab at the Wellness Center here in town. Life goes on–and he continues to heal.

Love,

Pam

---

13 Messages Posted Tuesday, September 16-17, 2008

I think of you two every day and send blessings.
Jeanie Frattallone

I am thrilled and encouraged by your healing. It is all a miracle! You have both been working so hard at healing; the glue to it all is your strong bond of love.
Love to you both,
Selma Holme

(Excerpts from our insurance policy–a very long document)

COVERAGE A–DWELLING and COVERAGE B–OTHER STRUCTURES

We insure against risk of direct loss to property described in Coverages A and B only if that loss is a physical loss to property.

We do not insure however, for loss:

. . . Damage caused by . . . Smog, rust, or other corrosion, mold, wet or dry rot . . .

We do not insure for loss caused directly or indirectly by . . . water which backs up through sewers or drains . . .

Wednesday, September 17, 2008

Note to Myself: Meeting w/Mike, contractor, again, re mold remediation.

Nancy remembers . . .

This was not an easy time for Pam. I could tell she was really tired, but she kept working hard to get things done at her house, and to make nutritious meals for Pete, trying to get him to eat. He was so skinny!

When she ran out of steam, she would sit on the love seat with a blanket clutched to her burning chest. I remember one day when I got home from work, she had fixed a wonderful casserole. Pete sat down at the table, looked at the food and said, "I can't eat this shit." Pam burst into tears.

Pete wouldn't normally act this way. It was part of the ICU psychosis syndrome. He forgot to be kind. I couldn't allow it, though, for Pam's sake. A few days later I made a chicken dish that had peas in it. Pete doesn't care for peas. He started to protest, and I said, "Listen here–you can eat this or you can go hungry. When my grandchildren are here I don't make two meals for them, and I'm not going to do it for you. You can eat this or you can go."

"I don't have any place to go."

"Yeah, think about it."

"How did you get to be so tough?"

"Somebody in my family had to be."

He didn't complain anymore. I got firm with him so this wouldn't become a pattern. I knew he would take it from me.

Update Thursday, September 18, 2008 at 7:49 a.m.

Yesterday, as usual, I read the Daily Word message from Unity Church to Pete. The theme for the message was "Courage." Among other things, it said, "I accept the blessings of change." Later in the day Pete asked me what the key word was. I told him. He said, "Courage." Several times throughout the day he simply said, "Courage."

I can only imagine how important courage is to Pete now. He can't drive. He can't walk very far. He gets confused. He swallows with great effort. He can't work. He tires very easily. He has no guarantees. For a guy who has always been strong and energetic, this is extremely difficult–and courage is critical.

He is a man of great courage and determination, though, and with many people who love him and support his healing, he will recover. He *is* recovering.

---

15 Messages Posted September 18-19, 2008

And Pete has your unfailing courage to shore him up when his falters. What a gift that is! We continue to hold both of you in perfect health.
Love,
Kerry Lytle

Peter, you have a deep unending stream of courage within you, where the Spirit of God dwells! If you ever feel your human supply of courage has run out, just drink from the well of Divine Courage, which will never fail you. Nor will Divine Love, Strength, Peace, and every other Good.

We are all here to remind you of that and to be a channel of all this Good, each in our own small, unique way.
Lots and lots of love,
Marty Rienstra

Thursday, September 18, 2008
Journal

Pete had his first session with Vicky Kerr, the speech therapist at our Wellness Center. She is very warm and kind, and encouraged me to sit in on the session.

Pete still has difficulty speaking clearly at times. He knows what he wants to say, but it doesn't always come out right.

> *"When I walk to the edge of all the light I have and take that step into the darkness of the unknown I believe one of two things will happen: there will be something solid for me to stand on . . . or I will be taught to fly!"*
> —*S. Martin Edges*

Update Friday, September 19, 2008 at 11:54 a.m.

Dear Ones—

Life flows on—and we make little steps along the way. Yesterday Pete had his first session with the speech therapist here in South Haven. She administered sections of an aphasia test, the same test that he had at U. of M. Hospital a couple of weeks ago. It tests his thinking processes and language. He did much, much better this time. Apparently his brain is creating new pathways where the old ones were damaged. There is still a long way to go, but this is very encouraging.

Some of you have commented that you see me as courageous, as well as Pete. I guess that is so. A long time ago I learned that I have many more reserves than I thought I had. We all do. When the difficult times come, somehow those reserves tap us on the shoulder and say, "Remember me?" It reminds me of a song I wrote a couple of years ago. Part of it goes like this:

> *Well, I've shed a tear or two with the troubles I've been through,*
> *And I wondered why it had to be.*
> *But I do what I have to do when there's nothing else to do,*
> *And there's always something there sustaining me.*
> *Inescapable love, irresistible grace,*
> *When I open my eyes, when I open my heart,*
> *It's all over the place.*
> *In the air that we breathe,*
> *And the smile on your face,*
> *Inescapable love, irresistible grace.*

Funny how my own lyrics have come back to me with new meaning in light of all that has happened to us this year. It underscores for me the belief that the things we create when we are in-spired are indeed co-creations.

So—yes—we have courage. And so do you. Maybe you don't even know it yet. I didn't. But I know now.

Love,

Pam

---

9 Messages Posted September 19-21, 2008

Pam, how true those words are! After my car accident I found the same thing to be true. People commented on both mine and Jack's courage, strength and good humor. You do it because you don't have a choice, and the caring people who love, support and pray for us make a huge difference. I can remember physically feeling lifted up while I was in the hospital right after my accident. I didn't know what it was until later, but it was the prayers of literally thousands of friends and friends of friends who sustained us. I know that you are feeling the same thing, and Jack and I add our prayers daily to the thousands who are holding you up to God.

Love,

Jo VandenBerg

What a beautiful song! And yes, I agree with you, creativity like this is truly inspired. It reveals Big Self at work through us, when the heart is open. Prayers of course, are with you steadily.

Judy Cassidy

Pam . . . Speaking of your songs and lyrics, I have your CD in my car player (have had for eight years!) and the words are healing to me each time I listen . . . Thank you for being you . . .

Betty McCormack

Pam, I loved the words to your song - How fitting then and again now! The love you and Pete share is deep and carries you through all that you are doing. It sustains you in many ways.

> My only caution as a caregiver—and you know I speak from experience, is—please pay attention to your needs too! Take time for yourself, have others relieve you, etc. I have a belief that I wouldn't be in my present situation of recurrence if I had paid more attention to the tension that was building up in me. And where does my tension rest in my body? Exactly where the affected lymph nodes are rearing their heads. I don't blame the situation on this, but rather on my inability to listen to my body sufficiently and to change my coping response so it didn't damage me.
>
> So far I am tolerating chemo and side effects amazingly well, supported by lots of alternative healing work, as well as lots of prayers and love from many sources.
>
> Take care. Jack and I send love to you and Pete.
>
> Selma Holme

Looking back . . .

Selma was so dear to share her advice with me—very dear, and very wise. Her own husband, Jack, had been facing some very serious health issues for years. The tension in her body took its toll, as did the tension in my body. For me it was primarily a delayed response. Have you ever worked like crazy, pushing hard to get something done, only to get sick once the whole thing was over and you were free to relax? That is what happened to me nearly two years after the transplant. I remember feeling as though the whole world was on my shoulders—and, as with Selma, the problem showed up where the tension had been held. I developed shoulder pain and tendonitis in my right rotator cuff and had several episodes of dangerously high blood pressure, irritable bowel syndrome, and other ailments after the first year.

Selma, dear Selma, passed from cancer a few months after posting this message. As I reread her precious postings, I know that I am being given the gift of her wisdom and support from another place altogether.

Friday, September 19, 2008
Journal

It's good to be here at Nancy Lou's, away from our contaminated home. When I go over to my house to try to restore order after months away, the very size of the task is overwhelming to me—and the "stuff" that needs to be put away—yikes! To prepare the house for the mold remediation I have to go through everything in the basement, our default dumping ground, and toss whatever is made of cloth, paper, or cardboard, plus anything else that has mold on it. That's going to take a whole lot of sorting. I also have to go through the other floors and get everything off tables, desks, shelves, etc., and remove all the curtains, towels, sheets, and pillows, and cover the beds with plastic. I think I should go over to the house and spend a half to one hour at a time, just putting things away right now.

But tonight my chest hurts again. Is it because I went to the house yesterday? Or would it have hurt anyway? I was in the house today just long enough to get a broom to sweep off the front porch, and I wore a mask. Hmmm . . .

This morning, as we were dozing in bed, Pete reached for me. He stroked my skin, and snuggled in ways he hasn't since he was hospitalized in June. We gave it a good try—but it didn't last. I don't know if that's due to his general condition or the meds he's taking. We'll see. I can wait. It was good to feel his arms around me in that way again.

I've been coaxing Pete to use more words when he wants something. He's been saying, "Water," or "Urinal" when he wants something. It feels like he is ordering me around, and I know it isn't a good pattern for him to establish, so I asked him to say, "Please," when he asked for something. I kept reminding him, like you do with a young child. After a while it became a bit of a joke. We were all tossing around "Please," and "Thank you," and really overdoing it. This afternoon, after Pete said "Water, please, please, please." Nancy Lou shot back, "Up yours." We all laughed like crazy.

Today we were all sitting around and Pete said, "May I please have some water? Up yours." We all roared, and it was like the sun pushing through the clouds. I know he's still in there. He's poking his way through.

We went to Nemo's for supper tonight—olive burgers and chicken dumpling soup. Not exactly heart-healthy fare, but Pete's gaining weight, which is wonderful.

Nancy Lou said that, back when Pete was in the hospital in Kalamazoo, he made her promise that she would look after me and see that I was all right.

She's been doing that ever since. Her good humor and kindness have been of enormous comfort to me.

Last night after Pete was asleep, she asked me what was the hardest thing for me to deal with. I thought for a moment, and then said that it was not knowing if Pete would get back to his old self. I really miss him. He's here–but he's not here. Sometimes he still looks like Jack Nicholson in "One Flew Over the Cuckoo's Nest." Sometimes he does inappropriate things. He doesn't remember to flush. He tends to parrot back things that I say. I'll say, "I think this is an absolutely perfect day." And he'll say, "Perfect day." I'll say, "We have some ice cream in the freezer," and he'll say, "Ice cream."

Other things. Little things. In the grand *scheme* of things, these aren't important at all, but to me they are little signals that he has a way to go before he is back to "normal," whatever that means now.

Update Saturday, September 20, 2008 at 10:53 a.m.

A couple of years ago we came to know Jerry, a retired school janitor, who lived a few blocks from our house. I first met him outside the post office downtown. He was leaning on his bicycle and looked like he could barely stand up. I asked if he was all right, and he said that he'd be okay. Then I asked if he was intending to ride that bike. He said he had to.

I could tell he was very ill, and I couldn't imagine that he could ride a bike, much less walk a block. I asked where he lived, and then told him I'd be happy to give him a lift. We put the bicycle in my trunk and I took him to his house, only four blocks from my own. Jerry said that he did odd jobs, repairs, and yard work if I ever needed any help. Once he got past this reaction to his recent chemotherapy treatment he would be much better, he said.

Jerry confided in me that he had several different kinds of cancer. He was not expected to live long. When he wasn't reeling from his treatments, though, he got around all right and was eager to work. I suspected that he needed the cash. Eventually he did do some work for me. He hung a new medicine cabinet, mowed the lawn, pulled some weeds. He seemed to be in much better shape then, and he was a hard worker. Every time he left, his parting words were, "God be with you in love."

As time passed, Jerry's health deteriorated. Pete lived with me then, and he and Jerry became friends. When Jerry was confined to a wheelchair, Pete took him for walks. We saved space for him on the bluff overlooking Lake Michigan for the 4th of July fireworks his last summer. He watched, bundled up in two blankets, his beautiful, dark brown face lifted up to the brilliant display.

One time, Jerry asked Pete to drive him to McDonalds to get a fish sandwich. Instead, Pete drove to the Thirsty Perch for a perch dinner take-out. Jerry was thrilled, like a child at Christmas time. Another time, Pete wheeled Jerry all the way out to the lighthouse at the end of the pier to drink in the spacious beauty of the great lake. On the way back they stopped at the concession stand for ice cream.

Jerry is gone now, and out of his pain.

Yesterday I wheeled Pete out to the lighthouse at the end of the pier. I couldn't help thinking that what goes around, comes around. "It all comes back to you," as my friend, Ellen, sings.

The people we saw along the way greeted us warmly—even more so than they might have otherwise, or so it seemed. I like to think that they saw Pete in the wheelchair with his mask on and something inside of them said, "There but for the grace of God go I." It is a gift that Pete can give right now, even without trying. He can help us all move into a place of deep gratitude for what we normally take for granted.

The body is a magnificent thing. Bless your body. Thank your body.

God be with you in love,

Pam

---

14 Messages Posted September 20-25, 2008

I'm reminded of a story from a friend who knew a successful but unsatisfied career woman in Chicago. One day she saw a man in a wheelchair. He'd thrown his head back to catch the breeze. He'll never know it, but he changed her life, brought her back, just being.

All good blessings this beautiful day,

Judy Cassidy

> . . . Continued prayers and blessings from a land in need of much healing. You two can pray for us too.
> Huge hugs,
> Karen and Steve Small (Nicaragua)

Nancy remembers . . .

I get up early most mornings to read my devotional and commune with God. I remember so clearly seeing Pam coming out of their bedroom with a urinal and carrying it into the bathroom to empty it. Those early days when they were here she did that four or five times a night. I don't think she got much sleep. She was heartbroken, exhausted, frustrated–but not angry.

Over time, we took to sitting together in the hearth room before I went to work, coffee in hand, chatting. We'd talk about our lives, the struggles, the joys, the irritations, the fears. It became a sacred time of deep friendship.

Pam remembers . . .

I really needed those conversations. I could tell Nancy anything, and she would keep it safe in her heart, and never judge me. It kept me sane.

Monday, September 22, 2008
Notes to Myself:
Today:

Pete–Speech Rehab 9:00
    Cardio Rehab–10:00
Pam–Meet w/city reps re sewer back-ups and
    damages–11:00

Tuesday, September 23, 2008
Pete–To Ann Arbor–Biopsy at U. of M. 12:30

Biopsy 9/23/2008: Rejection Level—1R (Mild Rejection)

Wednesday, September 24, 2008
Pete–Blood Draw, South Haven Hospital
 Speech 9:00
 Cardio Rehab 10:00

Friday, September 26, 2008
Notes for Doctor scribbled on a yellow post-it:
 Waiting for callback
 9:50 p.m.
 Coughing 26 times a minute
 Respiration 56
 Brought up copious amounts of clear, foamy spitum
 Short of breath
 Breathing fast and shallow

Looking back . . .

It's just a blur when I try to remember the week before Pete returned to the hospital. I know I took Pete in for speech therapy at the Wellness Center on Monday. Later that day I met with two men from the city regarding their part in the sewer back-ups that most likely caused the mold in our home. They told me their engineers had determined that the sewer system their contractors installed in 2004 was working as it should, and that the back-ups were caused by the "sewer service lead," the pipes from the middle of our front yard up to the house. Those pipes are the responsibility of the homeowner, they said. That absolves the city of any responsibility. The men were very cordial, and even offered to get some bids for me for replacing the sewer service lead, at our own cost, of course.

On Tuesday I drove Pete back to Ann Arbor for another heart catheterization and biopsy. It was a long haul for Pete–about three hours each way–so I bundled him up in blankets and brought a pillow, hoping he could sleep during the ride. I had what I thought was a bad cold, so I wore a mask. The last thing I wanted to do was infect him.

It felt strange to be wheeling Pete back into the hospital . . . a reluctant homecoming. The biopsy and heart cath took about three hours, and then we were on our way again. We were both tuckered out by the time we got back to Nancy Lou's.

On Wednesday I took Pete to the South Haven Hospital for a blood draw to check the levels of his anti-rejection meds, something that had become routine for us. Then Pete had speech therapy at 9:00 and cardio rehab at 10:00.

I was feeling lousy all week, congested and achy. My chest burned again. When Pete napped, I wrapped myself up in a blanket in the hearth room and dozed. I did my best to make meals and keep on top of Pete's meds, but I was so tired . . . Tom came by and checked me over. He said that I had bronchitis.

On Friday Pete didn't want to go in for speech and cardio rehab, so I called and cancelled. We were both under the weather. He had been coughing in the night for several days, and it seemed to be getting worse. Was it bronchitis? Did I give it to him? Should I have slept on the couch? Could his body fight this off? I felt sick and guilty–not a great combination.

Reverend Marty came for a visit that afternoon. She took Pete in his wheelchair down to gaze at the lake while I rested. After they returned, Pete's coughing grew worse. At one point he coughed up about one half cup of phlegm. I called the cardio team at the hospital and the doctor I spoke to said that when a heart transplant patient gets a cold, they treat it as they would for any other person–rest, fluids, etc. I had a feeling that this was more than a common cold, but I didn't want to overreact.

Pete got worse as the evening came on. He was coughing so much it scared me. I called to have the doctor paged again and waited for a response. Nancy Lou was home from work then, and she and I kept glancing at each other–What to do?

Early in the evening Pete finally fell asleep and stopped coughing. Nancy and I sat down with a glass of wine and took a few deep breaths. The storm had passed. Everything was going to be all right. Whew!

Pete woke up about ten minutes later, and began coughing even more. I called the doctor again. This felt really serious to me, but I'm not a doctor. What did I know? I paced the floor, waiting for the doc to call back. Pete kept hacking. I went into our bedroom to check on him, and when I came out, I heard Nancy call 911. God bless her.

The paramedics arrived within minutes, put Pete on a gurney, and hauled him out to an ambulance. When we got to the hospital, Nancy called her ex-husband, Jim, and asked him to come to the E.R. She was thinking ahead about transportation issues. Nancy waited for him in the waiting room and I went in with Peter.

The nurse in charge said that it was a good thing we brought him in when we did, because if we had waited another twenty minutes it might have been too late. Pete was unconscious, and his heart rhythm was all over the place. He looked frail there on the hospital table, my husband who played golf, bowled, and was proud of how fast he could run. The doctor, a tall, blond, serious-looking woman, stabilized him the best she could, and said that he would have to be transferred to a hospital with more resources. I asked that he be taken directly to U. of M. Hospital.

When the ambulance arrived, the driver said that I could ride along up front with him. Nancy Lou's plan worked well. She followed the ambulance in my car, and Jim followed her, so they could leave me with a car in Ann Arbor. By the time we got there, it was about 5:00 in the morning. Nancy and Jim checked to make sure that Pete was safely settled into his room and then left for the three hour drive back. Two recently divorced people, riding together for three hours in the wee hours of the morning to help out a mutual friend–now that is friendship!

Pete remembers . . .

I couldn't stop coughing. I was trying to clear my throat, and I couldn't do it. I was coughing up all this phlegm. I just wanted to stop, but I couldn't. It was terrible. I couldn't breathe. I remember the paramedics coming in and putting me on a gurney and wheeling me out to the ambulance. I don't remember going to the E.R., and I don't remember the ride back to U. of M. at all.

CHAPTER FIFTEEN

How Much Can He Take?

Beyond mountains, more mountains
–Haitian Proverb

Update September 27, 2008 at 9:03 a.m.

OH MY . . . NO postings lately because I've had bronchitis. I'm doing a little better with that, though.

Tough news: Last night Pete went into congestive heart failure. Long story short–after two ambulance rides we arrived again at the University of Michigan Hospital a little before 5 a.m. I'm grateful to Jim Gleason and Nancy Lou for helping me get here and lending their strong support.

Pete is now in the Cardiac ICU. He is sedated and stable. The staff here is still trying to determine what happened. Although the echocardiogram showed decreased movement in a part of the new heart, which sometimes indicates a heart attack, the EKGs and blood tests have not shown signs of a heart attack–at least not yet. His blood pressure and white count are okay. He has a breathing tube in. They will probably take the tube out and bring him out of sedation tomorrow morning. At this point I don't know any more than that.

I've been up for–oh, 26 or 27 hours now, so I'm going to try to find lodging and get some sleep. I'll post more when I know more. Thanks for staying in touch.

Much love,

Pam

---

33 Messages Posted September 27, 2008

Pam,

    Feel the loving network that is always there.

Love,

Nancy Green

"You gain strength, courage and confidence by every experience in which you really stop to look fear in the face. You are able to say to yourself, 'I have lived through this horror. I can take the next thing that comes along.' You must do the thing you think you cannot do."

–Eleanor Roosevelt

Update Sunday, September 28, 2008 at 3:37 p.m.

Thank you for the many postings today. It's a great comfort to me. I will surely read them to Pete.

He was semi-awake earlier today, but I could tell he was uncomfortable and exhausted. All I could do was hold his hand and soothe his forehead with a damp cloth. He looked frightened. He cried. Pete is sedated again now.

Twice they have removed the breathing tube and twice he has been unable to breathe without it due to lots of secretions. I was there just a bit ago when they did it for the second time. It was really hard to witness, because he got very red in the face and became extremely agitated, fighting to breathe. The tube was out for less than two minutes before they had to put it back in.

Everyone is very puzzled about what is causing all the fluid to build up in his lungs. There is speculation that he may have some sort of infection, but it hasn't shown up in the blood tests. Tomorrow the pulmonologist will probably take a look at his lungs with fiber optics to see what is going on. It's hard. We may be here for a while.

Love to you,

Pamela

---

43 Messages Posted September 28, 2008

Pam, I am here, sending you light energy and love. I hold you both in my heart and believe.
Much love,
Linda Steigenga

Pete remembers, telling Pam . . .

The second time I was admitted, I was coughing up a storm. When the ambulance guys came, that scared me more than the first time. I didn't know what was going on. I tried. I tried hard. I prayed. But it didn't seem to be enough. I was lacking something–at least I thought so. I said to myself, "There's plenty of people praying for me, and plenty of people donating their hard-earned money for my benefit. They shouldn't do it unless they see some results."

You were always encouraging me, Pam, and making me feel stronger than I was. I felt good when you were there. And when you were gone, I felt not so good.

Update Monday, September 29, 2008 at 8:29 a.m.

No news yet on Pete's condition. I was one hair's width shy of despair this morning when I checked the CarePages. There were 43 messages of love, hope, and constant prayer. I am restored. Thank you.

As my dear friend, Linda B. reminds us:

Hope steadily.
Trust unswervingly.
Love extravagantly.

21 Messages Posted September 29, 2008

And it all continues . . . holding you and Pete with tenderness.
Love,
Nancy Green

Believe!—Terry and Steve Vaughn

Divine Love knows only healing.—George & Jeannine Blake

My thoughts are with you and Pete. Your unflinching honesty, combined with your tenderness of heart pierces me. Thank you for including us. I know you will take care of yourself in the ways available to you.
Julie Ludwig

Trusting that which we do not know and understand right now . . . seeing you both as whole . . . and Loving you—Love with a capital L—through this part of the journey.
Go gently . . . knowing you are loved,
Linda Beushausen

My dears, I read all the CarePages. Some days I cry with you. I always pray with you.
Love—and hope,
Carol Thomas

We are so sorry about this setback, especially that Pete is afraid. We hope this resolves quickly so the waters of that big lake will resume soothing and healing. Pete might like to know that Armida and Patty cheered the Chicago White Sox on to victory at Cellular Field this afternoon. We were there, knowing Pete would appreciate the moment.
Love to you both,
Patty Walsh & Janos Szebedinszky

Pam, even though your strength amazes our humanity, we know you have only touched the tip of your source. One moment at a time . . . patience, courage, faith and love. We send you the beautiful, loving, healing energy of God.

Deb Lambert, Jaye, Zach and Josh Mann

Monday, September 29, 2008
Journal

I've been on a spiritual path for over twenty years now, reading extensively and attending workshops, conferences and seminars. I meditate, I pray, and I journal. I pay attention to what happens in my life and how it can help me grow in my awareness and consciousness. I try to be kind. Now I find myself in a life or death situation, and I can see how all this spiritual practice has an impact on my perception of what is going on. As I confront our situation, I am able to accept it as part of my life's path, and Pete's as well. I am waiting to see where it might take us, and I am resolved to stay in my loving.

This is a journey of the soul.

Update Monday, September 29, 2008 at 7:51 p.m.

The doctors have determined that Pete has pneumonia. Now it is a matter of getting rid of the fluid in his lungs and curing the infection with antibiotics and whatever else they decide will help. He remains sedated because he still has the breathing tube in, and it's very uncomfortable.

I'm not thrilled that he has pneumonia, but I am relieved that it's not a problem with the functioning of his new heart. He is still strong, and I *know* he will be able to get through this. It sure reinforces how vulnerable he is to infection, though.

I'm back in the same room at the Transplant House now. It's comfortable and close to the hospital. I'm trying to get as much rest as I can so that I can shake the last vestiges of bronchitis. It's tapering off, thank goodness. Yawn. I'm going to bed.

Much love to you,

Pam

20 Messages Posted September 29, 2008 after 7:51 p.m.

It's all so relative, isn't it? We are grateful for pneumonia, being that it could have been a heart problem! Well then, we are grateful!
Love,
Carol Johnson

Update Wednesday, October 1, 2008 at 7:29 p.m.

October–Wow. It doesn't seem possible. The months roll by, and here we are in Ann Arbor again. It's been more than three months altogether.

What we know now is that Pete has pneumonia caused by some sort of fungus in his lungs. He has been quite sedated since we arrived, so he doesn't communicate. (He did open his eyes a wee bit and lifted one finger to wave at Rev. Marty and John when they visited yesterday.) I miss the sound of his voice.

Since Saturday I have spent most of my waking hours in Pete's hospital room, reading, doing dozens of crossword puzzles, paying bills, just sitting, and waiting, waiting, waiting–for more news, for him to recover, for things to get back to "normal."

Life has a way of throwing us some curves, as we all know. My challenge today is to live in the *Now*–when it feels like I'm in limbo. (Actually, what could be more *Now* than limbo?)

I'm more than a little numb, but then I look at that man in the bed, that man who I love so much, and there is only compassion–compassion and hope.
Love,
Pam

24 Messages Posted October 1-2, 2008

Pam and Pete, try to stay strong. I have some experience in your area with struggles in my own life. One year ago I was given the gift of a visit from several angels. That experience has given me hope. Look for them. They are with you and Pete.
Michael Mayer

Oh Pam, you sound so tired! I wish I could just rock you like a mama would . . . Peace to Pete. Sometimes "now" isn't a fun place to be, it just is. Helping to hold the watch,
Jill Woods and Mary McCreadie

Update Thursday, October 2, 2008 at 5:35 p.m.

Dear Friends,

I spoke today with an infectious disease specialist here at the hospital who told me they have determined that Pete's pneumonia isn't due to mold after all. They believe the mold that showed up in the culture "crept in" from the environment in the lab and was not causative. Now they are calling it *bacterial* pneumonia and treating it accordingly. He still has a lot of secretions, so they have kept the breathing tube in. He opened his eyes a few times today, but he is still partially sedated. The cardiologist told me we can expect to be here for another 7-10 days.

As the fall chill creeps in, I am very grateful for the sweet days of late summer we had in South Haven. Pete was rolled down in his wheelchair to watch the big blue water every day. We both love that lake and draw inspiration and comfort from its ever-changing beauty.

Posted October 2, 2008

Remember the words from James Dillet Freeman's poem, "I Am There."

Do you need Me?
I am there.
You cannot see Me, yet I am the light you see by.
You cannot hear Me, yet I speak through your voice.
I am the love you can cling to.
I am your assurance.
I am your peace.
I am one with you.

This poem—read by millions around the world and left on the moon in 1971 for future space voyages . . . is held close in my heart and mind. In each of life's precious moments, God is there and you and Pete are never alone.

Jane Grady

I know what you mean about "one foot in front of the other." That is my life. Thank heaven for Hope/Trust/Love.

I love you two.

Jeanie Frattallone

Thursday, October 2, 2008

Journal

Nancy Lou thoughtfully tucked a book of crossword puzzles in my bag when we left for the hospital this last time. They are easy puzzles, but I don't think Pete could do them at this point. His brain is still too foggy. For want of something better to do, I picked up the book and did a puzzle. Then another. Then another. I think I've done about 40 by now. It keeps my mind occupied and out of worry-land, as I sit next to my silent, very sick man. I feel this sense of accomplishment when I can complete one page without looking at the answers in the back of the book. I guess it's just good news to have some good news. All I have to do is come up with a seven letter word that is a color and starts with "s." I can do that. Thank God there is *something* I can do.

Same day, later . . .

Through the twists and turns of life you encounter situations you would never have dreamed of facing. Sometimes you have to dig down deep to find the courage, strength, and commitment required of you. If you're lucky, you meet new people who help you along the way. Sometimes the new person you meet is yourself.

Same day, still later . . .

I have seen the bumper stickers that say, "I do what the voices in my head tell me to do." Everybody laughs, because those are the words of a psychotic, right? Well, *I* laugh when I see those bumper stickers, because I really *do* listen to the voices in my head, and I'm perfectly sane–well, *im*perfectly sane. It's my Inner Knower, my guide, intuition, Spirit, that Still, Small Voice within. It doesn't matter what I call it, but it ain't the lady next door. No, it is the God presence within . . . the "Big Self," the inner creative force that Judy Cassidy mentioned in her posting last month.

Some of you reading this will think all of this is a little too "woo-woo" for comfort. It may strike you as weird. Just relax with it. It's part of my journey, my experience.

You don't have to believe it. I don't mind.

Friday, October 3, 2008
Journal

As I rode in the ambulance to Ann Arbor last week, a message come through to me . . . that this was going to be hard, and that I should brace myself. Was that a gentle bit of guidance from Spirit or was it my own fear speaking? I don't know. Yes, I do.

It *is* hard. Pete can't talk. He's very weak. It seems to take every ounce of energy he has just for him to open his eyes. Day after day I come up to his room and sit with him. He seems unchanged and looks incredibly sad. I have a feeling he would just give up entirely if he could. I long to be able to hear him speak, to have him hold me in his strong arms, to talk with him about what's going on and what we can expect.

I have to figure out how to get $12,500, the latest estimate, so we can have the house cleaned up. I don't want to have to borrow any more money. We already have way too many payments each month.

Deep down I know that all of this is just "stuff." It has nothing to do with the essence of who we are and what our purpose is on this planet–but it still adds stress to what is already a very stressful situation. I want to run and hide.

Okay, Pam–It's time to test your belief in the Law of Attraction. Get it together. Everything you need is provided. Everything you need is provided. Believe. Trust.

Same day, later . . .

It occurs to me that many times in my life I have fumbled through putting some contraption or another together before giving up in exasperation and finally reading the instructions. It's a little bit like fumbling through life and then, when I finally find myself utterly incapable of coping, turning to God for guidance.

Same day, later . . .

Back when we were in South Haven, Nancy Lou suggested to me that I might want to think about getting a prescription for an antidepressant. I hadn't even considered that–but when I did, I realized that I was scraping bottom. I was so stressed and worn out, I couldn't shake the cold I had and it progressed into bronchitis.

The next day I had my prescription, thanks to Tom. Pete asked me what it was, and when I told him, he said that he thought perhaps he needed an antidepressant as well. He had been offered a prescription at the hospital when he was discharged, but had turned it down. Later, at home, he realized that he was having difficulty coping with his condition. He had *his* prescription the next day. The only difference I noticed in myself was that I didn't seem to be able to cry, and although I knew things were tough, I just kept moving forward. I didn't feel despair. I felt . . . there.

When Pete contracted pneumonia and we wound up back here at U. of M., I was still taking the medication. After a few days here I went off it because I couldn't feel anything. I was numb, moving through the days without emotion. I wanted to feel what I was experiencing, even if it was grief and pain.

Last night I realized that I was becoming a hermit. I didn't want to call anyone. I had taken to eating dinner in my room at the Transplant House so I wouldn't have to talk with anyone. I just wanted to hole up and go to sleep. Oh my–I realized–that's depression. So I went back on the medication last night. I guess I need if after all, at least for a while. This is hard.

I got a message last night from my guardian angel, Fiona. I became aware of her several years ago in a meditation. She told me that Pete would get better, and that we would be happy. That let me settle into a deep sleep.

Update Saturday, Oct 4, 2008 at 6:57 p.m.

We met four years ago today. This morning I watched Pete, his red-rimmed eyes sad and tired, a feeding tube in his nose, and his mouth propped open with a breathing tube. He has lost almost 50 pounds. Occasionally he lifted one of his hands, and it looked as if it weighed 100 pounds from the effort required.

The docs are concerned about the breathing tube being in for so long, which is not good. It's been a week now. Pete still has a lot of secretions and needs to be suctioned off frequently, so they don't know whether he will be able to breathe on his own without it. There is talk of a tracheotomy if Pete simply can't breathe on his own. That procedure carries a risk of damage to the voice box, but the breathing tube carries a risk of damage to the vocal cords.

If Pete couldn't sing again, it would be devastating to him. I ask you all to hold in your hearts and minds the image of him singing, with all his innate enthusiasm, his voice strong and clear. This is his passion, his precious gift. He has to be able to sing.

Much love,

Pam

---

28 Messages Posted October 4-6, 2008

. . . and he will!

Much love,

M (Mary James)

I hear Pete's song. It is his soul's song and will not be silenced. Fear not.

Sue Fischer

I remember that day four years ago, when you two met. And I remember that beautiful voice singing behind me. We were rehearsing the "Hallelujah Chorus." Pete was one of the few that could read music and really knew what to sing. We continue to see Pete whole, well, and singing with his robust enthusiasm. Blessings.

By Shirley Pressnell

Pam, fear not. No matter what happens, the soul filled with music always finds a way to sing.

Tammy Daniels

Update Sunday, October 5, 2008 at 6:17 p.m.

It's a bright, sunshiny day in Ann Arbor today. I went up to the hospital to see Pete before going to church. I think he's better today–less sedated and more responsive. They are working at getting rid of the fluid in his system, and it seems to be making a difference. He seemed comfortable when I left this evening.

At church today Lauren Lane Powell was the speaker and musician. I was pleased to see her, having met her several times in the past. Actually, she was Pete's choir director many years ago at the South Bend Unity Church. She knew Pete and me separately before Pete and I even met each other.

One of the things Lauren said that really struck a chord with me was that instead of asking, "Why is this happening to me?" when we encounter adversity–or what seems like adversity–we might better ask, "Why is this happening *for* me?"

Since everything that happens holds the potential for our growth and spiritual development, looking at it this way makes a lot of sense, and reminds me to look for the lessons and understandings that come from any difficult situation. To borrow a line from one of my songs, "In good time we will know what it's all about."

All is in divine order.

Love,

Pam

20 Messages Posted October 5-6, 2008

Attention all CarePage Friends:

There will be a Pam & Pete Benefit Concert Saturday, November 15, 7:30 p.m. at Foundry Hall in South Haven. Foundry Hall is located at 422 Eagle Street, right downtown. It's going to be an incredible concert with all professional entertainers. Put it on your calendars now!

Bring a carload, van load, caravan, or a bus. Let's raise the roof off this hall. It would be helpful if you could get the word out to your own church and to any organizations you belong to. Let's bring the whole town to the concert to support Pete and Pam in getting their home safe again.

Betty Smith

> *"Be patient toward all that is unsolved in your heart
> and try to love the questions themselves."*
> *–Rainer Maria Rilke*

Update Monday, October 6, 2008 at 7:17 p.m.

The tube is out! Glory be! This morning six doctors and nurses wrapped in sterile blue plastic gowns were able to remove Pete's breathing tube successfully. I watched through the window to his room. He is now breathing on his own and doing well. What a relief!

Pete has been advised to rest his vocal chords, as the tube goes right between them and they can be traumatized when the tube is put in or taken out. He wanted to say something, so I got him a piece of paper and a pencil. He scribbled three words: "I love you."

Right now he is resting quietly, looking a little scruffy with an eight-day beard, but smiling and comfortable. Now, with the tubes out, we can get him a shave!

I want to thank you all for your prayers and for holding in your minds and hearts a positive image of Pete singing. Surely you have helped him heal.

We had a visit today from Sally Brinkman, whom I've known since . . . well, let's just say it's been decades. Her mother was the nurse at Van Buren Youth

Camp when I worked summers there during high school and college. She was "Mom" to all of us on staff–a very kind and wise woman. I remember Sally as a young child, spending her summers at camp when her mother was treating our colds and scrapes and doling out vitamins. We share a special bond in that camp, where we all learned about leadership, loyalty, responsibility, and the gifts in working hard for something we believe in. Those lessons have stayed with me throughout my entire life–and have been particularly helpful these past few months.

We're blessed.

Love,

Pam

---

32 Messages Posted October 6-7, 2008

Your message, "Why is this happening for me?" has so resonated with me at this moment in my own journey. Thanks for sharing it.

I am so thrilled that the tube is out and Pete is breathing on his own. Congratulations! Such perseverance and tenacity!!

Love to you both,

Selma Holme

Update Wednesday, October 7, 2008 at 8:33 p.m.

Things are looking up. Pete is able to talk a little bit. He is breathing well on his own. He coughs some, but the docs say that is good, as he needs to clear the secretions from his lungs.

Lauren Lane Powell came to visit today. She does wonderful work with sound, vibration and healing. She brought with her a beautiful, 10-inch quartz crystal singing bowl, which she played with a wooden wand encased in suede. The sound is . . . well . . . ethereal. Lauren and I toned to the sound, and soon the entire room was vibrating to the beautiful resonance. Toning is the practice of using the human voice as an instrument for healing. We sustain a note, usually with a vowel sound, allowing the body to become a resonating chamber for the vibration of the tone. It is thought to help bring the body back into balance and harmony. When Lauren departed, she left behind the beautiful bowl for us. What a wonderful, precious gift!

I think that a few years ago I might have said, "Oh no, that's much too valuable. We can't accept that," but, as I've said before, I am getting better at receiving. So is Pete. Today we received the beautiful crystal bowl with deep gratitude both to Lauren, for her loving generosity, and to our Creator, the source of all abundance. The Universe supports us, and, by the way, you do too.

It is easier for many of us to give to others than to receive. When we are the ones receiving, it is at once humbling and uplifting. Pete and I have received so much in the past few months—donations, cards (over 200), postings on the CarePages (over 1200 and counting), visits, gifts and prayers. We are immensely grateful. Thank you for your many acts of kindness and love. It reinforces our understanding that we are all connected. It reminds us that we are loved.

Love,

Pam

---

14 Messages Posted October 7-8, 2008

. . . Tomorrow night is the healing circle at church; we will once again have Pete's photo and a prayer on a chair for him and send him distant healing.

Much love to you both,

Nancy O'Donohue

. . . Thank you for receiving with grace the gifts that God gives you through his human channels, as it allows the givers to be blessed as well. And when we say Yes! to Spirit, it automatically brings about more reasons to say Yes! yet again.

Love,

Joan Van Houten

Update Wednesday, October 8, 2008 at 7:38 p.m.

Good news! Pete was moved out of the Cardiac ICU this afternoon! He is now on a regular hospital floor in a single room (due to his being immune suppressed). This is definitely a step closer to being sent home. He is down to 140 pounds (from 196) and is still shaky standing up, but his body is recovering from the pneumonia, and I expect he'll be up walking soon. I think they will start giving him real food tomorrow instead of the puppy bottom pudding in a bag that now goes through a tube in his nose. He will welcome the change!

My sister, Connie, came today for a visit. We talked nonstop all afternoon, and then had dinner downtown at an Irish pub. It's good to have her company.

In the hospital gift shop I found a pair of earrings that say "Hope" on them. I'll be wearing them from now on.

Love,

Pam

---

16 Messages Posted October 8, 2008

Yes, . . . Hope UNSWERVINGLY!
This is wonderful, fantastic, terrific, magnificent, amazing, astonishing, marvelous, stupendous, supercalifragilisticexpialidoscious news!
Love you,
Linda Beushausen

Update Thursday, October 9, 2008 at 7:42 p.m.

Another promising day. Pete slept a lot, but he also walked about 20 feet with a little help from the physical therapist. He also passed the swallow test, so he will be getting real food now. He will need to regain his strength and stamina, but I'm confident he will recover.

Today, at one point, he reached for my hand and said, "Thank God for you."

All I could say was, "Thank God I still have you with me." We are truly blessed in our love for each other, and for all the tender times still ahead.

God is good.

Love,

Pam

Update Friday, October 10, 2008 at 8:46 p.m.

Pete slept most of the day, but between naps he walked a bit–twice as much as yesterday–and sat in a recliner for an hour or so. The cardiologist says we'll be here for a while longer. Tonight Pete was moved to the Cardiovascular Center, the same building where he had his heart transplant. I think they wanted him there a couple of days ago when he was moved out of ICU, but there wasn't a bed available then.

Sometimes this whole thing seems surreal. Hospital trays, white coats, blood pressure cuffs, wheelchairs–all with the backdrop the world's financial crisis and the presidential campaigns. I feel a little like Alice in Sunderland. With the externals of our lives upside down, I am grateful for a deep spiritual grounding. Without it, I think I would feel totally lost. With it, I take one day at a time and have hope for whatever will come next. Here's hoping you're coping well!

Love,

Pam

---

14 Messages Posted October 10-11, 2008

What you and Pete are going through really puts the financial "crisis" in perspective. I believe the "good" will prevail and that all is well!
Kerry Lytle

If it would help, we could keep you up to date: It's all illusion.
Dan Kivel

I love what you say here, Pam. The Sunderland. Your deep spiritual grounding, indestructible!
Judy Cassidy

Saturday, October 11, 2008

Journal

Now, with all the trappings of my normal life tossed aside, I wonder what is at the essence of who I really am. I know I am not the roles I have played–the conscientious student, the good wife, the girl with the guitar, the teacher, the hippy, the mother, the performer, the motivational speaker, the medium. I like to think that there is love at my core–and strength, and wisdom. I suspect many people think of me that way, but I'm not sure that I always own that. Sometimes I do. Today I do.

And who is this man that I care for, day after day, as he struggles to crawl back from the edge of death? He is kind–kind and comical, vulnerable, strong and tender. I love him with all my heart. I wonder why we have been brought together. I feel that together we have something to give, something to offer the world, and yet I don't know what that will be.

On a lighter note: I indulged in a "guilty pleasure" today, for which I feel no remorse at all. Pete was in and out of consciousness all day–mostly *out*. This being Saturday, I knew that he would normally opt for football games on the TV–but since he was out of it, I watched one chick flick after another, all day long–"When Harry Met Sally," "Terms of Endearment," "My Best Friend's Wedding" . . . He's too far gone to complain, or even care, and I don't think he'll remember this at all–but it was fun for me. I felt like I was really getting away with something. In fact, I believe I reached a saturation point. Imagine that.

Looking back . . .

I've often joked about Pete's chocolate craving, which I'm convinced came from his heart donor. And if the donor was a woman . . . couldn't he have taken on a predilection for chick flicks instead?

Update Saturday, October 12, 2008 at 8:32 p.m.

A beautiful day in Ann Arbor–summer's last whisper.

Pete is doing better. The respiratory therapist said that his lungs are more clear, which is *very* good news. I think he will be moved to 6A, the rehab floor, tomorrow–an important step. He is still very weak and a bit wobbly when he walks, even with a walker, but they do great work on 6A, the rehab unit. I remember that well.

Monday, October 13, 2008
Journal

It's easy for me to get bogged down, going up to the hospital day after day, seeing Pete make progress in Lilliputian increments and sometimes not at all. Outside the world keeps turning. Concerts come and go. Presidential campaigns get ugly. News of the economy gets more and more grim. The leaves turn and fall.

Sometimes I wake up at 4:00 in the morning and a list forms in my mind of the dozens of things I should be doing: paying bills (How?), writing thank you notes, getting birthday gifts (three October birthdays) for family, selling the Kalamazoo house. I'm so tired.

Oh—and when we get home—washing or tossing every bit of clothing and anything else made of cloth to get rid of lurking mold spores, sorting and throwing away or giving away the many things we don't really need, sorting through books—oh, will I have to throw out all our wonderful books? That makes me want to cry—wash the floors, the walls, the—everything. And dust everything.

Nancy Lou says I can't do that. I probably can't—but how in the world will it get done? I can't hire somebody to do it. I don't have that much money, and besides, who but me can decide what to keep and what to pitch? The church folks already did a massive job of cleaning back in July. Arghhhh . . . Sometimes it seems like it would be simpler just to light a match to it all.

This is a powerful lesson in attachment. I have a lot to learn about that. I'm very attached to that house, to many of the books, to some of the clothes. I have the family archives of documents, photos, memorabilia going back generations. How do I detach from that?

Pete is dozing in his bed, the feeding tube taped awkwardly to his right temple. Meanwhile, my mind races with an endless litany of things to worry about, and the occasional, fleeting rush of fear that I push out of the way. I'll deal with it later, I tell myself. Right now I'll just be here.

Sometimes it works. Today—not so much.

"Struggle is just another word for growth."
–Neale Donald Walsch

Update Tuesday, October 14, 2008 at 10:58 a.m.

Things are looking bright in Ann Arbor today. Pete is improving, slowly and steadily. He has good color, a decent appetite, and he coughs very little now. We had several great visits with staff today, all upbeat and promising. The physical therapy doc seems to think Pete will be going to the rehab floor soon, the nutritionist is sending goodies to fatten him up and the nurse is very interested in New Age books and ideas, so we had a lot to talk about. Pete took a stroll down the hall. All is well.

Last night I went to The Ark, a legendary coffee house here in Ann Arbor, to hear my friend and songwriting mentor, Jimmie Dale Gilmore. I was joined there by several other people who have taken Jimmies' songwriting course at the Omega Institute in upstate New York. I've taken the class six times, and have a deep respect for Jimmie and the process he facilitates. It was a warm reunion of friends, and a wonderful concert.

Plans are being made for a benefit concert for us November 15 at the Foundry Hall in South Haven at 7:30 p.m. Some absolutely fabulous talent will be performing–Star and Charlie, Carol Johnson, Elfi, Andru Bemis, Jim Hughey, Sandy and Larry Feldman, Great Lakes Grass and me! Pete and I are thrilled with the whole idea. It will help us immensely, and will be a real treat for all who attend. Circle the date!

I've been thinking about the concept of victimhood lately. It's really easy for me to slip into that role if I'm not careful. And Pete–well, Pete has every good reason to feel like a victim. It occurs to me that if we focus instead on what this experience has brought to us, the whole thing turns around. We have received a most wonderful outpouring of love and support from family and friends, a truly amazing gift to us! We have had the opportunity to take a deep look at our lives and our priorities and make some decisions about what is really important to us, and what we will want to do with the rest of our lives after Pete heals. Certainly, we wouldn't have chosen for Pete to get sick, or me either, but since that has happened, it is good to see that there are pearls of light and a new awareness amidst the grit of illness. We will get through this slice of time and have years of loving and living, hoping and giving yet ahead of us. Now that's a miracle! We're not victims. We're survivors.

October 15, 2008
Journal

I met a young woman walking the hall with her IV pole. She was preparing for her second heart transplant; the first one didn't take. That shook me up a little. I didn't tell Pete about her. He has enough to worry about.

I have enough to worry about too. Nancy Lou called me. She said that there is a strange odor in the room Pete and I used as a bedroom in her house. Her daughter-in-law thought so too. They did a thorough cleaning and vacuuming, but the odor persists. They can't quite figure out what the odor is, but Nancy is concerned that it might be mold, brought over in the clothes I have retrieved from our house.

I am *devastated*. It is enough that *our* house is contaminated. I just can't bear to think that we may have contaminated dear Nancy's house! I am beside myself. Nancy is going to have the room tested for mold. Oh dear God, what if I have brought it into Nancy's house? I wouldn't wish this on *anyone*. She has been so generous, so kind to us–I can't believe this. On top everything else that has happened, I just . . . can't . . . I can't bear it. Oh dear God, please! Please!

CHAPTER SIXTEEN

Trust Me

"When I'm trusting and being myself . . .
everything in my life reflects this
by falling into place easily,
often miraculously.
–Shakti Gawain

Update Thursday, October 16, 2008 at 9:11 a.m.

THINGS ARE UP and down here. The good news is that Pete says he's feeling great. I'm so glad to hear that coming from him! We don't know yet when he will be discharged, but it's likely to be soon.

The not-so-good news has to do with complications regarding our return to South Haven. Let's just say it's getting difficult and quite complicated. I have (another) lousy cold, which adds to the mix. Apparently my immune system is on vacation. Last night I prayed fervently for everything to work out well–and I received the message, "Trust me." Over and over again, as I wallowed in our problems, I heard the Still, Small Voice inside saying, "Trust me." That enabled me to slip into a deep sleep.

So—things *will* work out, but there are some challenges, so this is another great time for prayers, my dear friends. We need them.

Bless you!

Pam

---

23 Messages Posted October 16, 2008

Know that you can rest, surrounded by loving and living prayers that have been woven together for just such a moment as this. "Trust."
Love,
Joan Van Houten

E-mail, Thursday, October 16, 2008

Dear Pam,

You are certainly going through a trial of faith! I can understand why you are feeling so weary and overwhelmed.

Pam, you had no idea about the possibility of mold coming into Nancy's house on your clothes or whatever! I've never heard of such a thing, but whatever is going on, you bear no blame. I just join in believing with you that we are in God's hands, and that we can trust God. We are loved and cared for, and whatever is needed will be provided in the right form, the right way, at the right moment.

Lots of love and prayers,

Marty Rienstra

Update Thursday, October 16, 2008 at 8:27 p.m.

We received both good and bad news today. As in life, there seems to be a hilly landscape here. We were notified today that Pete has been approved for disability payments, beginning in December. That will help a lot.

Then we got the news that the contractors who will be cleaning our house of mold will most likely need to tear up and destroy all of our new carpeting.

Also to be destroyed: the new sofa and recliner, any other upholstered furniture, all curtains, linens, clothing, shoes, coats, mattresses, bedding, etc., throughout the entire house–basically anything we own that is not metal, glass, or plastic. I think we will be able to save some of the wood items. I guess we will be learning a lot about detachment. We'll be starting all over in some ways.

On another subject, Pete's potassium levels are too high now, and he can't be discharged until they get that under control. I am hoping I'll be feeling a lot better by the time he's ready to come back to South Haven, wherever we land. Right now he needs more assistance than I would be able to give him. Still, in general, I can see improvement with him, and that's encouraging. Tomorrow is his birthday–#57.

Everything will work out.

---

25 Messages Posted October 16-18, 2008

Happy Birthday to you (2x)

Happy Birthday, dear Pete

Happy Birthday to you.

Love ya both,

Joe Foster

Pete is here, alive, and on the mend! No material losses can ever overshadow that monumental fact. We will be awaiting word on how we can help replenish when the time comes.

Love,

Carol Johnson

Happy Birthday Pete! A tough place to celebrate, but keep in mind the celebrating which can come later.

Pamela, I have some furniture items, if you would like them. Let me gather a list and provide that, and if something is interesting, I'll get photos and you can choose. We will get you furnished somehow.

Be well. You are both in our thoughts.

Penni Casper

I remember you telling me not too long ago about your desire to simplify your life . . . So maybe this is a blessing in disguise. It is painful, and there is a definite sense of loss. However, everything from this point on is for you as a wife, as a partner with Pete, as a married couple. I hope you will find this challenge—of creating a new environment—a happy one and enjoy the process together.

Happy Birthday to Pete!

Sis

Update Friday, October 17, 2008 at 7:10 p.m.

Well, it wasn't exactly a blowout party, but I think Pete had a decent birthday. I got him a celebratory balloon so everyone who came in knew it was his special day. He got some dark chocolate, something he has been craving since his transplant, and a massage. Carol Johnson sent a great CD. The food service provided a birthday cake and gave me two passes so I could get his lunch and dinner at the cafe. It was a welcome change from tray food. We also had a visit from five teenaged Mennonite girls who sang beautifully for us. Pete had calls throughout the day from family and friends, including his son in Japan, wishing him a happy birthday. That was the best part!

Pete is walking about 30 feet at a time with a walker now, and is able to climb four stairs–very slowly. I don't know when he will be discharged, but I hope they let him get a little stronger first. I'm still coughing a lot and I get pretty tired. I want to be sure I am able to care for him adequately.

I've been thinking about Rachel Reenstra's experience when her apartment building went up in flames and she lost almost everything. She eventually came to think of that as a purification process. Pete and I are trying to look at our home situation in the same way. A new start. Clearing out the "stuff" of the past. Purification. I like that. Add to that the belief that the Universe will provide and–hey, we are going to be just fine. Much love to you,

Pam

Update Saturday, October 18, 2008 at 7:23 p.m.

Pete is stronger. Even his voice is stronger. Today he managed to stand up on his own from the bed. That's new. Then he walked on his own with the walker down the hall to the window. I followed with a wheelchair so he could sit down if he needed to, but he didn't need it. He seems more upbeat. I think he'll be ready to go home–wherever that is–soon. We're just taking this one step at a time, *trusting* that all will work out.

Thanks for your many postings of support and encouragement, and even furniture!

Love,

Pam

Update Sunday, October 19, 2008 at 6:49 p.m.

Sunday. I went to the Unity Church here again, where I now see many familiar faces and get my fix of hugs. The speaker talked about gratitude, something I've been thinking about a lot lately. A couple of days ago I had hit a new low emotionally. I had a lousy cold, was tired, discouraged and "stuck." Finally I started writing some long overdue "Thank You" cards. There are *many* to be written. After a few minutes I realized that my mood was shifting. In fact, my whole perspective shifted! It seems that when I focus on gratitude, there just isn't any room in my head for negative thoughts. It just fills up with love and joy. It's all good.

When I got up to the hospital today, Pete seemed even better than yesterday. He took three walks with the walker and no assistance at all. I didn't even follow with a wheelchair. The doc told him this morning that he will probably be discharged this week. That is great news, even though we don't know yet where we will be going. I just know something is going to work out.

Tonight I am swimming in gratitude. How about you? Come on in. The water's fine!

Love,

Pam

---

13 Messages Posted October 19-25, 2008

"Gratitude calms your fears, strengthens your courage, opens your heart for adventure—gratefulness heals . . . It is our courageous trust that life itself—kind or harsh, happy or sad—is good, if only we receive it as a gift."—Dr. Francis G. Lu

I am grateful, grateful, grateful! Life is good! Thanks for the reminder, Pam!
Kerry Lytle

I often repeat a mantra: I'm too blessed to be stressed.
Jeanie Frattallone

Sunday, October 19, 2008
Journal

Even with two people who love each other very much, there are things that go unspoken, protected in tender places like a scab you don't want to pull off too soon. Sometimes those thoughts spring out, caged lions set free.

Last night Pete said to me, "You'd be better off without me."

"What are you talking about?" I said, astonished.

"The life insurance," he said.

I won't pretend that I hadn't thought about what would happen if Pete were to die. My mind slipped into that territory several times, especially when he came so close. I knew he had a policy that would pay off our debts and leave me in good shape financially, but I also knew that it could never ease the pain of losing him.

I got right in his face and said, "You're right. I would have enough money–but I'd be miserable. I wouldn't have you." He looked doubtful, so I pressed on. "The one thing I am most grateful for in the whole world is that you are still alive. I would rather live in a one-room shack with you than in a beautiful mansion without you. Period. We're going to be just fine."

He smiled.

Update Tuesday, October 21, 2008 at 9:32 p.m.

We learned today that Pete will be discharged from the hospital tomorrow! For the first few days we are going to stay with my sister, Connie, and her husband, Jim, in Muskegon. They have a beautiful home on Mona Lake, and it will help us get acclimated to being outside of the hospital. Bless their hearts!

Then we hope to get down closer to home. There are a lot of things to take care of before we can get back into our house again. Sometimes it feels like I climb an entire mountain, only to find—another mountain. Still, I'm able to climb, thank God, and when I take the emotionality out of it, it is simply getting a big job done, one step at a time. We can't know at this point what is the meaning underneath all of this, but we know we will get through it—and we know we have each other, which is everything.

Pete is elated about being discharged. He has spent four months hospitalized this year. That's enough! He's getting stronger all the time, and the docs think he's just too healthy to be in the hospital. Yay!

Much love to all of you, and deep gratitude for your postings, and prayers,

Pam

---

24 Messages Posted October 21-22, 2008

This is wonderful news! Remember, keep one foot in front of the other and hold hands along the way.
Love,
Sue Kruizenga

Thursday, October 23, 2008
Journal

Today's headline: Markets Fall as Fears of Slump Span World
Thought: Maybe I should stop reading the paper.

Update Thursday, October 23, 2008 at 3:37 p.m.

We are in Muskegon now, staying with my sister and brother-in-law for a few days. Connie and Jim have really rolled out the red carpet for us. This will be a wonderful time for us to regroup. We plan to be back in South Haven Monday or Tuesday.

Pete did very well yesterday when we left the hospital. It was a long day, as we didn't get discharged and on our way until almost 6:00 p.m., and then we drove until almost 9. He's not used to being up–even sitting up–for that long, but he did well, and he even sat and watched a movie on TV with us all after we got here.

Today he took a walk with the walker–maybe 150 feet, and seems to be just fine. He'll be getting help at "home" from an occupational therapist, a physical therapist, and a visiting nurse for a while. Then, when he's ready, he'll resume cardiac rehab at the South Haven Wellness Center.

I'm feeling much, much better, and quite optimistic. The Universe has a beautiful way of supporting us.

Love,

Pam

Update Monday, October 27, 2008 at 9:36 a.m.

It's very peaceful here in Muskegon–a good time of reentry into the real world. Tomorrow we will be heading back to South Haven. Our dear friend, Nancy Lou will be hosting us in her home again. For a while we feared that some of the mold from our house may have contaminated her home by way of some of our belongings, but that has not turned out to the be case. Her house tested clear of mold, so we will be returning there. Enormous thanks to the wonderful friends who have offered us a place to stay.

Today Pete had visits from the traveling nurse and then the physical therapist. He is eager to regain his strength, balance and endurance, so he worked hard. Then he went right to bed again. He still tires quickly.

Yesterday I went to our own Unity Church in Douglas for the first time in months, and I was greeted with dozens of hugs, kisses, and squeals of delight! It was a love-filled homecoming for me and also a very special Sunday for the church, as it marked the changing of the mantle from one pastor to the other–two amazing and awesome women. The community we have there is strong and incredibly loving. We are blessed. Pete didn't come–it's too soon yet–but he sent his love, and I brought back many hugs for him.

We know that the prayers of many people have made an enormous difference in Pete's and my own healing. We are grateful beyond words, and look forward to whatever it is that God has been preparing us for. It's going to be phenomenal.

Love to you all,

Pamela

Tuesday, October 28, 2008

Journal

We returned to South Haven, and Nancy Lou's house today. It's good to be back. We still don't know what that strange odor was, but we're chalking it up to the fact that Pete was too weak to take showers regularly, and although I cleaned him up the best I could, it just isn't the same with a wash cloth. Nurse Nancy calls it "that old man smell." At any rate, Pete is stronger now, and better at showering with some help from me, so I think we have that issue licked.

We have to go to Ann Arbor again tomorrow for a biopsy–too much traveling all at once–but, there you have it. Pete says he's not going, but he will. He just likes to be able to say "No" once in a while.

Update Friday, October 31, 2008

I love it when Halloween is also a beautiful day. Hooray for the tiny vampires, ballerinas, and kitty cats! It's great to be back in South Haven, Pete is getting stronger every day, and I feel better than I have felt since May.

The work on our house will begin soon. The new contractor we're working with thinks we won't have to get rid of all the carpeting, curtains, linens, clothing, etc. He says that everything above the basement is contaminated from mold spores that travelled through the air ducts. That means the little buggers landed on horizontal surfaces, but aren't likely to have penetrated, so we are okay with items in drawers, mattresses that were covered with blankets, etc. We will have to wash or dry clean everything where the spores may have settled, and the ducts and the carpets will have to be cleaned, but we won't have to throw everything away, so we won't have nearly as much to replace as I originally thought. Isn't that wonderful?

Think I'll wheel ol' Wehle down to the bench where we can soak in the big lake and enjoy its magnificence. Hope you're enjoying this gorgeous day.
Love,
Pam

---

23 Messages Posted October 31 - November 2, 2008

Hi Pam and Pete,

So glad to hear that you're back here by the big blue water! It has wonderful healing powers. We will be at the benefit and hope to bring many more people with us! Looking forward to seeing both of you.
Love,
Cindy & Bob McAlear

What a wonderful uplifting note Pam. If I am up to it, Jack and I will work to make the 15th a possibility, bald head and all!
Love,
Selma Holme

On Gratitude: "I think it really is everything. All the research on gratitude is so powerful: You see that you can't be stressed and thankful at the same time. It's the way our brains and bodies are wired. So you focus on gratitude and you won't be stressed. It's the best stress reducer."
–Jon Gordon

Tuesday, November 4, 2008
Journal

Election day. Pete and I already voted with absentee ballots. Tonight–Victory! We are elated! Obama has won! There is hope!

E-mail, Wednesday, November 5, 2008

How are you guys doing? Obama won! And Indiana went democratic—amazing. I watched some of the election results come in on the TV here in Japan. They seemed to be interested in the election.

I'm still playing the same children's concerts over and over again. They are getting really boring now. I am going to try to go to Kyoto soon with some friends. I hear it is really beautiful, especially with the trees turning colors. The weather is still pretty nice—no snow here. I hope everything is well.

Love,

Paul

Update Wednesday, November 5, 2008 at 7:54 p.m.

Dear Ones–

Pete continues his healing journey. He is walking with a cane now sometimes, instead of a walker. This morning we went out for breakfast–our first true outing.

I'm spending a lot of time sorting, tossing, and packing in the basement at home, protected by an N-95 mask, plastic garment, booties, etc. It's a huge job, but I'm making progress. I have a couple of young people helping me out, which helps immensely. There is a 20-yard dumpster in the driveway, and we expect to fill it.

Update Saturday, November 8, 2008 at 6:24 a.m.

Pete is progressing. The O.T., nurse, and P.T. that visit twice a week are wonderful. Yesterday the O.T. gave him a book of Word Find puzzles to help him retrain his eyes and his brain. There are still some issues there. I do think, though, that his sense of humor is better than ever!

Work towards getting our house cleaned up is moving forward. The 20-yard dumpster in the driveway is huge. What an excellent opportunity to purge what should have been cleaned out years ago!

Pam

Wednesday, November 12, 2008
Journal

We rehearsed with Elfi today and started planning a new show. Imagine that! It felt good for the three of us to make music together again. Pete's breathing is still quite shallow, so he doesn't have the support he used to have when he belted it out like Gordon MacRae, but it will come. After rehearsal we had dinner with Brennan and Rachel, who are in Kalamazoo for a couple of weeks. It's so good to be with them!

Thursday, November 13, 2008
Journal

Pete reached for me in the night. Although we weren't able to arrive at the desired destination, the passion and pleasure were there, and I was taken, again, by how powerful sex can be. For us, it draws a nest of love and tenderness around us, binding us ever closer together.

Update Friday, November 14, 2008 at 7:41 p.m.

Pete is progressing, working with the visiting O.T., P.T., and nurse here at Nancy Lou's house. They're terrific. He seems more alert and his sense of humor has really kicked in. Pete is coming back. Thank God.

I've been working several hours every day getting our basement cleaned out and all the rooms in the house free of anything that might absorb mold spores. It's been quite a job–not much time to write. It's almost done, though, and ready to be remediated. We will have one very clean house! I can finally see the light at the end of the tunnel.

My dear niece, Wendy, sent me a lovely card and wrote that the cleansing of our house is sort of a metaphor for living the rest of our lives with intention, choosing carefully what needs cleaning up, what we will keep, and what we will leave behind. Ah, yes. Then she mentioned how great it would be if we could take each organ of our own bodies and remove it, give it a good cleaning, and put it back in! Wouldn't that be grand? Since we can't do that on a physical level, perhaps we can do it on a spiritual level. What needs cleaning?

Tomorrow night is the big benefit concert, and we are very excited! Wow! The lineup is fabulous, and they are *all* friends. It will be like a super duper birthday party and Christmas all rolled into one. Hope you can make it–but if geography or other matters get in the way, just know that we are grateful to you for all your support and loving prayers.

Love to you,

Pam

Update Monday, November 17, 2008 at 8:08 a.m.

Wow! What a weekend! Saturday night's benefit concert was amazing! The musicians were absolutely perfect, the house was packed, and the atmosphere was charged with love, compassion, and joy. We couldn't have hoped for a lovelier evening!

Pete was able to come, and when he was wheeled up to his front row vantage point, spontaneous applause filled the house. I think the biggest challenge in the evening for many was the "Please don't hug Pete" charge. He's immune suppressed, so we had to make do with hand shakes and conversations, but the love and concern for him was evident everywhere, and we both felt enveloped in the wonder of it all.

The concert, along with the bake sale and CD sales yielded over $3,000 toward our mold remediation at the house! Can you believe that? People were very generous. Our deepest thanks to all who organized, participated, attended, and donated. We now know first hand what community is all about, and we are grateful beyond words.

The second great event this weekend was Pete's triumphant return yesterday to our beloved Unity Church on the Lakeshore in Douglas. We were welcomed home with blessings, prayers, and celebration. This church is a very special, loving family, and it was healing just to step inside.

The third great thing was that I heard Pete singing in the shower this morning! About a month ago I told Nancy Lou that the day I heard Pete sing in the shower again, I would know that he was indeed well on the road to recovery.

Life is good, and every day on this planet is a blessing. This morning, snuggling in bed, we talked about how we might spend the next years of our lives, helping people find hope and a new relationship with Spirit in the face of difficult challenges. We can speak from experience, and hopefully repay some of the kindness that has been washing over us these past months.

Our love and deepest gratitude to you all!

Pam (and Pete too!)

---

21 Messages Posted Monday, November 17, 2008

What wonderful news! Thank you for allowing all of us to be a part of your special journey. I felt so privileged, as did many others, to witness the "sacred love" that was demonstrated Saturday night.
Love,
Linda LaRocque

Monday, November 17, 2008
Journal

First sticking snow today—about two inches worth.

Tuesday, November 18, 2008
Journal

Someone told me that the most moving moment in the entire benefit concert was when I took the stage to sing. Pete was seated up in front, and he stood up from his wheelchair and applauded enthusiastically. This set everyone off, and they all stood up, clapped and cheered. I felt my heart fill up with joy.

Wednesday, November 19, 2008
Journal

Message from Spirit: *Joy is love with wings.*

Brennan and Rachel are here tonight. We had dinner and talked and talked and talked. Hanging out with my grown-up son and his wife is a very treasured thing, indeed. They are a wonderful couple—bright, kind and fun. I miss them when they're in Montana. They love it there, though, and they have to be where their hearts take them.

Friday, November 21, 2008

Journal

I have a practice of meditative listening and taking dictation, for want of a better explanation. I sit silently and quiet my mind until all the chatter, lists, and to-do's fall away. Then I put my hands on the computer keyboard and ask, "What is it I should understand?" When words begin to form in my mind, I type them, as in taking a transcription.

I feel that I am inspired to write these words. At first, it seemed that the words were just for me. They brought me comfort, reassurance and guidance. They always seem wrapped in love. Today's message seems to be for more than just me, though. At the risk of being regarded as delusional or worse, I share them with you. If I am a messenger, I am just one of many—perhaps you are, too, in your own way.

Lessons in Loving

Dear Beloved,

I want you to listen very carefully to what I am about to say: You are a messenger. This is your purpose. I have much to say through you. It is essential that you pay attention, stay open and carry these messages to the world.

The first one is this: "Peace will not come to your planet until you and your people begin to grasp the basic truths of the universe. The most important of these is that we are all connected, and that what you do to anyone, you do to yourself." (Yes, Pam, I gave you those lyrics. You know that.) This is why it feels so good to be kind to others. It comes back to you in nonphysical and physical ways.

You have demonstrated this important principle by being open to receiving and by giving others the opportunity to give to you and Pete. Haven't you been amazed at the abundance, the love, the prayers that have come your way, like a river flowing? Don't slip into wondering if you deserve it. Everyone deserves it.

What you can do is "pay it forward," as the movie says. You can do that by sharing the message of your journey. That is another message: When you experience difficulty, heartache, illness, pain—you have the power to transform that experience into a spiritual one of depth and meaning. Of course, you also have the choice of going into despair and fear. You choose.

A third message is: Joy is where you make it. Happiness is a decision.

("What if what I do to you, I'm doing to myself?" is a line from my song, "One." I often feel that some of the lyrics to my songs are given to me, as if there is a sort of cosmic pipeline into my imagination. I've read about many other creative people describing the same sort of thing. It's magical, mystical, wonderful!)

Saturday, November 22, 2008
Journal

A curious thing–When I go to the grocery store, I ask Pete if there is anything he would like me to pick up for him. He invariably says, "Dark chocolate." He wasn't unusually fond of chocolate before the transplant. Now he wants it all the time.

Hmmm . . .

Update Monday, November 24, 2008 at 5:00 p.m.
Dear Friends, Family–

I brought Pete to Ann Arbor last night for another routine biopsy early this morning. Going up in the hospital elevator today he sang, "We're going up to the third floor! Which floor are you going to? Woo-woo." The other people in the elevator chuckled. They probably thought he was drunk–or completely daft!

This behavior is not new. Lately Pete has been talking incessantly, even when no one was listening, making up little songs and singing them everywhere, even in quiet spaces, and in general seeming rather giddy and extremely uninhibited–*way* over the top. Dr. Aaronson, who is taking care of Pete now, picked up on it right away, and whispered to me, "Manic." He admitted Pete to the hospital again–so here we are. Ironic, isn't it–to be hospitalized for being too happy?

The question is–what is causing this? Is it a problem with the meds? Is it related to the strokes? Does he have some sort of infection that is affecting the frontal lobe of his brain? They need to run some tests to get some answers.

Pete is very unhappy about being admitted again–he's had enough of hospitals–but when Aaronson explained that an infection in the brain could be fatal, Pete figured he'd better do as the doctor said.

So, we're back in Ann Arbor, grateful for the skilled staff here, and mindful that we have much to be thankful for this Thanksgiving. Life. May yours be blessed with love, laughter, and good food.

Love,

Pam

---

22 Messages Posted Monday, November 24-25, 2008

We will be thinking of you.

Kerry Lytle

Oh my . . . My heart goes out to you both.

Mary James

. . . Yes, get it all checked out. I think it's a good idea to be vigilant. Perhaps, like Commander Data in Star Trek Next G, someone surreptitiously installed a humor chip during the last rebooting. Chin up, what?

Love to all,

Richard Broadbent

Monday, November 24, 2008

Notes from Dr. Aaronson:

Eyes–hyperthyroid

Mania, Disinhibitions–possibly from steroids

Infection in frontal lobe?

Tests:

CT Scan

Spinal tap

Tuesday, November 25, 2008

Journal

Before we left for Ann Arbor for his routine biopsy this time, I surreptitiously threw a change of clothes in my bag. You never know, and I like to be prepared.

Glad I did. Instead of going to the Transplant House last night I slept on the sofa in Pete's room. The non-ICU rooms in the Cardiovascular Center are designed to accommodate such things. I'm hoping it will be a short stay . . . Thanksgiving is the day after tomorrow.

Pete has been undergoing a bunch of tests, including a spinal tap. The doctor told him all he had to do was to curl up in a "C" and the rest would be easy. Wrong. Pete has arthritis in the spot where the needle is supposed to go in, and telling from his response, the pain was excruciating. At the doctor's request, I was there to help keep Pete calm. He cried out and grabbed my belly, squeezing so hard I almost fainted. The doctor kept trying, over and over again, but apparently couldn't get the needle in properly. Pete was in agony. Finally, just before they were going to give him morphine, the needle slid into place, the cerebrospinal fluid was drawn, and it was all over. They will analyze the fluid for any kind of infection.

Whew! I'm glad that's over with.

Thursday, November 27, 2008
Journal

As it turned out, Pete was in the hospital for three days. The spinal tap results came back showing no infection. The problem must be with the meds. They tweaked those a bit, and asked me to monitor his behavior. Yesterday his discharge was delayed and then delayed again by CT scans and paper work and I don't know what else. We finally left for South Haven around suppertime. I'm glad we're back home. We did *not* want to spend Thanksgiving in the hospital.

Our usual Thanksgiving at Camp Friedenswald has been changed to every other year to accommodate in-laws. Pete's sons and mine are all scattered to the wind and unable to be with us. Nancy Lou is having dinner out of town with family, and I didn't have a chance to shop for Thanksgiving, so . . . we went to Big Boy. I always wondered who went to Big Boy for Thanksgiving. I guess it's people like us, with no one else to spend it with, no food prepared, whatever. The place was full.

I hope we never have to do that again. The food was okay, but it just seemed sad. As an Australian friend of mine would say, it was "rather a nonevent." I missed the lively conversation, the excitement, the celebration of Thanksgivings past with family. I am grateful, though–oh so grateful! I could have been a widow at this year's Thanksgiving. Pete is alive and healing! Life is good. I'll stop whining now. Next year will be better.

CHAPTER SEVENTEEN

Just Bumps in the Road

"The secret of making something work in our lives is, first of all, the deep desire to make it work; then the faith and belief that it can work; then to hold that clear definite vision in your consciousness and see it working out step by step, without a thought of doubt or disbelief."
—Eileen Caddy

Monday, December 1, 2008
Journal

PETE HAS ENTERED into a new phase. At first I was absolutely thrilled to have him speak at all. Now sometimes he talks and talks and talks to the point that I wish I could press "Mute" on him! He prattles on, recalling conversations that never happened. "He goes (Fill in the blank), and I go (Fill in the blank)." He interrupts people in conversations and interjects totally unrelated comments. He makes up little songs that are more annoying than charming. How can I find it annoying, when I'm so happy just to have him alive?

Tuesday, December 2, 2008

Journal

I presented a program for the Scott Club today on "Music that Heals." I think it went very well. I told them about music as medicine–how drumming relieves stress and improves concentration, about the effectiveness of the "Gifts of Art" music at the hospital, about how music therapy is useful for a full range of injuries and illnesses, including Parkinsons, Alzheimers, stroke and autism. I shared the tests that have been done with playing music with plants, and about the doctors in France who prescribe specific pieces of music three times a day for some patients. I spoke of the reports of cows yielding more milk when classical music is played in the barn, and of Masaru Emoto and his work with water and music.

One of my favorite stories to relate is about a group of Benedictine Monks in the south of France who became listless, tired, depressed quite out of the blue. No medical cause could be found. The monks had at one time gathered 8-9 times a day to chant, but Vatican II reduced the amount of chanting. When the monk's chanting regimen was restored six months later, the men returned to vigor and health . . .

Of course, I also sang for the ladies of the Scott Club. I love doing this kind of work.

Update Friday, December 5, 2008 at 9:03 a.m.

I am so sorry to be late in posting a new update. Pete was discharged on Thanksgiving Eve, and we arrived in South Haven at about 11 p.m. that night. His spinal tap (Ouch!) showed no infection, so the conclusion is that the cause of his recent behavior is either the medication (his thyroid levels came up high), stroke related, or both. He is doing well now, and the giddiness has subsided a little into a more reasonable range. We went out to dinner with some dear friends last night and he held court, telling stories and making everyone laugh. He's still a bit "high," but enjoying himself. We should all laugh so much!

Work is progressing on our house, and we hope to be back in soon . . . We had much to be grateful for this Thanksgiving, and as we approach Christmas, we both look for ways to give back, whatever that might look like.

Love & Blessings to you all,

Pam

15 Messages Posted Friday, December 5, 2008

Pamela,

    . . . I read today that laughter is like jogging for the intestines. Keep smiling. Many blessings to you and Pete . . .

Linda Garces

Update Tuesday, December 9, 2008 at 11:21 a.m.

Pete is a river flowing downstream to who he really is. Along the way he bumps into the occasional rock or fallen branch. He calls a glass a "jug," or he loses his balance and staggers a little. He has trouble with the TV remote and the zipper on his coat. But he keeps flowing downstream, and I am encouraged.

Sunday he managed a flight of stairs five different times. That is amazing. I think of a few months ago, when it took enormous effort for him to climb one step. He's coming back.

Sunday at our church's Christmas program he did a reading. He lost his place a few times, and faltered a little here and there, but he was surrounded by our loving church family, and everyone was pulling for him. The reading was, "Christmas in the Trenches," which is actually a song by John McCutcheon about a temporary and impromptu truce between British and German soldiers on a Christmas Eve battlefield during World War I. It's a tender, bittersweet story, and there wasn't a dry eye in the house. Several years ago Pete pledged to read the story every Christmas until we were out of Iraq and Afghanistan. He kept his pledge—and we were all very proud of him.

The other day we went to Captain Nemo's, a little restaurant downtown, and the owner was so happy to see Pete walking in the door, she treated us to breakfast. You know, people are just kind. We've learned that a hundred times over in the past few months, and we have felt tremendously blessed. As people have told us, the cool thing is that each person who gives from the heart is also blessed by his or her own generosity. It expands the heart when we give, whatever the gift might look like, and the world benefits from more love and joy. I can't think of a better example of win/win.

In the meantime, Pete flows downstream to his wholeness and fullness, and you all get to come along for the ride. Wheeeeee!

---

21 Messages Posted Tuesday, December 9-10, 2008

Gee, I was there and didn't hear Pete falter. I only saw a beautiful man on higher ground, being held by angels and having the time of his life!
Lin Speet

I can only imagine how difficult it has to be for you to see this wonderful man you love change, while at the same time try so hard to regain his losses. Calling a glass a jug reminds me of Jack when he gropes for words he has forgotten or no longer understands. I find myself ambivalent at some of those times, saddened by the loss and rejoicing at his determination to keep trying.

It is so wonderful that you have such a loving and supportive community surrounding you both. You are blessed.
Love to you and Pete,
Selma Holme

Tuesday, December 9, 2008
Journal

We laugh a lot, Nancy Lou, Pete and I. Last night over dinner, Nancy proclaimed that we should create nicknames for each other. Pete had already dubbed her "Zorro," from the book I'm reading. We both looked at Pete and the words that came out of my mouth were "Fancy Pants." I have no idea where that came from, but Nancy and I just howled. Pete was chagrinned, to say the least.

Then I asked Pete to stand up, and after a few protestations, he did. I swept up his shirt to reveal the scars from the incisions on his abdomen. Nancy's eyes popped out. "Wow!" She hadn't seem them before.

I figured he deserved his red badge of courage for those mementos. "Scar Belly!" I said gleefully. Pete liked "Scar Belly" a lot better than "Fancy Pants." When I left for a moment to use the bathroom, the two of them came up with my new moniker–"Hot Lips."

So now we are Zorro, Hot Lips, and Scar Belly, laughing and sharing this unique chapter in our lives. Beneath all the laughter is comfort, loving, and support. Pete and I are both eager to get back in our own home, but we will miss this special time with Nancy Lou very, very much.

"We're all bozos on the bus, so we might
as well sit back and enjoy the ride."
–Wavy Gravy

Wednesday, December 10, 2008

To the Family of the Heart Donor Who Saved My Life, (DRAFT)

My wife and I want to thank you and acknowledge your faith and compassion. We can only imagine the depth of your loss, and we hope you can imagine the magnitude of our gratitude.

We thought you might like to know a little about me, the transplant recipient. I am 57, white, six feet tall, and the father of two sons. Paul is 21 and just graduated from Indiana University at Bloomington this summer. He is currently playing bass in a symphony orchestra in Japan, where he will be for at least a year. Sean is 17 and a senior in high school in South Bend, Indiana. He lives with his mother.

In September of 2007 I married Pamela Chappell of South Haven, Michigan. That is where we currently live. Both Pamela and I are singers and have performed both separately and together. I do a Sinatra tribute. Pam plays guitar and writes some of her own songs. She has two grown sons and one granddaughter.

I had my own mortgage protection business when I collapsed at home June 4 of this year . . . I received my transplant on July 26-27, 2008 at the University of Michigan Hospital in Ann Arbor. It was a 14-hour procedure.

We haven't written to you before this because of some complications. I had two small strokes while I was on a life support machine before the transplant. It has been more difficult to recover from the strokes than from the transplant. I also got pneumonia, which necessitated another month in the hospital. That is why we haven't written to you sooner. We wanted to be able to tell you that I am doing great and am well on the road to recovery, which is now true.

We both believe that there is a higher power at work in our world, and that everything happens for a reason, even when it is difficult to understand what that reason might be. We are deeply sorry that your loved one died, and our hearts go out to you. We only hope that the huge gift of my second chance at life will be a comfort to you. We would love to hear from you if you would like to contact us. If not, we certainly understand.

With love and gratitude,

Peter Wehle

Thursday, December 11, 2008

Journal

Pete and I went for a session with Sherry Petro-Surdel today. She is a dear friend, a therapist, and co-pastor at our church. There has been much change in our lives in the last seven months (a bit of an understatement) and that takes some emotional work. Our roles as wife/caregiver and husband/patient keep shifting, and we thought it would help if we could talk it out with a professional. Sherry was very helpful.

Looking back . . .

We saw Sherry several times in the months that followed. She helped us navigate through the snares of married life as it moves from crisis to whatever normality is for us. Sherry is a gentle, wise woman, and a precious player in this wonderful Universe that provides so generously. She never sent a bill.

Update Friday, December 12, 2008 at 8:35 a.m.

We have good news for you all: Today Pete weighed in at 150 pounds. That means he has gained ten pounds since his transplant and all that followed. He had lost about 50 pounds and was looking skinny, so this is very good news! Perhaps his new craving for dark chocolate helps. It certainly might say something about the donor!

The other great news is that Pete has been officially discharged by the visiting physical therapist and occupational therapist. That means he's ready for outpatient cardio rehab, a real milestone. I think it helped that he did a little Fred Astaire-style dance with his cane for the O.T., who said that he has come "galaxies" since Thanksgiving. We are well aware that there is still a long road ahead of us in terms of full recovery, but that goal feels more attainable with each day.

We met with friend and therapist Sherry P. yesterday and began envisioning what the rest of our lives might look like, both as individuals and as a couple. Pete's heart transplant experience has brought us a powerful opportunity to examine our intentions, to look ahead with hope, and to go inside for the inspiration that is sure to come.

Enjoy this beautiful, white day!

Love,

Pam

Tuesday, December 16, 2008
Journal

I really look forward to Nancy coming home from work each day. It feels so good to laugh, and we do it a lot here. Nancy Lou is a real hoot. I swear she spends her drive time coming home from work thinking of funny stories to tell us. There is the one about the female patient who dubbed her "Lesbian-Crack-Whore-Bitch-Ass." We really howled at that one. I think we should get her new business cards with L.C.W. B.A. on them.

She told us about a patient's trailer, way out in the boonies, that has a sign on it: "This is no fucking flophouse. You can visit, but you cannot stay."

I love the quips she relays to us. One patient said, "I am just too pretty and too smart to be treated like an asshole any more."

Another said, "If you think I'm going to be the jackass in this rodeo anymore, you've got another think coming."

Then there is Nancy's intention to teach Pete how to cook. He is a reluctant learner. I'm told he lived on cream of wheat and carry-out pizza in college. Nancy coerced him into making a pumpkin pie with her. She was working on the crust, and she told Pete to use a whisk on the filling. "What's a whisk?" he asked. Another time she had him help her layer an English trifle. He really got into that. And once he actually pounded the meat for Swiss steak. Miracles do happen.

Nancy got out her Christmas decorations, including a sweet little white tree with beautiful glass ornaments. She has all the family stockings hung, and a Christmas teddy bear sitting on a little rocking chair. With all the laughs Nancy has given us, we figure we owed her a few, so we have been changing the teddy bear's position and location every day. When she comes home from work she may find him in the bathtub, or knitting, or mixing something (with a whisk!) in a big blue bowl on the counter. Once she found him (shocking!) with a rather large zucchini sticking out between his legs, and another time with two blue Christmas tree balls in the same spot.

It's working out well, here. Humor helps immensely. I think our real nicknames should be Larry, Curly, and Moe.

Nancy Lou remembers . . .

Sometimes we were just three little kids helping each other get through. It was a hard holiday that year.

Update Thursday, December 25, 2008 at 4:05 p.m.

Pete and I send you all a warm Christmas/Hannukuh hug with lots of love and gratitude mixed in. We have been blessed by your phenomenal support, prayers, and best wishes. Thank you from the depths of our hearts. It's a miracle that Pete and I have this Christmas together, and many more of them to look forward to.

Once again, I draw from something my dear niece, Wendy sent me:

"Christmas waves a magic wand over this world, and behold, everything is softer and more beautiful."–Norman Vincent Peale

Here's to a love-filled holiday, and the greatest New Year ever!

Love,

Pamela and Peter

> 15 Messages Posted Thursday, December 25, 2008
>
> May you experience many more happy Christmases together.
> Love,
> Martin Gruber

Saturday, December 27, 2008
Journal

Christmas Eve Day the transmission went out on my car. A few years ago that would have sent me into deep despair. *Where will the money come from to get it fixed? Do I need to get a new car instead? Oh my, then I'll have monthly payments again. I can't pay all my bills as it is! Yikes!*

When it happened, though, I just went straight into problem-solving mode, passing the emotion along the way, giving it a four or five second nod, and moving right on. I guess once you've looked death in the face and kept on breathing, transmissions seem like small change.

It's not that we have tons of money in the bank, or that it won't be a struggle–it's just that, in the grander scheme of things, it's *just not that important.* I'll simply deal with it. It's amazing to me that I can do that–Miss Cry-At-Telephone-Commercials–but I can, and I did. You can too.

> 25 Messages Posted Tuesday, January 27-30, 2009
>
> Where there is *love* there are miracles!
> Carol Thomas

"Just trust yourself. Then you will know how to live."
–Goethe

Tuesday, December 30, 2008

Journal

I'm in the waiting room of the CVC at the University of Michigan Hospital. Pete just went in for a routine heart catheterization and biopsy. The year is winding down. As I look back at it, it's almost as if it were someone else that wrote all these entries, walked this path.

Pete is much better now, but not completely well. He has some memory problems, has difficulty following basic instructions, and doesn't seem to sense when his behavior is inappropriate. He gives up easily when he can't do something right away.

He doesn't seem to realize how his behavior affects the people around him. Pete tends to be quite self-centered these days, which was not the case before he got sick. He likes to be waited on, something Nancy Lou and I are trying to bring to a halt. If he is corrected, he sulks or goes back to bed.

He's changed a lot, and yet glimpses of the old Pete do come through. I sure hope that this new Peter is temporary. It's not the man I married, and it would be difficult to live with for the rest of my life. Still, I love him so much, I can't imagine life without him. I just hope he evolves back into the caring, tender Pete I married just a few months ago.

CHAPTER EIGHTEEN

Life Unfolding

"You have done what you could—some blunders and absurdities have crept in. Forget them as soon as you can. Tomorrow is a new day. You shall begin it serenely and with too high a spirit to be encumbered with your old nonsense."
–Ralph Waldo Emerson

Saturday, January 3, 2009
Journal

THIS MORNING NANCY Lou found Pete in the front room in his pajamas, robe, winter coat and boots. He was getting ready to go out and shovel the snow. A man's job . . . She wouldn't let him. Nancy can be very tough.

Looking back . . .

Nancy remembers: I think "mean" was Pete's term. But that was such a glimpse of the real Pete–a gentleman. How I treasured it!

Sunday, January 4, 2009

Looking back . . .

Jeanie died on this date. I didn't know until three months later. She'd been on my mind a lot, so I called Penny Baker to ask her how she was and Penny said, "She died." Jeanie Frattallone, bundles of energy, smiles, and one enormous heart. I knew she had been dealing with breast cancer for a long time–years. The last time I saw her was at our wedding. She asked someone to take a picture of her with the bride and groom, something she'd made a practice of doing at every wedding for years. She seemed pale and thinner than usual, but she had her arm around me in the picture, and her smile was radiant. You've read her encouraging postings in this book. Jeanie, rooting for us, praying for us . . .

Ah, Jeanie . . . I didn't know.

Monday, January 5, 2009

Journal

I pray every night for God to help me stay in love with him. Sometimes it's easy. Other times, irritation, impatience, and frustration gnaw away at me, and I remember falling out of love with my first husband. I don't want this to happen with Pete. Yes, he's ornery and self-absorbed these days, but I do love him–very, very much. I think maybe all I have to do is decide to keep doing that. I think.

January 8, 2009

Journal

We went to the store to pick up a few things. Pete wanted to walk this time, rather than ride in one of those electronic carts. I had to go to the far side of the store to get a cartridge for my computer printer, so I suggested that we meet at the flour/sugar/spices aisle–aisle eight–and he could look for the demerara sugar we like in our coffee. His pace is rather slow these days, so I figured I could get the cartridge and be at aisle eight by the time he reached there.

When I got to the sugar aisle, there he was, standing in the middle of the aisle, looking a little lost. "Did you find the sugar?" I asked.

"What sugar?" he said.

"Remember, I asked you to look for the demerara sugar?"

"Oh."

"Do you remember me asking you?"

"No."

"It's okay, honey. Here it is, right here. I was just wondering."

Saturday, January 10, 2009
Journal

Puffy white flakes are coming down steadily outside. There are about six inches on the ground and more expected, but inside Nancy Lou's house it's cozy and snug. Pete has gone back to bed after a breakfast of turkey sausage and scrambled eggs. I have a feeling of contentment and peacefulness.

I had a call from Sue Fischer yesterday, and she said that her heart went out to me. "I probably shouldn't say this, but I think you'll understand. It's just that Pete is not the same man you married. That must be really hard. I bet you miss him."

No, he is not the same, and I do miss him. Still, he is better from day to day, and I have great hope that he will return to normal—that he will make a full recovery.

Normal. Hmm . . . I don't really know what "normal" means. I truly don't expect that things will ever be the way they were before all of this. For one thing, we are both not the same physically, and will be dealing with that for the rest of our lives. Or will we? I should probably get that thought out of my mind.

Nancy Lou told me about being at a healing seminar when the leader asked, "Who among you is experiencing a disease or condition that needs healing?" No one spoke up. Finally he had everyone in the circle take a turn and tell if they had something that needed healing. Apparently it was an unusually healthy group because no one spoke up. Finally it came around to Nancy, and, hearing no one else speak up, she said, "Well, I do have glaucoma." The leader had everyone circle around Nancy and lay their hands on her, praying for her healing.

Nancy returned to her opthamologist shortly after that and he said, "Well, this is strange. There is no sign at all of glaucoma. What have you done?" She has had no recurrence of the condition.

So—maybe that was a "coincidence," and maybe not. Maybe, if we can muster up enough faith, Pete and I can be healed. I'd like to think so. I've read and heard many, many stories of this sort of thing happening. Would people just make them up? Or does believing it can happen make it happen? Maybe that's what people call a "Godincidence."

Same day, later . . .
To Peter:

Do you realize that we have created a loving space? Not a physical space, but a spiritual space that surrounds us and goes with us wherever we go. It's you and me and Spirit, and love, all of which are one in the same–and it goes with us everywhere.

We are blessed.

And in this loving, we have the potential to spill over to the rest of the world, which is sorely in need of loving.

This is joy.

> *"When I see the waves of Lake Michigan toss*
> *in the bleak snowstorm, I see how small*
> *and inadequate the common poet is."*
> *–Ralph Waldo Emerson*

Tuesday, January 13, 2009
Journal

For three days solid we couldn't see where the big lake ended and the sky began. It was all just a veil of steely gray. The ice floes are forming early this year, luring careless teens to climb out on them. I remember Connie falling in one year. It was one of several miracles in my big sister's young life that she survived. Today the temperatures are plunging into bitter cold. I walked the two blocks from Nancy Lou's to our house to shovel the sidewalk and our porch so we could get our mail, but it was so cold, I didn't last long. The rest of the snow can wait.

Pete is sleeping now. He sleeps a lot. I wonder about how things will be in the next year or two. Last night he was coughing in the night, and I immediately started making a mental list of the things I would need to throw in a bag if we had to rush him to the hospital again. I wonder if our lives together will always be like that—waiting for the next shoe to drop. He's better today, though, and life goes on.

Sometimes I can't remember what he was like before. He gets confused. He has a tough time turning on the TV with the remote. He can't follow simple directions—*on the first shelf, to the right*—and he says the weirdest things in conversations. He interrupts people and then says something vaguely related to the discussion ten or twenty minutes ago, but totally off track now. It's as if he gets lost and can't follow a thought path, so he just throws in whatever is on his mind and hopes it fits in. His jokes get progressively worse. It's frustrating—for both of us.

Thursday, January 15, 2009
Journal

My, my can that man consume dark chocolate! It's fascinating to me. I've heard about such things happening with transplant recipients, so I looked into the matter. Cellular memory is a controversial concept, but an intriguing one in view of the many, many accounts of organ recipients who have taken on behaviors, traits or tastes that can be attributed to the donor.

I read about the man who received a heart from an artist and suddenly began producing beautiful landscapes and drawings of wildlife. In her memoir, *A Change of Heart*, Claire Sylvia relates how she started to like beer, green peppers and fried chicken, none of which she liked before her heart and lung transplant in 1988, but all of which were favorites of the 18-year-old boy who was her donor. There is even the report of a ten-year-old girl who was murdered. Her heart was given to an eight-year-old girl who subsequently had nightmares of a man murdering her. Eventually, through her description of the man, the police were able to apprehend the murderer.

There are many such accounts that doctors and other scientists are hard pressed to explain. One explanation is that of cellular memory—the concept that all the body's cells have their own memories, including information about our tastes, personalities, and histories, and that the transplanted organ retains the cellular memory of the donor at least for a time. Some spiritual mediums suggest that the new behaviors and tastes of transplant recipients represent the presence of the spirit of the deceased donor. You can imagine how scientists love that idea!

It may be that we never know for sure whether cellular memory exists, but every time Pete downs another dark chocolate bar, I wonder.

Monday, January 19, 2009
Journal

I took Pete to Mishawaka, Indiana today to have a neuropsychological evaluation. We wanted to get a handle on whether Pete has any brain damage from the strokes back in July, and if so, how much, and is there anything we can do to help rewire his brain.

Dr. E. did separate interviews with Pete and me and thirteen tests of one sort or another with Pete. It took hours. I was in the room for a couple of the tests, and I could tell that he has made some good progress since he left the hospital, but there are clearly some deficits in his reasoning, memory, and problem-solving. I hope we will get some information that will be useful.

Tuesday, January 20, 2009
Journal

Today's headline: Obama Sworn in as 44th President

Wednesday, January 21, 2009
Looking back . . .

I've mentioned my medium friend, Margie Towne Kivel. I took classes from her for six years and developed my own mediumship gifts. Years ago I was given a message for her–I saw her in a wedding gown, getting married. Margie had a rough first marriage, and said that she didn't ever wanted to get married again. She wasn't looking for a mate, but sure enough, less than a year passed after the message I gave her, before she became the wife of Dan Kivel, also a medium, and also a spiritualist minister. I had never seen her so happy! She knew he had some health issues–he'd had a heart attack–but he was full of vitality and life, and the two of them were very much in love. Margie moved to the Detroit area, so I didn't see her very much after that, but she remained a close friend of the heart. I knew Dan too–a great guy. He posted encouraging messages often on the CarePages.

He died on this date. Oh, Margie, I'm so sorry . . . And then, a few months later, there were three: On September 13 of 2009 we lost our dear friend, Selma, who had been undergoing treatment for cancer for quite a while. I always thought of Selma as a model for how to live one's senior years. She had just taken her granddaughter on a trip to Greece. She and her husband, Jack, travelled a lot, were in a folk dancing group, and kayaked, among other things. Such dear folks. Jack is not well himself. I don't know how he'll do without Selma.

First Jeanie, then Dan, and then Selma–three of our most loyal supporters when Pete was in the hospital, cheering us on, encouraging us, praying for us–and now they are gone from here . . . and Pete has survived. Life's funny, isn't it . . . You never know.

Wednesday, January 21, 2009
Journal

I helped Pete compose his second letter to the heart donor's family. He couldn't send the first one because it had too many details about our lives, and we've been told that we can't reveal anything that would make us identifiable. I don't really know why that is, but, anyway, we drafted a second letter today.

I hope the family responds. We'd really like to know about the donor. We joke a lot about the few clues we have. The doctor told me that the main valve of the donor heart was too small, so they had to use a pig valve in the transplant surgery. Then there is Pete's new craving for dark chocolate. So—we figure his donor was a woman. I wonder if we'll ever know for sure.

Wednesday, January 21, 2009
To the Family of the Heart Donor Who Saved My Life,

My wife and I want to thank you and acknowledge your faith and compassion. We can only imagine the depth of your loss, and we hope you can imagine the magnitude of our gratitude.

I thought you might like to know a little about me, the recipient. I am 57, married, and the father of two sons. One is 21 and the other is 17.

I haven't written you before this because of some complications. I had two small strokes while I was on a life support machine before the transplant. It has been more difficult to recover from the strokes than from the transplant. I also got pneumonia, which necessitated another month in the hospital. I didn't write to you until now because I wanted to be able to tell you that I am doing great and am well on the road to recovery, which is now true.

We are deeply sorry that your loved one died, and our hearts go out to you. We only hope that the huge gift of my second chance at life will be a comfort to you. We would love to hear from you if you would like to contact us. If not, we certainly understand.

With love and gratitude,

Peter

P.S. From Pete's wife–You have given us more years together, a precious and blessed thing. I am immensely grateful to you and to your loved one who made this possible. Pete is my shining star, a courageous, intelligent and funny guy with a very loving nature, and much to give to those around him. Thank you again, and bless you!

> *"Your life is a sacred journey. And it is about change, growth, discovery, movement, transformation, continuously expanding your vision of what is possible, stretching your soul, learning to see clearly and deeply, listening to your intuition, taking courageous challenges at every step along the way."*
> *–Caroline Adams*

Update Sunday, January 25, 2009 at 4:02 p.m.,
Phoenix, Arizona

It's been a month since I posted anything–mostly because there hasn't been much news until now. Pete continues to improve, step by step, and I'm doing pretty well too. We both still need a lot of rest, though, and about a million vitamins, etc., every day. We haven't moved back home yet. The contractor and his crew did all the cleanup and follow-up testing on our house, but the testing showed that there was still too much mold remaining. They went back in last week and are confident they will be able to zero in on the problem areas soon.

When we got married in September of '07, we bought a time share in Sedona, Arizona, where we honeymooned. As times got tough and money got tight last summer, we tried to sell it, but had no luck with that. (Anybody want to buy a great time share?) In December we decided we might as well use our one week before it expired—so we planned to do that in January. Then some dear friends offered us a second time share week they weren't going to be able to use, and—here we are in beautiful, warm Arizona!

We're in Phoenix with Pete's sister and brother-in-law for a few days, and then we'll head up to Sedona. This morning Pete actually hit a few balls at the driving range. He had a little difficulty focusing on the ball, as his vision has been impacted by the strokes, but he liked the feel of a golf club in his hands again. His endurance is improving, and he is gaining weight. I'm hoping that a couple of weeks out of the ice and snow will be just the medicine he needs right now. I've been asked to sing at the Unity Church of Sedona next Sunday, so that will be great fun, too.

We'll be returning on Friday the 13th of February, and hopefully we'll be able to move back into the house soon after.

Much love and many rays of sunshine to you!

Pam (and Pete too!)

Update Tuesday, January 27, 2009 5:12 p.m.

Just a quick note to let you know that Pete and I are celebrating the six month anniversary of his heart transplant today. Now he is walking with just a cane, cracking jokes, growing a beard and soaking up the Arizona sunshine. We are truly blessed. Life is so precious! Tell someone you love them.

Love,

Pam

Monday, February 2, 2009—Sedona

Journal

I sit at the computer tonight with Pete sleeping in the bed beside me. He still sleeps a lot, often shutting down before 8:30 p.m. He is improving, but it is a very slow process. He takes stairs at a slow pace with his cane. He walks haltingly, and occasionally staggers a little, off-balance and unsteady. I know he hated it this morning when I hauled all of our luggage down the flight of stairs to take them to the car. He feels that "the man" should be doing that, but he can't. Not yet.

He's done very well on this trip, though. Apart from the fact that he needs a lot of rest and sleep, he has been quite active. We walked a fair amount when we went to Red Rock Crossing the other day, he shot a few balls at the driving range with his brother-in-law, Bob, and he ambled all the way from the car to the ruins at Montezuma's Castle.

Marty asked me Saturday how I've been dealing with all of this. I told her that the hardest thing for me is that he is not the man I married . . . and yet he is. So much has changed, and yet at the soul level–the heart level–he is the same man, and I love him deeply.

Sometimes I get tired.

Saturday, February 7, 2009–Sedona
Journal

A few days ago I went to Angel Valley with some Michigan girlfriends that are here in Sedona now. Angel Valley is an inspirational retreat and learning center quietly nestled between several mountains south of Sedona. It is a secluded, welcoming, desert oasis, full of surprises and breathtaking views of the towering mountains and of Oak Creek that meanders through them. The center has two labyrinths, a chakra path, and much more.

The labyrinth is a patterned path, usually somewhat circular in design, that dates back at least as far as ancient Egypt. There has been a resurgence of interest in the Labyrinth in recent years, especially among those interested in metaphysics, as it is symbolic of wholeness, inviting the walker into transformative prayer. Unlike a maze, the labyrinth has only one path, often stones arranged on a flat piece of land. There is no puzzle to solve except for the puzzles inherent in one's awareness. One simply follows the winding path to the center of the labyrinth, representing perhaps the deepest self, and then out again. Walking the labyrinth is a moving meditation, a metaphor for life's journey. Some people pose a question before entering the labyrinth, or ask for guidance. Some are in prayer for the entire walk. The experience tends to open avenues of intuition and creativity, and, depending on the person's intention, may lead to new understandings, revelations, and self-awareness. It is a personal pilgrimage.

I approached the larger of the two labyrinths with reverence, walking slowly and steadily. The winding pathway brought to mind the twists and turns in my life. Each stone that lined the path seemed to represent a person or situation that had been significant for me. At each turning in the path, there was a little hourglass shaped pattern of pebbles which for some reason reminded me of my creative works–the songs, the writings, the performances. Infinity in tiny little pebbles–simple expressions of my own life in the hugeness of all that is.

I continued walking, meditating, through childhood, adolescence, marriage, children, divorce–always searching, always absorbed in music. Images danced through my mind–my father teaching me how to tie my shoes, my first menstrual period, singing Joan Baez songs in a campfire ring, Brennan as a baby, fitting between my elbow and wrist, Phil standing center stage and singing "Gary, Indiana" in his eighth grade choir concert, taking community education guitar lessons, receiving my divorce papers, taking third place in a songwriting contest at Wheatland Music Festival, struggling with forgiving an old friend for choosing sides when I got divorced, holding Mama's hand when she passed, discovering a new way to think of God. Suddenly I slowed down, sensing that I had reached the point in my path when I met Peter. I stepped very slowly then, soaking in a bright, warm feeling of love and deep belonging. With another turning came the beautiful September evening when we got married. I remembered the silk flowers in my hair, and the huge ball of sun that set right on cue over Lake Michigan. It was a time brimming with joy and optimism. I felt Pete's warm and strong arms encircling me. Everything was so good!

In time, though, I reached the turning when Pete got sick, and our happiness morphed into something close to despair. Step after step after step . . . Mountain after mountain. So tired. So tired. Eventually there followed a time of healing for both of us, and I relaxed, feeling the tension like so many heavy blankets, fall off my shoulders. That brought me to my present, my Now. It felt serene and comforting. Pete and I walked together, and life was good. We had everything we needed. I walked for a while, then, through quite a few turns, always moving forward.

Suddenly, a good time later, there was another turn. It felt heavy, dark and full of sorrow. I knew at once that it was when I would lose Peter. I stopped, feeling a huge cavern of loss. I hadn't seen it coming, but there it was. I knew.

After that, I walked slowly, plodding along. The creative works represented in the hour glass pebbles were dark and pitted. Grief. I just wanted to rest, but

I had to keep walking. In time, and with a few more turnings, I began to feel a slow return to balance and a new level of acceptance and peacefulness. It seemed that those days were to be particularly rich in a creative sense.

When I finally reached the center of the labyrinth, it became clear to me that the center represented my own transition. That was it, this time around. Done! Fini! I was curious about what will come after that—what will happen when my spirit leaves this body—but at that point I just couldn't keep going, walking the outward path. I checked in with Spirit. *I don't want to go any further. Is that okay? I mean—can I just stop for now?* And right away I understood that it was my choice, and I chose to stop. I carefully stepped over the rows of life stones and walked away. I had learned about as much as I could absorb at that time, as much as my heart could hold.

Update Monday, February 9, 2009 at 8:39 p.m.—Sedona

Snow is falling steadily outside. Maybe this is Nature's way of helping us make the shift from Arizona back to Michigan. Most of our time here it has been sunny and warm, rather like early fall in Michigan. We've had wonderful visits with friends and family, and we've soaked up the healing sun and the vibrations of this wonderful place.

We are very grateful to our friends who have gifted us with a week at their time share, and those who have given us excursion train tickets, dinners out, and their presence. Pete and I are both healing, thanks to all the love that surrounds us.

A few days ago we got the news that our home in South Haven has been successfully remediated from the mold, and the post-testing indicates that it will be perfectly safe for us to move back in when we return to Michigan. Yay!

We are flying back to Michigan on Friday the 13th, and plan to take Saturday to rest a bit and get packed at Nancy's. Then we will move back into our home on Sunday afternoon. If any of you are in the area and would like to come join the move-in party, just show up at our house. With several pairs of hands, it won't take long, and there is no heavy lifting to speak of.

So much love heading your way!

Pamela

Tuesday, February 11, 2009–Sedona
Journal

I love it here. I was honored to sing at the Unity Church of Sedona Sunday. Monday we drove north to Flagstaff to see the white buffalo, which are considered sacred by most Native Americans. We had a birthday party for our friend, Donna, and with Claudia and Bob we had a day trip to Jerome, a historic copper mining town once known as the wickedest town in the West. Now it's an artist community and a National Historic District, and, the residents say, a ghost town. Our friends Lou and Lin gave us passes for the Verde Canyon Railroad, a ride that took us from Clarkdale to Perkinsville at about 12 miles per hour through canyons, an old mining town, and past a ghost ranch. It was a warm, breezy day, and the ride was relaxing and very picturesque.

Pete is holding up well through all of this activity, although he does need to take a couple of naps during the day. He's *very* glad to be away from winter in Michigan.

CHAPTER NINETEEN

Learning How to Live Again

"The paradox of living purposefully is to relax and love what
I have, and get going to create what I want."
Mary Hayes-Grieco

Update Sunday, February 15, 2009 at 8:02 p.m.–Michigan

TODAY, TWENTY OR more folks showed up to help us move back into our house and get settled in. We started out by circling up and asking Nancy O'Donohue to lead us in a blessing/prayer. Then we all sang, "Thank you for this house, Spirit . . ." with many a verse, as Nancy smudged the entire house for us. People brought food, new sheets and pillows, smiles, laughter, and tons of loving energy. With their cheerful, efficient help, we did the entire job in under two hours. We were all like little worker ants, and we laughed a lot.

Again Pete and I are overwhelmed by the love and support of our wonderful friends. Thank you so much, those of you who helped. You were/ are awesome!

Thanks also to Nancy Lou, who welcomed us to her home and took us in like stray cats. We had a great time at her house, and will be bonded forever as family.

And now, after eight months away—it's good to be home!

Love to you all,

Pam

Monday, February 16, 2009

Journal

Today we received the report from the neuropsychological evaluation Pete had done in Mishawaka last month. Here are some observations and conclusions from the report:

Mr. Wehle presents as a slim Caucasian male of average height, with medium-length, thinning, gray hair, moderate facial stubble (he is growing a beard), casually though appropriately attired, evidencing satisfactory grooming and hygiene, and appearing his chronological age. He was alert, attentive, oriented, pleasant, and cooperative. Gait is somewhat slow, though he seemed reasonably steady when on his feet, and also seemed comfortable when seated. I did not detect fine motor dyscontrol. Speech was spontaneous, fluent, non-paraphasic, and non-dysprosodic, slightly rapid though not pressured, and also slightly slurred from time to time. There was no idiosyncratic word use. Thought processes were grossly intact, though he tended to be moderately tangential, and also repeated himself with modest frequency. He was a good historian. Affect was stable, spontaneous, and appropriately reactive. Eye contact was well maintained. He evidenced good social skills. Regarding test-taking behavior, he attended well to tasks, gave forth what appeared to be an optimal effort, and did not become unduly frustrated in response to apparent failure (in spite of occasionally uttering mild expletives). He did appear to become noticeably tired toward the end of a moderately lengthy test session (three hours), though this did not appear to impact significantly upon his performance. Rapport was easily maintained. The resultant data are viewed as valid and reliable.

Bearing in mind that neuropsychological findings are not definitive, these results are none the less suggestive of globally moderate impairment. This implicates psychomotor and cognitive speed, mental flexibility and "tracking," cognitive fluency (both verbal and figural), visual-spatial constructional and perceptual skills, executive planning-organization, visual concentration/"vigilance," and abstract reasoning/

novel problem-solving. Per the latter, he is somewhat concrete and slow to "catch on" when engaged in trial-error learning-problem solving endeavors. He does not benefit consistently or efficiently from feedback as a means of modifying his responses, once his initial responses have proven unsuccessful. Rather, he tends to be somewhat inflexible, and somewhat perseverative in his response pattern . . .

In practical terms, Mr. Wehle appears to be able to function reasonably satisfactorily on a daily basis in a somewhat structured/supportive environment. However, he may continue to require assistance in more complex activities, e.g., of a financial nature. Also, his problem-solving skills are clearly impaired, and he should not be expected to understand abstract/complex in unfamiliar subject matter. He will need extra time and support in terms of problem-solving when confronted with tasks or situations that contain even a modicum of complexity. He certainly should not resume driving at this time, or likely in the near future. His visual status may need to be monitored. His performance on various visual graphic tasks actually was suggestive of somewhat greater tendencies to "neglect" stimuli in the left visual field. In any case, this might be monitored, possibly via contact with an occupational therapist. I would also recommend that he continue with speech/language/cognitive therapy. Hopefully, with time, this might facilitate improved attentional/information processing capability, among other things . . .

Lastly it may help to re-examine this gentleman neuopsychologically in approximately six months. This is deferred to his physicians and his treating clinicians.

Friday, February 20, 2009
Journal

Pete is better in so many ways—but there are still things that I notice. Last night he woke up very early in the morning and said me, "I gah go botrm." He can say, "I have to go to the bathroom," very clearly, but it seems to take considerable effort and concentration. His default language setting is often a sort of slurred approximation of the intended message.

He also has difficulty with memory, reasoning, and understanding. I'm sure in time it will improve, but we don't know how much.

Monday, March 2, 2009
Notes from Pete's Speech Therapy Session:
Ask O.T. to help with visual field, especially on the left

Possibly some psychological counseling to help deal with "things"
Slurred speech–practice exaggerating articulation
Learning how to live again . . .

Tuesday, March 3, 2009 (Square Root Day)
Journal

It shows up in little things. He drives once or twice, and I notice that he overshoots our driveway, coming in over the curb. He goes through two checks before he is able to write the third one correctly. Sometimes he takes half of his pills in the little cubicle of his pill sorter, leaving the rest. He picks up a book to read and sets it down again after two or three minutes. He can't focus.

No big deal, any of these things. I just notice.

Pete remembers . . .

The Shoreline Wellness Center is a beautiful, new facility only ten minutes from home. The rehab department is adjacent to the general workout area, so when we went, Pam would exercise on the other side, and check in on me once in a while. When I was in cardiac rehab, everybody was really helpful. Dr. Dotson was on site in case of an emergency. It was good to know that she was there if I had any serious problems.

The staff was great. There was Fred–a friendly, funny guy. I wise cracked with him a lot. He could dish it out and take it in. I asked about his kids–he has four, a houseful. Pam gave him her children's CD. Jamie and Diane were there too, recording what I was doing and cheering me on. It was a jovial bunch. We did a lot of joking and laughing. It made it more fun.

First I had to do a stress test. Then Fred had me start slowly. I stretched at the stretching station and then I walked the track with a heart monitor on, starting with one rotation and gradually building up. I would signal to them as I passed by, "One, two," eventually getting up to "Ten."

I did a real light routine on the treadmill–zero level, not very far. Then they started me on other machines–arm machine, peddling machine, etc., so there was a routine. They had me drink some water, then work another machine. I was asked how many calories I had burned and what level of exertion was required–strong, middle, or light.

They took my blood pressure before I began, between machines and at the end of each session. I got to a point where they put me on weights. Fred encouraged me to do a little bit more each day.

I came home exhausted every time and went to sleep right away. After being hospitalized for so long I was weak, and I didn't like that, so I really pushed myself. It was hard work, but every day I got a little stronger. Considering what I'd been through, this was a piece of cake.

I liked talking with the other people in rehab. Everybody had had surgery or a stent or something. I was the first person they had there who had a heart transplant, so they watched me closely. If I was tired, they told me to stop. I was never in any problems physically.

Emotionally, I accepted what I had to do because I knew it was for the best. I knew I had to do it even if I didn't want to. I looked around and saw people there, generally older than me, and I was grateful that I was able to do what I did. If I had been older, I might not have been able to do it. If they can do it, I can do it, I thought.

It was good to see the same people every day. Fred, Jamie, Diane and I used to laugh a lot. I really liked the people there. I never thought of quitting. It gave me something to do—out the door activity, which was good.

E-mail, Tuesday, March 10, 2009

Marty—

We're settling in a little bit at a time, but we're far from organized. Pete is making good progress, and for the first time in a long time I am beginning to hope again for his full recovery. He is getting stronger cognitively and physically. Thanks be to God . . .

I'm coping okay. Being half-unpacked is unsettling, but I'm trying to just let it be. I hope Pete will be able to kick in with a little more help around the house as time goes by. Right now, I do it all, and it's a bit much.

I'm really looking forward to seeing you and John too. It was wonderful to have that time with you in Sedona. Michigan misses you. Take care.

Love,

Pam

E-mail Reply, Tuesday, March 10, 2009—Sedona

Pam,

Thanks for the update Pam. Are you sure Peter is doing what he could right now to help you? Remember our talk about that? If it's too much for you right now, he needs to know that and figure out with you a good approach that lets him do what he can do, since every little bit helps. Right? You have a soft heart, and I am guessing you tend to take on a bit more than you should, out of love, of course. But remember my psychology professor's sage advice: "If you overfunction, others will underfunction." You know!

. . . I am so glad you are able to hope to see Peter fully recovered. I will join you in that vision.

Love,

Marty

Thursday, March 19, 2009

Journal

This business of loading up the pill sorters has become a sort of ritual for me. I have a routine. Once a week I pull out of the closet two grocery recycle bags of medications, one for each of us. I have two grids I made up that show which pills are taken upon waking, at breakfast, at lunch, at dinner and at bedtime; the dosage; the color and shape of the pills; and the purpose. I go through the list for Pete, getting all the little pills in the right compartments. I make a note of whatever I need to reorder. Then I do mine; I have almost as many as he does. It takes a while.

Today I had Pete watch me do his meds. We went line by line on his grid, as I showed him how I do it. I don't think he can do it by himself yet, as he gets confused when it comes to any task that has several steps, but I'm hoping in time he will get it.

New thought: The lake is stunning this morning, steely blue with whitecaps rushing in from the Southwest. I'm so glad we'll be home for the first few days of spring.

March 31, 2009

Journal

I'm 62 today! Eligible for Social Security. Thank God. I do.

Saturday, April 4, 2009

Journal

There are definite gains—and definite deficits. I do think Pete is improving, but it is agonizingly slow—probably more so for him than for me.

For example, when we went to Panera for coffee, Pete picked up his paper cup and tried to put on the sleeve that prevents your hand from getting too hot holding the cup. He tried and tried, and finally gave up, saying, "It doesn't fit." He couldn't figure out that he was holding the sleeve upside down.

We have agreed that he will do the dishes—the one thing, so far, that he will do to help me around the house. Yesterday he rinsed and put two or three items in the dishwasher and then went into the other room. I asked him if he was done. He said, "Oh, is there more?" I honestly do not think he left the rest of the dishes in the sink intentionally. He *wants* to "pull his weight," as he says, but he kind of gets lost in the doing.

I find myself in the awkward position of having to remind him to do things many times a day:

"Would you mind picking up your clothes in the bathroom and putting them in the hamper?"

"Could you please bring your dirty dishes back to the kitchen?"

"Did you take your noon meds?"

In some ways it's like working with a child. I don't like taking the mom role with him, but sometimes it seems necessary. I'm sure he doesn't want to evolve into a spoiled kid whose "mother" does everything for him—and I certainly don't want that for myself, either.

Yesterday he tried to make some calls to settle a pension issue. He kept getting the wrong number, over and over again. Finally, he turned and asked, "Is it me?"

Most of the time we laugh it off. We reaffirm how far he has come. But still—it must be hard. And, I'll admit, when I'm in a hurry or really tired, it can be exasperating for me.

Saturday, April 11, 2009

Journal

There has been a lot going on lately—some of it around me, and a lot of it within me. All week we've had workers here from dawn to dusk, putting on a new roof. The sounds of the generator, the pounding, and the ladders clanking on the side of the house have been our constant companions.

With the new roof, we had to empty the attic, so we are surrounded by boxes and bins and there is a ton of dust, settling and floating through the air and from there into my allergic body. Every time we pull down the collapsable attic door in the hallway ceiling upstairs, clouds of dusty little fibers sprinkle down and find new homes, gradually spreading throughout the house on our shoes and pant legs. We hired a young man to come in and clean out the old insulation in the attic, some of which was probably installed in 1927 when the house was built. It's all loose and very dusty. He and a couple of his friends filled dozens of bags with the crud, and there is still more to go.

Now it's Easter weekend, so we are left with the mess—and the formidable task of cleaning up afterwards. It's a bit overwhelming. No—let me reframe that—It's just something to do. It's just something to do. Pete did the dishes last night. That helped. We can do this.

I'm concerned about Pete. The doc changed his medications because his tacro (Prograf) levels were very high. Pete has very little appetite, and he sleeps much of the day. He has missed a couple of cardio rehab sessions because he was just too tired to go. The thing I worry about the most is his mind. Sometimes he has no recall whatsoever of things we have talked about. Is he just not paying attention, or does he have some significant gaps in his gray matter? Will he eventually return to his former intellectual level?

E-mail, Tuesday, April 14, 2009

Debra Dear—

Things are moving along here. Pete is more "with it" cognitively and is getting stronger physically. There are still some gaps in his mental processing—primarily problem solving and memory, as far as I can tell. When I think of how he was just three months ago, though, it's clear he has made good progress.

I know this is a tough time for him, because he can't do much. He says, "I should be working," but there is no way he could do that now. He has difficulty helping with simple things (dishes, dusting) around the house. Of course he says that's because it's not in his DNA! (Is it in mine? Yours?)

Most of my time is spent in taking care of his needs—meds, appointments, cardiac rehab, meals, keeping the house afloat, medical bills, etc. I do squeeze in a little time now and then to write, and I've been able to sing a couple of times at area churches.

Spiritually I waver between a vague sort of fatigue and a fervent commitment to what I consider to be a sacred trust. My role as Pete's caregiver is the top priority right now, and I know there will be more time for me as we progress. We had a "date" Saturday night, which was really nice—just a meal out and a movie—but it felt more like husband and wife than patient and caregiver—and that was good for us.

How are things going for you? I'd love to know. I look forward to a big hug and a conversation with you one of these days. Sunday I sang at the Unity Church in South Bend and a very kind woman whose name I've already forgotten came up and introduced herself as part of the "Debra Basham Group." She was so happy to meet us after having read all my postings that you so kindly passed on to the fellowship gang. I saw tears in her eyes. It was a very sweet encounter. We never know how far the ripples extend, do we!

Love and Blessings,

Pam

Journal

On Healing and Dying

This is how I see it: The body's natural desire to heal is evidence of God's presence within. We get a cut, we bleed, the blood clots, a scab forms and eventually it all heals, sometimes with a scar of remembrance. A woman goes through childbirth, stretching her body in incredible ways, and then afterwards, the body goes back to, if not exactly what it was before, at least a state that can be considered "normal." I had thyroid cancer more than three decades ago, and here I am, alive and kicking. Pete went through incredible trauma to his body and now he walks, talks, and functions, with the heart of another person beating inside his chest. It's a miracle. It's grace. Our bodies want to heal. That healing impetus is God within.

Before all of this happened with Pete, I used to think of the God presence within as a spark or a flame. I envisioned it somewhere in the area of the heart, or perhaps the third eye, between the eyebrows. Now, when I think of our body's natural tendency to heal, it seems to me that God's presence must be there in every cell of the body—not just a spark, but a luminous, pulsing presence. God within, and all around us too. It's mind boggling. It's awe-inspiring.

What about those who don't heal? What about those who experience chronic illness or incapacitating injuries? What about Elfi, who can't see? People with Alzheimer's disease? Inoperable cancer? Quadriplegics? I think that there are things each of us needs to experience in order to evolve in our consciousness or in order to facilitate another person's growth. Perhaps Pete needed to be convinced of his own worthiness, or of the presence of unconditional love. He experienced both of these things in very dramatic ways when he was in the hospital. Perhaps he is meant to help others by encouraging organ donation. We don't know yet. I do know that his crisis and recovery led me to a much deeper, fuller awareness of the divine presence—so—who knows? Maybe part of the reason was to help me evolve.

Because of our limited perspectives, it may be difficult for us to grasp any possible purpose for one's pain and suffering, but that doesn't mean the purpose isn't there. I can only say that everything happens for a reason. We may not grasp that reason now, or even in this lifetime, but what happens serves a purpose. Argue science with me if you wish, but some things can't be measured and weighed, tested and proven. Believing that is what I call "faith."

Then comes the big part: The value or damage in any experience depends upon the response. Illness and pain can make a person bitter and defeatist, or it can bring out courage, faith, and the determination to move beyond the physical to create a life worth living. This is a huge step in the evolution of consciousness, and it's a choice. Every day it is a choice. Every moment.

And what of those who die? What about the child who dies of cancer? The young father killed in a drive-by shooting? Women who die in childbirth? How can we make sense of deaths that seem to be random, premature, or pointless? Again, our perspectives are limited. I like to think of the difference between the eagle, soaring high above the prairie, and the ant, busily carrying crumbs somewhere, far down below. Maybe we are ants, unable to grasp it all from our perspective. It can be very challenging for those left behind to imagine how the passing of someone they love can have meaning or purpose . . . but it does.

As for those who pass—I feel that each being leaves this earth plane at just the right time—when the purpose for being here is fulfilled, when the time is right to move forward to another dimension. We don't really die, of course. We continue. We move on. And when we shed our earthly bodies, that God presence leaves the cells of that body, and, like a heavenly passport, travels with us to the New.

CHAPTER TWENTY

Choosing, Losing, and Love

"Between stimulus and response there is a space. In that space lies our freedom to choose our response. In those choices lie our growth and our happiness."
—Stephen Covey

Update Saturday, May 2, 2009 at 8:39 a.m.

A FEW DAYS AGO I was thinking that it might be time to sign off from the CarePages. Pete had finished his program of cardio rehab and was about to be discharged from speech/cognitive therapy and occupational therapy as well. He started voice lessons to get ready to perform again. He was making jokes and complaining about the economy. In short, things were settling down into a new normal.

There were some things I was still concerned about, though. He seemed very tired and napped most of the day. He had almost no appetite, and some nausea that didn't seem to go away. Sometimes just the smell of food made him queasy. He lost a precious 12 pounds and was down to 148 or so.

Then on Tuesday of this week, the left side of his neck started hurting–*really* hurting. Sometimes it got so bad he would cry out in pain. Tylenol didn't seem to help much at all. By Thursday he was finding it impossible to sleep because of the pain. Then the welts appeared. Friday morning the left side of his neck was red and covered with dime-sized blisters. He has shingles.

It just doesn't seem fair. (Of course, then, I am reminded of Wendy's fourth grade teacher who said, "If life were fair, we wouldn't need wheelchairs.") Pete is in some serious pain. Yesterday morning I packed a bag in case we would have to go to the hospital in Ann Arbor again, as a nurse had hinted on the phone. Our dear friend and family doctor, Tom, made a house call around noon. He conferred by telephone with a doctor from the cardiac team at U. of M. Fortunately, he convinced the cardiac doc that we could treat Pete here at home. Pete began his medication regime for the virus yesterday afternoon. He had insisted that he would *not* go back the hospital. I knew it would be hard to persuade him otherwise. He's had enough of that.

Yesterday afternoon Tom came back to the house and gave me a shingles immunization. One of us has to be healthy. Throughout the day, I was reminded about Lauren Lane Powell's message last summer: "Why is this happening for me?"

This weekend I was supposed to attend an annual convention in Grand Rapids for The Delta Kappa Gamma Society International, a society of key women educators. I am a member, and was slated to sing at three different times and was in charge of selling some items to benefit a grant fund. With two phone calls and the help of loving, loyal friends in the organization, I was able to pull out of the commitment gracefully and hopefully with no hard feelings. It was hard to cancel on something I enjoy so much, though.

Instead of conventioning, I puttered around the house a lot, keeping busy–trying to put things right, I suppose. I had to do *something*. Once, as I passed Pete's recliner in the living room, where he was resting, I heard him mumbling something, so I moved a little closer. He was saying over and over, "Why is this happening for me?" Another mountain. Here we go. He does have the will, though, to fight. Last night he told me, "I don't want to say goodbye." Holding back the tears as best as I could, I assured him that he wasn't dying, and that we will have many years together.

This is hard. Please, once again, pray for us. We are so grateful for your ongoing support. The power of prayer is—well, it's everything.

Love,

Pamela

P.S.—In case you're interested—I didn't know much about shingles, but I've heard horror stories about how painful it can be. This is what I've learned from reading on the Internet and talking with the doctor: (Skip this part if you're squeamish or if you already know about Shingles. I haven't told Pete about most of this yet. He has enough to deal with right now.)

Shingles is caused by the same virus that causes chickenpox. The virus can live, inactive, in the body for many years. If it becomes active again, it can result in shingles. Having a weakened immune system due to anti-rejection meds has made Pete more vulnerable to the virus. The shingles rash usually lasts up to 30 days. It's typical for the rash to occur on only one side of the body. For most people, the pain associated with the rash lessens as it heals.

Shingles has the potential to be serious. This pain can range from moderate to severe, and vary from tenderness of the skin to a burning, throbbing, shooting or stabbing pain. For some people, it may lead to long-term pain that can last for months, or even years. As you get older, your risk for long-term nerve pain may increase. For many people, the pain is so severe that the touch of soft clothing or even a slight breeze against the skin can be painful. Other potential complications include scarring, bacterial skin infections, decrease or loss of vision or hearing, paralysis on one side of the face, and muscle weakness. We hope and pray and affirm that Pete will have none of this.

---

37 Messages Posted Saturday, May 2-4, 2009

I believe this too will pass and the strength and fortitude of your faith will lead you through. I pray that the pain lessens and the medicine assists with the shingles. I know this to be true.

Love,

Barbara Corcoran

Wow, just when you thought you were out of the woods! Okay—here's another affirmation. The ego loves to answer questions: "What are the infinite possibilities that Pete will get through shingles with ease, joy, glory and little discomfort?"

Shirley Pressnell

. . . I see healing happening in others because of your journey in ways that only your journey can provide . . . I have to tell you, part of me is pissed off at a Universe that allows this to keep happening "for" you. Then I forgive . . . again.

Love always,

Lauren Lane Powell

"Are you encountering difficult challenges?
That means you're ready for great things."
–Ralph Marston

Tuesday, May 5, 2009
Journal

We're back into patient/nurse mode again, and we're both more than a little tired of this. Pete keeps saying he's sorry, as if he chose to get sick. He feels bad about me missing the convention this weekend. And–it's only ten days before I planned to go to Virginia. I probably won't be able to go. That will be sad. Very sad.

On the other hand, I just can't think of leaving him here without adequate care–that means me. He needs me. This is where I need to be, both to help him, and for my own peace of mind. Right now I'm waiting to hear from the pharmacy that his prescription for Vicodin has been called in and prepared. He is so miserable!

I miss Pete. He's here, but he's out of it most of the time. He slurs his speech again, and sometimes I can hardly hear him. He is eating a bit now, though. Our neighbor, Karen, brought over a hot apple pie, which we ate with gusto. Comfort food.

May 12, 2009

Journal

To go to Virginia or not to go to Virginia . . .

I don't know. I don't want Pete to feel abandoned—or to go if he really needs me here. I *do* want to go because of the creative juices that always flow for me at the gathering, and for the wonderful friends there . . . and I could use a break. But then, Pete could use a break even more. I think I've decided not to go on Friday—but maybe later, depending on how he feels.

Shingles is nasty. Painful. All Pete does is hurt and sleep, except when I can coax him to eat a little. He weighed in at 142 this morning. I joke about how there are much easier ways to lose pounds! Pete is depressed. Of course he's depressed. He's been very, very sick for almost a year now. That's a long time. He was just about to turn the corner and join the real world again when this shingles thing erupted.

I've heard that a man's identity is more tied up with his work than a woman's. I know that's a sweeping generalization, but there is at least some truth to it—and I think it's true for Pete. He's worked all of his life, and then suddenly there is no work, there is no paycheck, there is no feeling of usefulness. He went from being top salesman on his team to having to depend on a nurse to wipe his butt. How demoralizing is that?

He wants to work again. He took a one-night class on doing voice-overs, and he thinks he would like to do that. He could work from home, and we already have the equipment he would need. He did some voice-over work years ago for a radio station in Indiana. With his warm voice and acting experience, I think he'd be very good.

Pete depends on me to prepare meals for him, to remind him to take his meds, to get groceries, to pay bills—As Nancy Lou said, "You're doing all the work for both of you. No wonder you're tired." That is true, and I know Pete doesn't like it. He would like to do more. He's just so tired, and so depressed that he sleeps and sleeps and sleeps.

How can I leave him to go to Virginia when he's like this?

Tuesday, May 19, 2009

Journal

Some people think that I am this sweet, loving wife and caregiver who has sacrificed everything to be at her beloved husband's side as he moves through his pain and fatigue to–perhaps–recovery. Sometimes I'm like that. Today I don't feel like that at all. I feel disgruntled and down. I think it's burnout.

I have heard, "Take care of yourself," about five million times by now. I try to do that, but I often find myself at the short end of a very long stick, wondering how I can enjoy the things I used to enjoy and still be there for Pete.

I was planing to leave for Virginia last Friday. I'm part of a songwriting group that meets the week before Memorial Day every year. We call ourselves the "Omega Survivors," giving credit to Jimmie Dale Gilmore's songwriting workshops at Omega Institute for Holistic Studies in upstate New York, where the whole thing began. We gather at an old 4-H camp near Charlottesville, Virginia, to focus on songwriting, collaboration, and renewing our friendships. The week culminates in a concert, usually featuring songs we have written that week. I packed everything up–tent, sleeping bag, guitar, song ideas, thesaurus, maps, directions, books on CD, etc. I had a huge pile in the entryway, waiting to be loaded into the car.

I arranged for friends to check in on Pete, and had a schedule of "Pete's Pals," all of whom seemed delighted to be able to step up and help. I had another friend who was going to call Pete five times a day to remind him to take his medications.

Thursday, Jim Gleason arranged to take Pete to a movie in the afternoon. Pete got up and showered. Then he called to me from upstairs. I went to the staircase to see what he wanted. "You go to the movie with Jim. I'm too tired." He was trembling, bracing himself on the banister. "I'm just not up to it."

Pete doesn't get out of bed at all without my urging him on. Some days he stays in his pajamas all day. He doesn't seem to get hungry at all, and I just knew that he wouldn't eat, even with all the provisions I had stocked up for him. He is down to 141 pounds.

I was awake until after three in the morning, struggling with the decision, and no matter how I look at it, the answer is the same–*I'm not going to Virginia.*

I'm incredibly sad about this. I needed this—a little break, some time away. It's been almost a year now of 24/7 caregiving.

Pete encouraged me to go, saying he would be just fine, but in the night, I kept thinking about the what-ifs. What if Pete had to go back into the hospital? I would be a two-day drive away. What if he forgot to take his medications, or accidentally took the wrong ones? What if he didn't eat? He's just skin and bones right now. He gets dizzy when he stands up. What if his depression gets worse and worse, and he thinks I have abandoned him? If I did go, I would be so worried about him, I don't think I could enjoy myself. The what-ifs are just too big. *I'm not going to Virginia.* Sigh.

I keep thinking of all the things Pete has given up. He's had it much worse than I have, no contest. Of course, he didn't have a choice. I do, and I choose to stay. He needs me. I'm really down. Whining. Good grief, I'm whining. I don't like myself like this, but this is where I am. God help me get out of here!

> *"Life is unstable. Get used to it."*
> *–Christiane Northrup*

Update Friday, May 22, 2009 at 5:37 p.m.

Well, it's back to our old home away from home, University of Michigan Hospital. Pete's cardiologist wanted to see him because his case of shingles was going on too long and—well, getting out of control. We came in this morning and Pete was admitted to the hospital again.

The docs think we will only be here "a few days," whatever that means. He will be given IV antibiotics, which should speed up his recovery. He's miserable right now with lots of blistery lesions that are extremely painful to the touch all over the left side of his neck, jaw, cheek, shoulder, chest and upper arm. He's extremely tired too.

I am hopeful that this more aggressive treatment will help him to bounce back. They will be able to ease his pain with more powerful pain killers here too.

I'm doing okay. I feel well, and I'm glad I didn't go to Virginia as planned. The toughest thing is that Pete's younger son, Sean, graduates from high school tomorrow—and we'll miss that. Sigh. Ah well, life goes on, and we're grateful for that!

Much love to you all from both of us—

Pete and Pam

---

35 Messages Posted Friday, May 22-26, 2009

Last night, when holding you in sacred space, I saw a loving angel gently minister to you by lovingly applying a cooling golden salve to Pete's body, covering all of him with golden healing and holy medicine from heaven. The two of you were surrounded by a gentle golden light and nestled in a comforting healing space, lifted and carried by grace through yet another challenge.

With much love,

Joan Van Houten

Saturday, May 23, 2009

Journal

University of Michigan Hospital, sixth floor, Area B, Room 6124. There's a sign on the door warning pregnant women not to enter without first speaking to a nurse. The left side of Pete's neck is swollen and red, and he has crusty lesions in his beard and scalp. There are angry-looking red welts about a half inch in diameter rising out of the skin on the left side of his shoulders, chest, back, neck, upper arm, all following the affected nerve pathways. That's what shingles do.

He is in a lot of pain. The night before we came here he whimpered all night in his sleep. And he is down to skin and bones. Yesterday he weighed in at 139, dripping wet. When he looked in the mirror, he broke down and cried. I overheard the doctor refer to him as "anorexic." The flesh on his arms sags and wrinkles like my mother's did when she was eighty.

The infectious disease doc who admitted Pete yesterday said that he would probably only be here for a few days. It's Memorial Day weekend. Scenes of barbecues, beaches, family get-togethers and traffic conditions flash across the

TV suspended from the wall. It's another holiday in the hospital. In about an hour, Pete's son, Sean, will graduate from high school. We just learned that he is salutatorian of his class and he'll be giving a speech at the ceremony. Pete keeps murmuring, "I'm sorry, Sean." He *so* wanted to be there! He is about as depressed as I've ever seen him.

A young man came in to draw blood early this morning. He was handsome in a Latin or Italian sort of way, with a mass of thick black hair and deep, intense brown eyes. We got to talking, and he told us that he had been born with hemophilia, and had spent seven years in and out of this hospital. He'd also had both hips replaced here. Working here is how he gives back. He told Pete that there were times that he just wanted to give up and chuck it all, but he didn't. "I tell you, man, you've gotta stay positive. That's what's gonna save you. There's a reason you're alive. God has a plan for you." His parting shot was, "God bless you both."

In *Conversations with God, Book I,* I've read that we all have the potential to be messengers. God, Spirit, Creator–whatever name you want to assign to the great source energy–works through us. And so here was this young man, drawing Pete's blood, and leaving in his casual conversation a profound, yet simple message for both of us to absorb. I wonder if he knows he's a messenger.

Update Sunday, May 24, 2009 at 2:04 p.m.

Pete is resting quietly with a little help from morphine. He's starting to itch, so being able to sleep through that is a blessing. Oh, and good news–the doc thinks we may be able to go home tomorrow. We shall see. Many of Pete's lesions are crusting over. At this point he is contagious to the touch. The good news is that his appetite is picking up a little. It's so good to see him eat! I bought some smaller pants for him, as the ones he has were falling off him. His waist is only 31 inches. I had to go to the boys' section of the store to find a belt small enough!

I went to the Unity Church of Ann Arbor this morning, and had a warm welcome from several folks who remembered me. One was a very special fan of mine who tells me she listens to my CDs all the time. We celebrated her 91st birthday this morning.

I'm glad we're here for now. Pete's getting great care and good, strong meds. This morning, thinking of the work by Dr. Emoto of Japan, I wrote LOVE and HEALING on Pete's water cup. He'll get through this.

Thank you for your prayers. They matter. Big time.

Love,

Pam

---

19 Messages Posted Sunday, May 24-25, 2009

Just wanted you to know that the Omega Survivors' crew down in Charlottesville, Virginia, from which I just returned, has shared your situation, evoked you both in celebratory remarks, and sent you all the love and prayers and transformational vibes we were capable of!

Love and best wishes,

Jeep Rosenberg

We prayed for you this morning together with the chaplains and during church. You are so loved and supported, and we are affirming that Pete's innate health and wholeness is manifesting itself very quickly and thoroughly. We are seeing you both sitting on the Big Lake, watching the sunset with great delight in perfect health.

And for you Pam, a huge dose of Amazing Grace to see you over another bump on the road.

So much love,

Marty Rienstra

Come home soon to continue making beautiful music together.

Love,

Michael Helms and Sue Bensinger

E-mail, Sunday, May 24, 2009

Hi Dad and Pam,

I just read that you have gone back to the hospital. Are you still there? I hope you are getting over the shingles as quickly as possible. How are you doing? I got your latest care package the other day. It made me very happy. Thank you. I already finished the macaroni and cheese, Oreos, and pretzels.

The Fig Newtons and Goldfish are next. I'm waiting to get some friends together to make the pizza.

I can't stop thinking about coming back home in August. I can't wait to see you. I have been a little lonely here. Recently I have been watching Youtube videos about Japan on Sachiyo's computer. I saw some about World War II. Really awful things happened. It is strange that I am here now in Japan and playing music when 60 years ago there was a war going on between our two countries.

I miss you. Daiji ni suru . . . Take good care.

Lots of love,

Paul

Update Monday, May 25, 2009 at 8:10 p.m.

Dear Ones,

Again I am lifted up by your wonderful postings. Thank you so much! It helps to keep us going. (I hit a wrong key there, and typed: "It helps to keep pus going." Well, the pus *is* going–and that's a good thing!)

The doctors here in Acute Care have decided to keep Pete for another day or two. They want to be sure that no new lesions form and that the pain is under control. A couple of times today Pete picked at a crusted over-spot and then cried out, bending over in agony. Obviously he needs a) a little more time here and b) to stop scratching. That's hard, because the lesions itch something awful.

We took a little wheelchair stroll down to the courtyard this afternoon and had some ice cream to observe the holiday. Later, when Pete was watching a war movie on TV, I saw him tear up. He's such a tenderhearted soul. I'm sure he was thinking about his father, who served in WW II. Now his son is living in Japan, playing in a symphony orchestra, and dating a Japanese girl. Don't you love the symmetry, the irony of that?

We both keep trying to focus on "Why is this happening for us?" rather than "to us," and looking forward to what is in store for which we have been more than adequately prepared. I know he will come through this and move on to great health and happiness, and I'll be there, sharing it with him.

Blessings to you all on this day when we remember those who have gone before . . . and we are so blessed by the ones we love who are here, in the flesh, today.

Love,

Pamela

"The Obstacle is the path."
–Zen Proverb

Tuesday, May 26, 2009

Journal

The doctor left the decision to Pete–go home today or tomorrow. His antibiotics were changed from IV to oral form, and his pain medication was adjusted. If Pete stays another day they can monitor how he does with that. Pete opted to stay until tomorrow.

Today, Tuesday, is calm. Pete is twitching and making little noises in his sleep, busy in some other dimension, I suppose. He seems better, though. We didn't find any new lesions this morning, and the old ones are crusting over. He asked me to put some more Calamine lotion on, so the itching is still bothersome. He takes one medication for pain and another for itching. I'm grateful that he can sleep so much. It makes the time pass for him.

Update Friday, May 29, 2009 at 11:34 a.m.–South Haven

Dear Ones,

We are home again, enjoying the lake. Pete's Pals have gotten organized and are bringing us meals. What a blessing that is! Thanks so much to you, wonderful friends!

Pete is still very tired and sleeps a lot, but most of the lesions from his shingles are crusted over and falling off–a good sign. He's still contagious to the touch right now, but becomes less so each day.

I can only imagine the full range of emotions that have gone through this sweet man's mind. Next week it will be a year since his heart went into failure and our lives changed dramatically. Now he is redefining who he is, what his goals are, and what he wants to do for the rest of his life. In that sense, it's an awesome opportunity, although it doesn't always feel that way.

Love,

Pamela

---

22 Messages Posted Friday, May 29, 2009

Dear Pam and Pete,

. . . I'll think of you on your porch, enjoying the sweetness of the mornings and the beauty of the sunsets.

Much love to you both,

Sharon Jensen

Friday, May 29, 2009–South Haven

Journal

Before we went to the hospital this time, Pete was in such incredible pain he said, "Now, if I die, you do know where the life insurance papers are, right?"

I knew he was going to get over the shingles, but *he* didn't know it. He thought all of this suffering was going to take him out of this life. I tried to reassure him, but I could see the resignation in his face. I wanted to cry for him, but I was beyond tears.

For me, it was a relief to be at the hospital. I knew he would get the usual excellent care there, and the guesswork of caring for him at home would be over. At the hospital I was his coach, his cheerleader, his wife. At home, I'm everything, and sometimes I'm just flying by the seat of my pants.

We're back home now, and Pete is much better than he was a week ago. He is still very tired, and sleeps a lot, but the lesions are smaller and crusting over. There are some raw spots on his neck where he has picked at them. I hope they don't scar. He can't seem to keep his hands off his neck. When he gets up from bed, the sheets look like they are full of crumbs, but it is really dead skin and scabs.

Meanwhile, I am preparing for several gigs. Sunday there is a "Peace Pizazz" at Bronson Park in Kalamazoo. It's a peace event for children, an alternative to the Memorial Day observations. I will be singing my "Peace Canon" with the Covert Middle School Choir. I only rehearsed with them once, but they sounded great. I'll also sing a few other peace songs. Then Tuesday night I'll join several others to do a program for the local historical association. In a couple of weeks I'll be doing the music for a three-day conference on spirituality.

It feels good to be performing again. It makes me feel fully alive. There is a greeting card I found at Angel Valley that I framed and hung in our bedroom. It says, "May the song in your heart always touch the souls of those who surround you." This is my dream.

CHAPTER TWENTY ONE

Strange Wrapping Paper

"The transitory ups and downs are merely tiny threads in the overall fabric of your life. Each one ultimately adds to the richness of your experience."
–Ralph Marston

Monday, June 1, 2009
Journal

I AM GRATEFUL. Immensely, tremendously, fabulously, remarkably, wonder-fully grateful. Pete is here, getting stronger and healthier every day. He is right here, by my side. Sometimes I wake in the dark of the night and just reach over to touch him in his sleep. He is here. I am beyond happy. I used to think I would live alone into my senior years, but no, Pete is here. I am happy. Thank you, God.

Wednesday, June 3, 2009

Journal

I've been trying to get things in order at home–to simplify, and let go of things I no longer need, want, or use. Digging into my closet in our bedroom I found a number of things that didn't need to be squeezed in there. Way back in a corner was an ancient pink globe for a converted oil lamp that once hung in my bedroom in another house, another time. It went to the attic. There was a box of old clothes to be worn when painting . . . and then there was the mink coat my grandmother gave Mom, and Mom left behind when she passed.

I smiled. Grandma had married a second time after Grandpa died, and her second husband, a retired postmaster whom we called Grandpa Edwin, doted over her lovingly. I remember a day when I visited them and he said to me, "Doesn't my Mary look pretty today?" They were both in their eighties at the time, and Grandma basked in the glow of her husband's affection, something that had not been openly demonstrated in her first marriage. Grandpa Edwin gave her a mink wrap, an extravagance such as she had never known in all of her thrift shop years. She wore it to church proudly and treasured it until the day she passed.

The mink went to my mother then, and Mom wore it on occasion too, although wearing animal pelts was becoming politically incorrect. Today, there it was, hanging in the back of my closet. I won't wear it, but I couldn't just throw it out–it meant so much to Grandma. So I wrapped it lovingly in tissue paper, placed it in a box, and stowed it away for now.

What else shall I stow away? Give away? Hold on to?

Saturday, June 6, 2009

Journal

Pete and I decided to go to the "Celebrate Your Life Conference" in the Chicago area this weekend. There was an impressive lineup of presenters, and we both thought the spiritual focus might give us a lift. It turned out to be a remarkable weekend for both of us.

Internationally known psychic medium and author, James Van Praagh was the keynote speaker for one of the general sessions. I had read several of his books, but I hadn't seen him work in person, so I was excited. Pete was tired and opted to sleep this one out at the hotel.

James talked a bit about his life as a medium and then launched into his work. He spoke with several people in the crowd of–oh, over 1,000, I would say. Then he said, "Who is it that recently packed up her mother's fur coat and put it in a box." I froze. No one spoke up. Finally I stood. "That's you?" he asked.

"Yes," I said. "I wrapped it up and put it away last week."

"Okay," he said. "So this message is for you. I'm seeing a lot of clutter–books everywhere, on shelves, on tables, on the floor. Is that right?"

"Yes, unfortunately." I always seem to be reading four or five books at a time, and I have them all over the place.

"Clean up the clutter," he said. "It's too messy."

"I prefer to think of it as creative," I joked.

"Well, you may be very, very creative, but clutter can interfere with that. You have to give it space." He continued. "There are a lot of your mother's things around you. She's passed, right?"

"Yes, I live in her house."

"I'm seeing a lot of your mom's costume jewelry–boxes of it."

"Yes," I gulped.

"Who's Sara?"

"Sara is my brother's granddaugher."

"So Sara would be your mother's great granddaughter."

"Yes."

"Give the jewelry to Sara."

"I can do that," I said.

"I'm seeing some dishes–tannish, with a pattern around the edges."

"Sara's mother has those," I said, amazed. They were cream colored, with a gold wheat pattern around the edges. Grandma had given them to my mother, and I had passed them on to Wendy, Sara's mother.

"Your mother is very energetic, full of vitality and enthusiasm. There's lots and lots of love coming to you from her. She mentions your writing."

"I'm writing a book right now." I had already begun work on the book you are holding in your hands. The audience murmured. They were as impressed as I was. "This work you're writing–she says it's important for you to finish it. Sometimes you have a tendency to start things and then not finish. Is that right?"

"Uh, yes, sometimes."

"Clear away the clutter and finish what you're working on! That's what she's saying."

James also mentioned that there was another opportunity for Mom to get married before she married my father. I remember her telling me about that.

"Who had some kind of surgery in the neck area?"

"That would be me–thyroid cancer surgery about thirty years ago. My father had the same surgery the same day as I did, but his wasn't cancer."

James said thank you, the audience applauded, and he moved on to another person in the crowd. I sat down, shaking. Although I have long believed in mediumship and psychic phenomena and have worked with both myself, to receive such a wonderful message from my mother through someone of the stature of James Van Praagh was a huge thing for me. Wow.

"I think that all things are Spirit and are derived from Spirit.
When you look at life from that perspective,
it takes on a whole new meaning."
–James Van Praagh

Sunday, June 7, 2009
Journal

What a weekend! We went from workshop to workshop, hearing some of the great spiritual teachers of the day, absorbing wonderful concepts and being challenged to expand and deepen our awareness. Pete and I had a one-day workshop with Neale Donald Walsch, author of *Conversations with God* and other books.

We had a workshop with John Holland, who is also an internationally known psychic, medium, and author. He gave a message to both Pete and me that was very accurate, ending the session by asking Pete if he had seen a cardiologist lately.

Here are a few quotations from the conference that were meaningful to me:

"There is only the unfolding, the opening, ever happening. All else are thoughts–lollipops for the mind."
–Neale Donald Walsch

"Women don't really hit their stride until they're 60."
–Christiane Northrup

"You can either be there for everybody or be there for your soul–and which do you think better serves the world?"
–Cheryl Richardson

"You are an extension of God. You have a purpose here."
–Alan Cohen

"Do the next moment with all your heart and see what happens."
–Elizabeth Lesser

"You're never learning anything unless you're uncomfortable."
–Sonia Choquette

"If this issue were to last forever, what quality would I have to develop in order to have peace of mind?"
–Michael Beckwith

"Without intention, external events bounce you around."
–Michael Beckwith

"Pain is a gift in strange wrapping paper."
–Darren Weisman

"Until we forgive, we will keep giving our future up to the past."
–Robert Holden

Sunday, June 14, 2009

Journal

I was the music leader for the Coptic Conference at Olivet College this weekend. It was a great opportunity for me to share my music and its message with others. I love doing this kind of work, and the people there responded very positively. They've already invited me back for next year's conference.

The Coptics are a spiritual group dedicated to world peace and unity among peoples, religions and nations. They explore universal truths and personal empowerment and teach principles of balanced, positive and joyful living. I have been to two Coptic events over the years, and was pleased to be asked to sing at this conference.

A bonus for providing the music for the weekend was being able to have Pete come along and for both of us to be able to attend all the sessions, which ranged from Hopi and Mayan prophesies to Christian mystics, numerology, and spiritual power.

Pete was "conferenced out" by the time Sunday rolled around. He was exhausted and slept all the way home.

Monday, June 15, 2009

Journal

Three Breaths

At the Coptic Conference I learned from Rabbi Chava Bahle the following greeting from the Hebrew tradition:

When you greet a loved one, take three deep breaths, saying . . .

1. *I will not always be here.*
2. *You will not always be here.*
3. *That makes this moment especially precious.*

I love this.

Wednesday, June 17, 2009

Journal

Busy. Busy. Busy. Pete saw the opthamologist Monday to see if the sarcoidosis has affected his eyes. Apparently not. Tuesday we went to Ann Arbor for another heart catheterization, biopsy and an echocardiogram. That was a long day. Then there were dentist appointments on Wednesday. (When am I supposed to pay bills, do laundry, reorder meds, and clean house?) Company is coming this weekend. Whew!

I know I'm supposed to take care of myself, but . . . how? When?

> *"Sit in a comfortable, safe place and allow your attention to drift inward. Ask yourself, "If I let love lead me in this situation, where would I go and what would I do next?"*
> –John-Roger

Monday, June 22, 2009
Journal

He doesn't know how exhausted I am.

I'm hiding out at the South Haven Memorial Library—I've escaped. It's not quite a vacation, but it's away from the house. I don't think I have anything left to give. I am depleted.

It's very hot and muggy out. I don't do well in heat. It's cool here in the library, and nobody even knows I'm here, thank God. We have visitors this weekend—Phil, Katlyn, McKenzie, Sean, and not staying at the house but visiting, Wendy, Andy, Hannah, and Sara. I love them all—and I'm overwhelmed—not by them, but by life.

People ask me how Pete's doing. He's—okay. The shingles blisters have healed, although the skin left behind on his neck and shoulders is still an angry red. The results from last week's biopsy came in and his rejection level was zero. Zero is as good as it gets. All the labs came back normal. So why is he so exhausted?

He's tired all the time, and weak too. He's also depressed and frustrated because he can't do much of anything. He wants to work, play, mow the lawn, sing, go somewhere, but his body won't let him do very much before he just has to lay down and rest.

Every so often he says, "You'd be better off without me," or "I'm a burden to you." I try to convince him that I love him so much that I would be miserable and lonely without him, and besides, who would make me laugh? I remind him that he would give me the same care if it were me, instead of him. I mean it when I tell him these things. They are not lies, but I'm not sure that he believes them.

He shuffles when he walks, and his clothes hang on him like they do on the old men in nursing homes. He sighs. He cries—often and briefly. He's also emaciated. Naked, he looks like the pictures of survivors from Auschwitz. Truly. I'm not exaggerating. The scars from his open heart surgery and the tubes from the life support machines add to the effect. He has no appetite. I have to coax him to eat, and even then, I have minimal success.

So he gets frustrated, and so do I. He lays in bed or on the couch, and from there tries to get me to fix everything in his very small world. He doesn't know how exhausted I am.

"Where are my glasses?"

"Did the guy call about when he's going to repave the driveway? Why not?"

"Did you get an e-mail from Paul?"

"The lawn is a mess. When is Phil going to mow it?"

"There are sticks all over the yard from the storm. They need to be picked up."

"Where are my meds?"

"Did you call (fill in the blank)?"

This morning when I couldn't find the graduation card I had picked out for Sean, Pete mocked me, with a sort of fourth grade playground "Na-na-na-na-na-na," sound, which felt to me like he was saying that I was a lousy personal secretary. Suddenly I am back with my first husband, feeling abandoned, used, unappreciated and criticized. Same buttons, different man. Sean was right there, watching his father act like a jerk, treating me without respect.

"I quit!" was on the tip of my tongue, but of course I didn't say it. Of course.

For months now I have dipped deeply into reserves I didn't even know I had, and I am grateful that I have been able to be strong for Pete and do the things that needed to be done. But today—today I don't feel so strong. I'm scraping bottom. I feel tired, sad, and unappreciated.

I just want to go on vacation. It's been more than a year now, since I began doing everything for both of us, and I'm tired. I need a break.

A Message from Spirit:

Everything you need to know is written inside your soul. You just have to search for it and find it. You are the well of wisdom. Most people don't know that. They just bumble through life, learning from the outside as they go along. The greatest thing is to learn from the inside. That's where God dwells.

I get up.
I walk.
I fall down.
Meanwhile, I keep dancing.
–Rabbi Hillel

Update Tuesday, July 7, 2009

Just a quick note to let you all know that Pete is getting better. The long, painful battle with shingles is over except for some tightness in the skin where the lesions were. His energy is picking up, and he even drove the car by himself to the post office yesterday–his first solo venture in over a year.

I've had a few challenges myself lately. It seems that the stress of the past year has shown up in my body in the form of irritable bowel syndrome. I'm under a doctor's care, though, and I hope with reduced stress and a careful diet I will have this under control soon.

We are so blessed to be in our home overlooking the tranquility and beauty of Lake Michigan! We often have our meals on the front porch, watching the kite surfers and sailboats, listening to the laughter of little children playing in the water. It's a wonderful place for Pete to regain his strength and energy.

We both hope you are enjoying this beautiful summer and that your health is just perfect. We are immensely grateful for your love and support.

23 Messages Posted Tuesday, July 7, 2009

Dear Pam and Pete,
    What wonderful news! I was thrilled to see you both at the 4th of July parade on Saturday. To see Pete jump up and wave like a kid brought tears to my eyes . . .
Linda LaRocque

"If you have made up your mind to find joy within yourself,
sooner or later you will find it."
–Paramahansa Yogananda

Wednesday, July 8, 2009
Journal

Pete is coming back. He sings in the shower again. He makes jokes. He is still weak and *very* skinny, but he's coming back. Yesterday, twice, he suggested we go for a walk. We only went a few blocks each time, but it was a good sign. South Haven is beautiful this time of year, and a great place for walking.

This past couple of weeks I've been dealing with irritable bowel syndrome (IBS). I was in a lot of pain the first few days. Dr. Tom has me on a regimen now to try to get it under control, and I'm supposed to avoid stress. It's no wonder that the various crises of the past eleven months showed up in my body, this time in the colon. I guess you could say that I've had enough of this shit. I really did need a break. Caregiving is not a walk in the park.

After a few days of the IBS, when I felt like I had a cucumber up my rectum, and had cramping almost to the point of going to the emergency room, I got very discouraged. I didn't take my regular medications because I felt too sick. I fell apart in tears at the simplest things. I got really discouraged and depressed, wondering if this would be with me for the rest of my days. I couldn't do the things I wanted to do, the things I felt needed to be done. I hated being sick.

Then I thought of Pete. He's been sick for over a year now, unable to do most of the things *he* would have liked to do. He nearly died several times, and in living must have wondered if he would always be this weak, this "disabled." I've almost always believed that he would recover and resume a sense of normalcy in his life, but I know there were times when he couldn't hold that belief himself. Bless his precious new heart–he has suffered so! During my brief illness, I could glimpse how devastating it has been for him, and I have an even deeper respect for the strength and courage he has shown. I also find it easier to forgive when he is irritable. Good grief, it's understandable!

Twenty years ago this month I went to Detroit to hear Louise L. Hay speak. She has done a great deal of work with self-esteem, healing, and affirmations. This morning I ran across my notes from that lecture. I think perhaps I need to take them to heart, as it appears that I need healing too. Funny how sometimes our body has to get our attention in rather unpleasant ways.

Steps to Love Yourself

1. *Stop all criticism. Choose nurturing thoughts.*
2. *Don't scare yourself. Switch to a positive image whenever a negative one appears.*
3. *Be gentle, kind, and patient with yourself. Consider your life a garden. What will you grow?*
4. *Be kind to your mind. Gently change your thinking. Take time to relax. Tell yourself, "I love you. All is well." Meditate. Create positive visualizations.*
5. *Praise yourself. Allow yourself to accept good. Feel that you deserve all good. Ask yourself, "What meaning does your life have? How much are you willing to do to improve your life?"*
6. *Support yourself.*
7. *Be loving to your negative patterns. Let go of them lovingly. Use humor. Laugh.*
8. *Take care of your body. Do mirror work: Look into your own eyes in a mirror, say your own name, and tell yourself, "I love and accept you exactly as you are."*

For many years I've been working on these steps and others I have learned along the way. At this particular time it's good to have a reminder. I know that

I have to nurture myself if I am to be any good to anyone at all, and if I am to fulfill my purpose here. There are songs to be written and sung, this book to be written and shared, people to love and nurture, and joy to be embraced. I have to take care of myself so I can do these things.

Looking back . . .

Everything looked grim then, but it was temporary. Once I got some more rest, and things calmed down at home, I felt better, and my health improved. It took nearly two years after the transplant for me to feel the stress in my shoulders let up. (You could tell I was stressed out, because I seemed to be wearing my shoulders as earrings.)

Wednesday, July 15, 2009
Journal

I am concerned more about Pete's mind than the rest of him now. I think he is on the path to recovery in the physical sense. He has some trouble, though with thinking things through. Memory, reasoning, understanding, communicating–they all seem much more difficult for him now. Strokes are strange things.

It shows up in things like being able to follow basic directions. I still have to show him how to use the pause button on the TV remote, for instance. I think I've shown that to him at least five times. He doesn't remember. Or I'll tell him something that is, at least to me, important, and when it comes up again in conversation he doesn't remember it at all. That could be selective listening. Hard to tell.

Sometimes I have to explain to him what is going on because he doesn't pick up on nuance or implications.

Pete is fully able to function now, and will do all right at this level, but for his sake, I hope new synapses in his brain keep firing. I suppose I should be honest and admit that it's for my sake too.

Update Sunday, July 26, 2009 at 1:15 p.m.

Today is the one year anniversary of Pete's heart transplant! They say the first year is the hardest, so maybe now we can relax. I remember that night well. Many of you held us in prayer all night from wherever you were.

Thank you for your wonderful support during this most challenging year. Pete is now gaining weight and feeling stronger every day. He is more like his old self in every way. We are so very blessed!

Love,

Pam

Looking back, Pete says . . .

I'm changed from all I've been through. I realize that life is more than it seems. I know it. I respect people who have faith. I have faith too. I don't always say it, but I try to be it, to act from a place of integrity and forethought.

I have a sense that we don't die, and that I'm a part of everything. I used to think that you died and that was it, but I don't think so now. It's a beginning. I always believed there was something greater than me. It's awesome.

Grateful

I am so grateful
For the blessings in my life.
I am so grateful
For the blessings in my life.
The cup is full to overflowing.
Look at me, you'll see it's showing,
I'm so grateful, grateful, grateful,
I'm grateful,
Grateful for the blessings in my life.

©2005 Pamela Chappell

"Now, how may I serve?"
—Sal Sapienza

EPILOGUE

"If you touch a single soul, it's as if you changed the world."
–Old Hebrew Saying, as told by Sandy Feldman

THIS ACCOUNT OF Pete's heart transplant and our journey as we moved through this time has to end somewhere, and it seems appropriate for me to close the story at the one year post-transplant mark. It's been a remarkable experience for both of us, and it continues, as Wendy says, in all its ordinary splendor.

After the bumpy first year, our challenges eased up and Pete became healthier. We had one more rather scary challenge in September of 2009 when Pete's white blood cell count dropped way below where it should be. He had to be quarantined at home until the count was back within a healthy range. But like everything else, that was temporary. He got better.

We have not heard anything from the family of Pete's heart donor, and we respect their right to anonymity. We just hope they can sense the depth of our gratitude.

As I write this, we are well past the second year anniversary of the transplant. It's true that the first year is the hardest; things are much better now. We went to Florida for a few weeks last winter, and Pete played 18 holes of golf–*well*. He mows the lawn, hauls out the trash, works out at the gym, and is chomping at the bit to get back to work. I still can't get him to cook, but then I never could. (I might as well ask him to eat peas.) He still needs his rest, but then, so do I. We're not exactly spring chickens. We travelled in 21 states in 2010, and Pete did the bulk of the driving. One excursion was to Montana, where Pete and I were able to hold our new grandson, Henry. Dreams do come true.

Pete continues his affair with dark chocolate, which I'm sure has helped him get back up to a healthy weight. His voice is coming back, strong and true.

I ran across some notes I took from a reading my medium friend, Margie, gave me shortly before Pete and I were married:

She saw a dove, representing love, and a musical note. There were two people, mates, walking a path together leading to the future. It would not be without its challenges. She saw marriage, music, and blessings as our destiny, and said that life brings us challenges as gifts leading to our upliftment. Our choice is how we respond to the challenges.

Pete and I have weathered more storms in two years than some couples face in forty. The trivial irritations and painful moments wash away with each new sunset, and our love and commitment to each other is firm.

As I look back on the past two years, I realize how many things I have learned. Some of these things were already in my belief system, but it's different now that I have lived them. Now I don't just believe—I *know*.
I know . . .

. . . that the Universe provides.

. . . that, even when it does not appear so, all is well.

. . . that prayer is more powerful than I had ever imagined.

. . . that worry is a waste of valuable energy and is harmful to the soul.

. . . that asking for help gives others the opportunity to experience the joy of giving.

. . . that abundance often comes from totally unexpected sources.

. . . that we can change our thoughts in an instant, and in doing so, change our lives.

. . . that setting priorities is best done from the perspective of what love is calling us to do.

. . . that taking care of ourselves is a sacred responsibility.

. . . that what we focus on expands.

. . . that kind words can mean the world to a person struggling with challenges.

. . . that we are truly all connected.

. . . that there is enough.

. . . that I am enough.

. . . that music has powerful potential for healing.

. . . that peace of mind can be found in the midst of turmoil.

. . . that God is everywhere and in all things.

These lessons have been a gift, enriching my life many, many times over. I have experienced what has been referred to as a "downward upward journey." Pete and I feel exceedingly grateful to be alive, to have each other, and to be able to share our story with you. As someone once told me, "As one of us heals, we all heal." We hope this is true for you.

Breathless Hearts

By Peter Michael Wehle

I sing out to the memories of breathless hearts,
Shouting their thanks
In one glorious voice.
They are magical.
Listen, oh listen,
And you shall truly see the forgiven,
And all that is unforgiven.
From my heart,
The one borrowed,
I live now.
I can breathe in the Spirit around me every day.
I am so grateful!
I am so here!
Thank you to someone I will never know . . .
Or will I?

© 2011 Peter Wehle

RESOURCES

Abraham	www.abraham-hicks.com
Celebrate Your Life	www.mishkaproductions.com
Pamela Chappell	www.pamelachappell.com
Coptics	www.thecopticcenter.org
Daily Word	www.dailyword.com
For Pete's Sake	www.forpetessakethebook.com
Karen Drucker	www.karendrucker.com
Masaru Emoto	www.masaru-emoto.net
Louise Hay	www.louisehay.com
Carol Johnson	www.caroljohnsonmusic.com
Ralph Marston	www.greatday.com
National Institutes of Health (NIH)	www.nih.gov
Omega Institute for Holistic Studies	www.eomega.org
Lauren Lane Powell	www.singforyoursoul.com
Unity	www.unity.org
Neale Donald Walsch	www.nealedonaldwalsch.com

All original songs mentioned in *For Pete's Sake* may be heard at:
www.forpetessakethebook.com with the password: <peteandpam>.

'The Prayer for Protection' by James Dillet Freeman,
is printed with permission from Unity (see above).

Note: The websites indicated above are current at the time of publication.

The songs mentioned in this book are listed below.
Please refer to the Resources page to learn how you
may listen to the songs free of charge.

Songs Mentioned	Date
One	May 2004
Peace Canon	May 2004
Please and Thank You	July 7, 2008
Everything is Alright	July 8, 2008
Joy in my Heart	After July 14, 2008 Posting
Peace Canon (repeat)	After *Looking Back*, July 14, 2008
Send Out More	July 30, 2008
May We Be Healed	August 23, 2008
May We Be Healed (repeat)	August 27, 2008
Inescapable Love	September 19, 2008
Peace Canon (Repeat)	October 31, 2008
One (Repeat)	November 21, 2008
Peace Canon (Repeat)	May 29, 2009
Grateful	July 26, 2009

Pete and Pam watch sun set at their wedding,
September 2007

Pete prior to transplant

The Wehle Vigilantes wait during transplant surgery

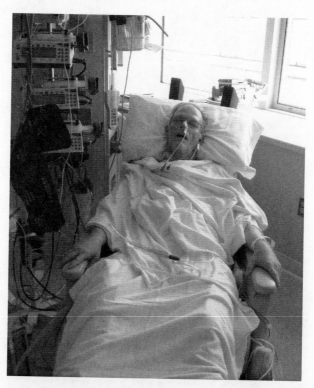

Five days post transplant, August 1, 2008

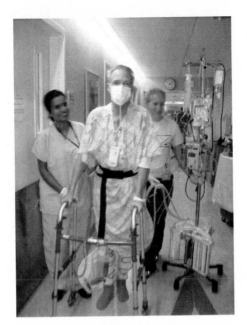

Pete walks

Pam whips the basement into shape, November 5, 2008

Pete stands from wheelchair to applaud Pam at Benefit
Concert, November 15, 2008

Pam and Pete at Benefit Concert, November 15, 2008

Sedona, February, 2009

Author Pamela Chappell is also a singer/songwriter with several CDs to her credit. *For Pete's Sake* is her second book. An ordained minister with the International Metaphysical Ministry, Chappell is also a motivational speaker. She teaches workshops in various aspects of spirituality and serves as a music leader and performer at conferences, conventions and other events. She has performed at the United Nations Headquarters in New York City and for former President Jimmy Carter. She resides in Michigan with her husband, Pete Wehle.

Ms. Chappell may be contacted at <pamela@pamelachappell.com>.

Order Form

Quantity		Price	Your Price
	For Pete's Sake	$20	

Also Available

	Joy in my Heart CD	$15	
	Coming Down Easy CD	$15	
	Inner Journey CD	$15	
	Everything is Alright CD	$15	
	A Little Sunshine CD	$15	
	A Little Sunshine for Teachers–Book & CD	$25	
	Shipping/Packaging/Tax	$3.50 per CD $5.00 per book	
	Total Order		

Ship to: _____

Address: _____

_____

Phone: _____

E-mail: _____

Please make your check or money order out to:

Pamela Chappell   Phone: (269) 637-3781

And mail to:

Pamela Chappell, Big Blue Water Productions

P.O. Box 287, South Haven, MI 49090

For more information: www.pamelachappell.com

Edwards Brothers, Inc.
Thorofare, NJ USA
September 12, 2011